COMPUTER PROGRAMMING

THIS BOOK INCLUDES:
LEARN PYTHON +
SQL PROGRAMMING+ARDUINO PROGRAMMING

By Damon Parker

LEARN PYTHON

A CRASH COURSE ON PYTHON PROGRAMMING AND HOW TO START CODING WITH IT.
LEARN THE BASICS OF MACHINE LEARNING AND DATA ANALYSIS

SQL PROGRAMMING

THE ULTIMATE GUIDE WITH EXERCISES, TIPS AND TRICKS TO LEARN SQL

ARDUINO PROGRAMMING

THE ULTIMATE GUIDE FOR MAKING THE BEST OF YOUR ARDUINO PROGRAMMING PROJECTS

LEARN PYTHON

A CRASH COURSE ON PYTHON PROGRAMMING AND HOW TO START CODING WITH IT.
LEARN THE BASICS OF MACHINE LEARNING AND DATA ANALYSIS

By Damon Parker

Table of Contents

Introduction

Congratulations on purchasing *Learn Python: A Crash Course On Python Programming And How To Start Coding With It. Learn The Basics Of Machine Learning And Data Analysis,* and thank you for doing so.

The following chapters will discuss the core concepts of Python coding to help you kick start your coding journey. You will also learn the fundamentals of data analysis and machine learning technology. You will start this book with the key features and advantages of learning to code Python as well as the history of how Python programming was created. In the first chapter of this book, you will find instructions on how to install Python on your operating systems (Windows, Mac, and Linux). The concept of Python data types is presented in exquisite detail with various examples of each data type. In Python, variables are at the heart of every syntax. You will learn how to create these variables and assign desired data type to them. This chapter also includes comprehensive lists of a variety of built-in functions and methods supported by Python.

The chapter 2 of this book titled "Python Coding" will introduce you to the basic concepts of writing efficient and effective Python codes, focusing on various programming elements such as Booleans, Tuples, Sets, Dictionaries and much more. Each concept is explained with standard syntax, relevant examples, and followed by exercises to help you test and verify your understanding of all the concepts. You will also learn how to write "if" and "else" statements to retrieve desired information from your data. The concept of "for" and "while" loops are explained with explicit details in an easy to understand language.

In chapter 3 titled Data Analysis and Machine Learning with Python, you will learn the basics of big data analysis and the fundamental machine learning algorithms. This chapter also includes brief overview of various renowned machine learning libraries such as Scikit-Learn, NumPy, Matplotlib, SymPy and Pandas among others. A detailed walkthrough with an open-source database using illustrations and actual Python code that you can try hands-on by following the instructions in this book. A number of Python coding tips and tricks have also been provided that will help you sharpen up your Python programming skillset or get familiar with the coding if you are new to Python coding.

There are plenty of books on this subject on the market, thanks again for choosing this one! Every effort was made to ensure it is full of as much useful information as possible; please enjoy!

Chapter 1: Introduction to Python

Python is a high-level programming language, commonly used for general purposes. It was originally developed by Guido van Rossum at the "Center Wiskunde & Informatica (CWI), Netherlands," in the 1980s and introduced by the "Python Software Foundation" in 1991. It was designed primarily to emphasize readability of programming code, and its syntax enables programmers to convey ideas using fewer lines of code. Python programming language increases the speed of operation while allowing for higher efficiency in creating system integrations. Developers are using Python for "web development (server-side), software development, mathematics, system scripting."

With the introduction of various enhancements such as "list comprehension" and a "garbage collection system," which can collect reference cycles, the Python 2.0 was launched in the last quarter of 2000. Subsequently, in 2008, Python 3.0 was released as a major version upgrade with backward compatibility allowing for the Python 2.0 code to be executed on Python 3.0 without requiring any modifications. Python is supported by a community of programmers that continually develop and maintain the "CPython," which is an open-source reference implementation. The "Python Software Foundation" is a not for profit organization that is responsible for managing and directing resources for developing Python programming as well as "CPython."

Here are some of the key features of Python that render it as the language of choice for coding beginners as well as advanced software programmers alike:

1. **Readability**: Python reads a lot like the English language, which contributes to its ease of readability.
2. **Learnability**: Python is a high level programming language and considered easy to learn due to the ability to code using English language like expressions, which implies it is simple to comprehend and thereby learn the language.
3. **Operating Systems**: Python is easily accessible and can be operated across different Operating systems including Linux, Unix, Mac, Windows among others. This renders Python as a versatile and cross-platform language.
4. **Open Source**: Python is "open source", which means that the developer community can seamlessly make updates to the code, which are always available to anyone using Python for their software programming needs.
5. **Standardized Data Libraries**: Python features a big standard data library with a variety of useful codes and

functionalities that can be used when writing Python code for data analysis and development of machine learning models. (Details on machine learning libraries will be provided later in this chapter)

6. **Free**: Considering the wide applicability and usage of Python, it is hard to believe that it continues to be freely available for easy download and use. This implies that anyone looking to learn or use Python can simply download and use it for their applications completely free of charge. Python is indeed a perfect example of a "FLOSS (Free/Libre Open Source Software)", which means one could "freely distribute copies of this software, read its source code and modify it."

7. **Supports managing of exceptions**: An "exception" can be defined as "an event that can occur during program exception and can disrupt the normal flow of program." Python is capable of supporting handling of these "exceptions," implying that you could write fewer error-prone codes and test your code with a variety of cases, which could potentially lead to an "exception" in the future.

8. **Advanced Features**: Python can also support "generators and list comprehensions."

9. **Storage governance**: Python is also able to support "automatic memory management," which implies that the

storage memory will be cleared and made available automatically. You are not required to clear and free up the system memory.

Applications:

1. Web designing – Some of the widely used web frameworks such as "Django" and "Flask" have been developed using Python. These frameworks assist the developer in writing server-side codes that enable management of database, generation of backend programming logic, mapping of URL, among others. Machine learning –A variety of machine learning models have been written exclusively in Python. Machine learning is a way for machines to write logic in order to learn and fix a specific issue on its own. For instance, Python-based machine learning algorithms used in development of "product recommendation systems" for eCommerce businesses such as Amazon, Netflix, YouTube and many more. Other instances of Python-based machine learning models are the facial recognition and the voice recognition technologies available on our mobile devices.

2. Data Analysis–Python can also be used in the development of data visualization and data analysis tools and techniques such as scatter plots and other graphical representations of data.

3. "Scripting" –It can be defined as the process of generating simple programs for automation of straightforward tasks like those required to send automated email responses and text messages. You could develop these types of software using the Python programming language.
4. Gaming Industry –A wide variety of gaming programs have been developed with the use of Python.
5. Python also supports the development of "embedded applications."
6. Desktop apps–You could use data libraries such as "TKinter" or "QT" to create desktop apps based on Python.

Installation Instructions for Python

You can follow the step by step instructions to download and install Python on a variety of operating systems. Simply jump to the section for the operating system you are working on. The latest version of Python released in the middle of the 2019 is Python 3.8.0. Make sure you are downloading and installing the most recent and stable version of Python and following the instructions below.

WINDOWS

1. From the official Python website, click on the "Downloads" icon and select Windows.

2. Click on the "Download Python 3.8.0" button to view all the downloadable files.

3. You will be taken to a different screen where you can select the Python version you would like to download. In this book, we will be using the Python 3 version under "Stable Releases." So scroll down the page and click on the "Download Windows x86-64 executable installer" link as shown in the picture below.

- Python 3.8.0 - Oct. 14, 2019
  Note that Python 3.8.0 *cannot* be used on Windows XP or earlier.
  - Download Windows help file
  - Download Windows x86-64 embeddable zip file
  - Download Windows x86-64 executable installer
  - Download Windows x86-64 web-based installer
  - Download Windows x86 embeddable zip file
  - Download Windows x86 executable installer
  - Download Windows x86 web-based installer

4. A pop-up window titled "python-3.8.0-amd64.exe" will be displayed.

5. Click on the "Save File" button to start downloading the file.

6. Once the download has completed, double click the saved file icon, and a "Python 3.8.0 (64-bit) Setup" pop window will be displayed.

7. Make sure that you select the "Install Launcher for all users (recommended)" and the "Add Python 3.8 to PATH" checkboxes. Note – If you already have an older version of Python installed on your system, the "Upgrade Now" button will appear instead of the "Install Now" button, and neither of the checkboxes will be displayed.

8. Click on the "Install Now" button and a "User Account Control" pop up window will be displayed.

9. A notification stating, "Do you want to allow this app to make changed to your device" will be displayed, click on Yes.

10. A new pop up window titled "Python 3.8.0 (64-bit) Setup" will be displayed containing a setup progress bar.

11. Once the installation has been completed, a "Set was successful" message will be displayed. Click on the Close button, and you are all set.

12. To verify the installation, navigate to the directory where you installed Python and double click on the python.exe file.

MACINTOSH

1. From the official Python website, click on the "Downloads" icon and select Mac.

2. Click on the "Download Python 3.8.0" button to view all the downloadable files.

3. You will be taken to a different screen where you can select the Python version you would like to download. In this book, we will be using the Python 3 version under "Stable Releases." So scroll down the page and click on the "Download macOS 64-bit installer" link under Python 3.8.0, as shown in the picture below.

- Python 3.7.5 - Oct. 15, 2019
  - Download macOS 64-bit/32-bit installer
  - Download macOS 64-bit installer
- Python 3.8.0 - Oct. 14, 2019
  - Download macOS 64-bit installer
- Python 3.7.4 - July 8, 2019
  - Download macOS 64-bit/32-bit installer
  - Download macOS 64-bit installer
- Python 3.6.9 - July 2, 2019

4. A pop-up window titled "python-3.8.0-macosx10.9.pkg" will be displayed.
5. Click on the "Save File" button to start downloading the file.
6. Once the download has completed, double click the saved file icon, and an "Install Python" pop window will be displayed.
7. Click on the "Continue" button to proceed, and a terms and conditions pop up window will be displayed.
8. Click Agree and then click on the "Install" button.
9. A notification requesting administrator permission and password will be displayed. Simply enter your system password to begin installation.

10. Once the installation has been completed, an "Installation was successful" message will be displayed. Click on the Close button, and you are all set.

11. To verify the installation, navigate to the directory where you installed Python and double click on the python launcher icon that will take you to the Python Terminal.

LINUX

- **For Red Hat, CentOS, or Fedora**, install the python3 and python3-devel packages.
- **For Debian or Ubuntu**, install the python3.x and python3.x-dev packages.
- **For Gentoo**, install the '=python-3.x*' ebuild (you may have to unmask it first).

1. From the official Python website, click on the "Downloads" icon and select Linux/UNIX.

2. Click on the "Download Python 3.8.0" button to view all the downloadable files.

3. You will be taken to a different screen where you can select the Python version you would like to download. In this book, we will be using the Python 3 version under "Stable Releases." So scroll down the page and click on the "Download Gzipped source tarball" link under Python 3.8.0, as shown in the picture in the next page.

- Download Gzipped source tarball
- Download XZ compressed source tarball
- Python 3.8.0 - Oct. 14, 2019
  - Download Gzipped source tarball
  - Download XZ compressed source tarball
- Python 3.7.4 - July 8, 2019
  - Download Gzipped source tarball
  - Download XZ compressed source tarball

4. A pop-up window titled "python-3.7.5.tgz" will be displayed.

5. Click on the "Save File" button to start downloading the file.

6. Once the download has completed, double click the saved file icon, and an "Install Python" pop window will be displayed.

7. Follow the prompts on the screen to complete the installation process.

Getting Started

Now that you have the Python terminal installed on your computer, we will now see how you can start writing and executing the Python code. All Python codes are written in a text editor as (.py) files, which are then executed on the Python interpreter on the command line as shown in the code below, where "smallworld.py" is the name of the Python file:

"C: \Users\Your Name\python smallworld.py"

You can test a small code without writing the code in a file and simply executing it as a command-line itself by typing the code below on the Mac, Windows or Linux command line, as shown below:

"C: \Users\Your Name\python"

In case the above command doesn't work, you can use the code below instead

"C: \Users\Your Name\py"

Indentation – To understand the Python coding structure, you must first understand the significance of indentation or the number of spaces before you start typing the code. Unlike other coding languages where "indentation" is added to enhance the readability of the code, in Python, it is used to indicate a set of code. For example, look at the code below

If 6 > 3:
        print ('Six is greater than 3')
There is indentation prior to the second line of code with the print command. If you skip the indentation and write the code as below, you will receive an error:

If 6 > 3:

print ('Six is greater than 3')

The number of spaces can be adjusted but must be at least single-spaced. For example, you can execute the code below with higher indentation, but for a specific set of code same number of spaces must be used, or you will receive an error.

If 6 > 3:

        print ('Six is greater than 3')

Adding Comments – In Python, you can add comments to the code by starting the code comment lines with a "#", as shown in the example below:

#Add any relevant comment here
print ('Small World)

Comments are also used as a description of the code and not executed by the Python terminal. It is important to remember that if you put a comment at the end of code like the entire code line will be skipped by the Python terminal as shown in the code below. Comments are extremely useful in case you need to stop the execution when you are testing the code.

print ('Small World')   *#Add comments here*

You can also add multiple lines of comments by starting each code line with "#," as shown below:

#Add comment here
#Supplement the comment here
#Further add the comment here
print ('Small World')

Python Variables

In Python, variables are used to store data values without executing a command for it. You can create a variable by simply assigning desired value to it, as shown in the example below:

A = 100
B = 'Patrick'
print (A)
print (B)

A variable may be declared without a specific data type. The data type of a variable can also be modified after it's initial declaration, as shown in the example below:

A = 100 # A has data type set as int
A = 'Nick' # A now has data type str
print (A)

There are certain rules applied to the Python variable names as follows:

1. Variable names can be short as single alphabets or more descriptive words like height, weight, etc
2. Variable names can only be started with an underscore character or a letter.
3. Variable names must not start with numbers.
4. Variable names may contain underscores or alphanumeric characters. No other special characters are allowed.
5. Variable names are case sensitive. For example, 'height,' 'Height' and 'HEIGHT' will be accounted as 3 separate variables.

Assigning Value to Variables

In Python, multiple variables can be assigned DISTINCT values in a single code line, as shown in the example below:

A, B, C = 'purple,' 'red,' 'blue'
print (A)
print (B)
print (C)

OR multiple variables can be assigned SAME value in a single code line, as shown in the example below:

A, B, C = 'purple'
print (A)
print (B)
print (C)

Python Data Types

To further understand the concept of variables, let's first look at the Python data types. Python supports a variety of data types as listed below:

Category	Data Type	Example Syntax
Text	*"str"*	'Small World' "Small World" """"Small World""""
Boolean	*"bool"*	'True' 'False'
Mapping (mixed data types, associative array of key and	*"dict"*	'{'key9' : 9.0, 6 : True}'

value pairs)		
Sequence (may contain mixed data types)	*"list"*	'[9.0, 'character', True]'
	"tuple"	'[9.0, 'character', True]'
	"range"	'range (10, 50)' 'range (100, 50, 10, -10, -50, -100)'
Binary	*"bytes"*	b 'byte sequence' b 'byte sequence' bytes ([120, 90, 75, 100])
	"bytearray"	bytearray (b 'byte sequence') bytearray (b 'byte sequence') bytearray ([120, 90, 75, 100])
	"memoryview"	
Set (unordered, no duplicates, mixed data types)	*"set"*	'[9.0, 'character', True]'
	"frozenset"	'frozenset ([9.0, 'character', True])'

Numeric	"int"	'54'
Numeric	"float"	'18e9'
	"complex"	'18 + 3.1j'
Ellipsis (index in NumPy arrays)	"ellipsis"	'...' 'Ellipsis'

To view the data type of any object, you can use the *"type ()"* function as shown in the example below:

A = 'Purple'
print (type (A))

Assigning the Data Type to Variables

As mentioned earlier, you can create a new variable by simply declaring a value for it. This set data value, in turn, assigns the data type to the variable.

To assign a specific data type to a variable, the constructor functions listed below can be used:

Constructor Functions	Data Type
A = str ('Small	str

World)'	
A = int (99)	Int (Must be a whole number, positive or negative with no decimals, no length restrictions)
A = float (15e6)	Float (Floating point number must be a positive or negative number with one or more decimals; maybe scientific number an 'e' to specify an exponential power of 10)
A = complex (99j)	Complex (Must be written with a 'j' as an imaginary character)
A = list (('blue', 'red', 'green'))	list
A = range (1, 100)	range
A = tuple (('blue', 'red', 'green'))	tuple
A = set (('blue', 'red', 'green'))	set
A = frozenset (('blue', 'green', 'red'))	frozenset
A = dict ('color' : 'red',	dict

'year' : 1999)	
A = bool (False)	bool
A = bytes (54)	bytes
A = bytearray (8)	bytearray
A = memoryview (bytes (55))	memoryview

EXERCISE – To solidify your understanding of data types. Look at the first column of the table below and write the data type for that variable. Once you have all your answers, look at the second column, and verify your answers.

Variable	Data Type
A = 'Small World'	str
A = 99	int
A = 29e2	float
A = 99j	complex
A = ['blue', 'red', 'green']	list
A = range (1, 100)	range
A = ('blue', 'red', 'green')	tuple
A = {'blue', 'red', 'green'}	set
A = frozenset ({ 'blue', 'green', 'red'})	frozenset
A = ['color' : 'red', 'year' : 1999}	dict
A = False	bool
A = b 'Welcome'	bytes

A = bytearray (8)	bytearray
A = memoryview (bytes (55))	memoryview

Output Variables

In order to retrieve variables as output, the "print" statements are used in Python. You can use the "+" character to combine text with a variable for final output, as shown in the example below:

'A = 'red'
print ('Apples are' + A)'

OUTPUT – 'Apples are red'

A variable can also be combined with another variable using the "+" character as shown in the example below:

'A = 'Apples are'
B = 'red'
AB = A + B
print (AB)'

OUTPUT – 'Apples are red'

However, when the "+" character is used with numeric values, it retains it's function as a mathematical operator, as shown in the example below:

'A = 20
B = 30
print (A + B)'

OUTPUT = 50

You will not be able to combine a string of characters with numbers and will trigger an error instead, as shown in the example below:

A = 'red'
B = 30
print (A + B)

OUTPUT – N/A – ERROR

Python Built-in Functions

Like most programming languages, Python boasts a number of built-in functions to make your life easier while coding a software program. Here is a list of all such built-in functions:

Function	Description
abs ()	Will result in the absolute values of the numbers.
all ()	Will result in True if all items within an iterative object are true.
any ()	Will result in True if any item of the iterative object holds true.
ascii ()	Will result in a readable version of an object and replace non-ascii characters with escape characters.
bin ()	Will result in the binary version of the numbers.
bool ()	Will result in the boolean values of indicated objects.
bytearray ()	Will result in an array of bytes.
bytes ()	Will result in bytes objects.
callable ()	Will result in True if a specific object is callable or else results in False.
chr ()	Will result in a character from the indicated Unicode code.
classmethod ()	Will convert any method into class method.
compile ()	Will result in the indicated source as an object, ready for execution.
complex ()	Will result in a complex number.

delattr ()	Will delete specific attributes (property or method) from the indicated object.
dict ()	Will result in a dictionary.
dir ()	Will result in a list of properties and methods of the specific object.
divmod ()	Will result in the quotient and the remainder when one argument is divided by another.
enumerate ()	Will take a collection and result in enumerate objects.
eval ()	Will evaluate and execute an expression.
exec ()	Will execute the indicated code (or object)
filter ()	Uses a filter function to exclude items in an iterative object.
float ()	Will result in floating point numbers.
format ()	Will format the indicated value.
frozenset ()	Will result in a frozen set object.
getattr ()	Will result in the value of the indicated attribute (property or method).
globals ()	Will result in the most recent global symbol table as a dictionary.

hasattr ()	Will result in True if the indicated object has the indicated attribute.
hash ()	Will result in the hash value of the indicated object.
help ()	Will execute the built-in help system.
hex ()	Conversion of numbers into hexadecimal values.
id ()	Will result in the identity of an object.
input ()	Will allow user input.
int ()	Will result in an integer number.
isinstance ()	Will result in True if the indicated object is an instance of the indicated object.
issubclass ()	Will result in True if the indicated class is a subclass of the indicated object.
iter ()	Will result in an iterative object.
len ()	Will result in the length of an object.
list ()	Will result in a list.
locals ()	Will result in an updated dictionary of the current local symbol table.
map ()	Will result in the indicated iterator with the indicated function applied to each item.
max ()	Will result in the largest item of an

	iteration.
memoryview ()	Will result in memory view objects.
min ()	Will result in the smallest item of an iteration.
next ()	Will result in the next item in an iteration.
object ()	Will result in a new object.
oct ()	Converts a number into an octet.
open ()	Will open files and result in file objects.
ord ()	Conversion of an integer representing the Unicode of the indicated character.
pow ()	Will result in the value of a to the power of b.
print ()	Will print to the standard output device.
property ()	Will retrieve, set, and delete a property.
range ()	Will result in a sequence of numbers, beginning from 0 and default increments of 1.
repr ()	Will result in a readable version of objects.
reversed ()	Will result in a reversed iteration.

round ()	Rounding of a number.
set ()	Will result in new set objects.
setattr ()	Will set attributes of the objects.
slice ()	Will result in a sliced objects.
sorted ()	Will result in sorted lists.
staticmethod ()	Will convert methods into a static method.
str ()	Will result in string objects.
sum ()	Will sum the items of iterations.
super ()	Will result in an object representing the parent class.
tuple ()	Will result in tuples.
type ()	Will result in the type of objects.
vars ()	Will result in the _dict_ property of objects.
zip ()	Will result in a single iteration from multiple iterations.

Python Built-in String methods

There are a number of built-in Python methods specifically for strings of data, which will result in new values for the string without making any changes to the original string. Here is a list of all such methods.

Method	Description
capitalize ()	Will convert the initial character to upper case.
casefold ()	Will convert strings into lower case.
center ()	Will result in centered strings.
count ()	Will result in the number of times an indicated value appears in a string.
encode ()	Will result in an encoded version of the strings.
endswith ()	Will result in true if the string ends with the indicated value.
expandtabs ()	Will set the tab size of the string.
find ()	Will search the string for indicated value and result in its position.
format ()	Will format indicated values of strings.
format_map ()	Will format indicated values of strings.
index ()	Will search the string for indicated value and result in its position.
isalnum ()	Will result in True if all string characters are alphanumeric.
isalpha ()	Will result in True if all string

	characters are alphabets.
isdecimal ()	Will result in True if all string characters are decimals.
isdigit ()	Will result in True if all string characters are digits.
isidentifier ()	Will result in True if the strings is an identifier.
islower ()	Will result in True if all string characters are lower case.
isnumeric ()	Will result in True if all string characters are numeric.
isprintable ()	Will result in True if all string characters are printable.
isspace ()	Will result in True if all string characters are whitespaces.
istitle ()	Will result in True if the string follows the rules of a title.
isupper ()	Will result in True if all string characters are upper case.
join ()	Will join the elements of an iteration to the end of the string.
ljust ()	Will result in a left-justified version of the string.
lower ()	Will convert a string into lower case.

lstrip ()	Will result in a left trim version of the string.
maketrans ()	Will result in a translation table to be used in translations.
partition ()	Will result in a tuple where the string is separated into 3 sections.
replace ()	Will result in a string where an indicated value is replaced with another indicated value.
rfind ()	Will search the string for an indicated value and result in its last position.
rindex ()	Will search the string for an indicated value and result in its last position.
rjust ()	Will result in the right justified version of the string.
rpartition ()	Will result in a tuple where the string is separated into 3 sections.
rsplit ()	Will split the string at the indicated separator and result in a list.
rstrip ()	Will result in a new string version that has been trimmed at its right.
split ()	Will split the string at the indicated separator and result in a list.

splitlines ()	Will split the string at line breaks and result in a list.
startswith ()	Will result in true if the string starts with the indicated value.
strip ()	Will result in a trimmed version of the string.
swapcase ()	Will swap the alphabet cases.
title ()	Will convert the first character of each word to upper case.
translate ()	Will result in a translated string.
upper ()	Will convert a string into upper case.
zfill ()	Will fill the string with the indicated number of 0 values at the beginning.

Python Random Numbers

A "random ()" function does not exist in Python, but it has an embedded module called "random" that may be utilized to create numbers randomly when needed. For instance, if you wanted to call the "random" module and display a number randomly between 100 and 500, you can accomplish this by executing the code below:

import random

print (random.randrange (100, 500))

OUTPUT – Any number between 100 and 500 will be randomly displayed.

There are a number of defined methods in the random module as listed below:

Method	Description
betavariate ()	Will result in random float numbers between 0 and 1 based on the Beta distribution.
choice ()	Will result in random elements on the basis of the provided sequence.
choices ()	Will result in a list consisting of a random selection from the provided sequence.
expovariate ()	Will result in a float number randomly displayed between 0 and -1, or between 0 and 1 for negative parameters on the basis of the statistical exponential distributions.
gammavariate ()	Will result in a float number displayed between 0 and 1 on the basis of the statistical Gamma distribution.

gauss ()	Will result in a float number displayed between 0 and 1 on the basis of the Gaussian distribution, which is widely utilized in probability theory.
getrandbits ()	Will result in a number that represents the random bits.
getstate ()	Will result in the current internal state of the random number generator.
lognormvariate ()	Will result in a float number randomly displayed between 0 and 1 on the basis of a log-normal distribution, which is widely utilized in probability theory.
normalvariate()	Will result in a float number randomly displayed between 0 and 1 on the basis of the normal distribution, which is widely utilized in probability theory.
paretovariate()	Will result in a float number randomly displayed between 0 and 1 on the basis of the Pareto distribution, which is widely utilized in probability theory.

randint ()	Will result in a random number between the provided range.
random ()	Will result in a float number randomly displayed between 0 and 1.
randrange ()	Will result in a random number between the provided range.
sample ()	Will result in a sample of the sequences.
seed ()	Will trigger the random number generator.
setstate ()	Will restore the internal state of the random number generator.
shuffle ()	Will take a sequence and result in a sequence but in some random order.
triangular ()	Will result in a random float number between two provided parameters. You could also set a mode parameter for specification of the midpoint between the two other parameters.
uniform ()	Will result in a random float number between two provided parameters.
vonmisesvariate()	Will result in a float number randomly displayed between 0 and 1 on the basis of the von "Mises distribution", which is utilized in

	directional statistics.
weibullvariate()	Will result in a float number randomly displayed between 0 and 1 on the basis of the Weibull distribution, which is utilized in statistics.

Python Built-in List methods

Python supports a number of built-in methods that can be used on lists or arrays, as listed in the table below:

Method	Description
append ()	Will insert an element at the end of the list.
clear ()	Will remove all the list elements.
copy ()	Will result in a replica of the list.
count ()	Will result in the number of elements with the indicated value.
extend ()	Will add the elements of a list (or any iterator), to the end of the current list.
index ()	Will result in the index of the first element with the indicated value.
insert ()	Will add an element at the indicated position.

pop ()	Will remove the element at the indicated position.
remove ()	Will remove the first item with the indicated value.
reverse ()	Will reverse the order of the list.
sort ()	Will sort the list.

Python Built-in Tuple methods

Python supports a couple of built-in methods that can be used on tuples, as listed in the table below:

Method	Description
count ()	Will result in the number of times an indicated value appears in the tuple.
index ()	Will search a tuple for the indicated value and result in the position of where the value is found.

Python Built-in Set methods

Python also supports a variety of embedded methods that can be used on sets that are listed in the table below:

Method	Description
"add ()"	Will add an element to the set.
"clear ()"	Will remove all the elements

	from the set.
"copy ()"	Will result in a replica of the set.
"difference ()"	Will result in a set that contains the difference between 2 or more sets.
"difference_update ()"	Will remove the items from a set that can be found in another, indicated set.
"discard ()"	Will remove the indicated item.
"intersection ()"	Will result in a set that is the intersection of couple other sets.
"intersection_update ()"	Will remove the items from a set that are not present in another indicated set.
"isdisjoint ()"	Will determine if intersection exists between two sets.
"issubset ()"	Will determine if the identified set contains another set.
"issuperset ()"	Will determine if a different set contain the identified set or not.
"pop ()"	Will remove an element from the set.
"remove ()"	Will remove the indicated element.
"symmetric_difference	Will result in a set with the

() "	symmetric differences of the two indicated sets.
"symmetric_difference _update () "	Will insert the symmetric differences from the indicated set and other sets.
"union () "	Will result in a set containing the union of sets.
"update () "	Will update the set with the union of the indicated set and other sets.

Python Built-in Dictionary methods

Python also supports a large number of built-in methods that can be used on dictionaries that are listed in the table below:

Method	Description
clear ()	Will remove all the elements from the dictionary.
copy ()	Will result in a copy of the dictionary.
fromkeys ()	Will result in a dictionary with the indicated keys and values.
get ()	Will result in the values of the indicated key.
items ()	Will result in a list containing a tuple for every key-value pair.

keys ()	Will result in a list containing the keys of the dictionary.
pop ()	Will remove the elements with the indicated key.
popitem ()	Will remove the key value pair that was most recently added.
setdefault ()	Will result in the values of the indicated key. In case the key is not found, a new key will be added with the indicated values.
update ()	Will update the dictionary with the indicated key value pairs.
values ()	Will result in a list of all the values in the dictionary.

Python Built-in File methods

Python also supports a large number of built-in methods that can be used on file objects that are listed in the table below:

Method	Description
close ()	Will close the file
detach ()	Will result in a separate raw stream.
fileno ()	Will result in a number representing the stream, per the operating system processing.

flush ()	Will flush the internal buffer.
isatty ()	Will result in determination if the file stream is interactive.
read ()	Will result in the content of the file.
readable ()	Will result in determination if the file stream is readable or not.
readline ()	Will result in one line from the file.
readlines ()	Will result in a list of lines from the file.
seek ()	Will modify the position of the file.
seekable ()	Will result in determination if the file permits modification of its position.
tell ()	Will result in the current position of the file.
truncate ()	Will change the size of the file to the indicated value.
writeable ()	Will result in determination if the file permits writing over.
write ()	Will write the indicated string to the file.
writelines ()	Will writes a list of strings to the file.

Python Keywords

Python contains some keywords that cannot be used to define a variable or used as a function name or any other unique identifier. These select Python keywords are listed in the table below:

Method	Description
"and"	Logical operator.
"as"	For creating an alias.
"assert"	To debug.
"break"	For breaking out of a loop.
"class"	For defining a class.
"continue"	For continuing to the next iteration of a loop.
"def"	For defining a function.
"del"	For deleting an object.
"elif"	For use in conditional statements, similar to "else if".
"else"	For use in conditional statements.
"except"	For use with exceptions, so the program knows the steps to follow in case of an exception.
"FALSE"	One of the data values assigned only to Boolean data type.
"finally"	For use with exceptions, this set of code would be executed regardless of any occurrences of an exception.
"for"	Used in creation of a "for loop".
"from"	For importing particular part of a module.
"global"	For declaring a global variable.

"if"	For making conditional statements.
"import"	For importing desired module.
"in"	For checking a specific data value within a tuple or a list.
"is"	For testing two variables that may be equal.
"lambda"	For creating an anonymous function.
"None"	For representation of null data value.
"nonlocal"	For declaration of a non-local variable.
"not"	Logical operator.
"or"	Logical operator.
"pass"	Will result in a null statement that would not be executed.
"raise"	Used to raise an exception to the statement.
"result in"	Used for exiting a function and resulting in a data value.
"TRUE"	One of the data values assigned only to Boolean data type.
"try"	Used for making "try except" statements.
"while"	For creating a "while loop".
"with"	Used for simplification of the handling procedure for exceptions.
"yield"	For terminating a function and resulting in a generator.

Chapter 2: Python Coding

In the previous chapter, you learned the basics of Python syntax, the concept of Python Variables and Comments, as well as details of various built-in Python methods and keywords that serve as a prerequisite to the learning of Python programming. In this chapter, we will be looking at the nuances of how to write efficient and effective Python codes, focusing on various programming elements such as Booleans, Tuples, Sets, Dictionaries and much more. So let's get started.

Python Numbers

In Python programming, you will be working with 3 different numeric data types, namely, "int," "float" and "complex." In the previous chapter, you learned the details of what these data types entail, but below are some examples to refresh your memory.

Data Type	Example
Int (Must be a whole number, positive or negative with no decimals, no length restrictions)	*36 or 3.14*

Float	29e5
(Floating point number must be a positive or negative number with one or more decimals; maybe scientific number an "e" to specify an exponential power of 10)	
Complex (Must be written with a "j" as an imaginary character)	99j

EXERCISE – Create variable "a" with data value as "3.14", variable "b" with data value as "9e2" and variable "c" with data value as "-29j".

USE YOUR DISCRETION HERE AND WRITE YOUR CODE FIRST***

Now, check your code against the correct code below:

```
a = 3.14      # int
b = 9e2       # float
c = -29j      # complex
```

```
print (type (a))
print (type (b))
print (type (c))
```

Note – The # comments are not required for the correct code and are only mentioned to bolster your understanding of the concept.

Converting one numeric data type to another

As all Python variables are dynamic in nature, you will be able to convert the data type of these variables if needed by deriving a new variable from the variable that you would like to assign a new data type.

Let's continue building on the exercise discussed above.

```
a = 3.14        # int
b = 9e2         # float
c = -29j        # complex


#conversion from int to float
x = float (a)


#conversion from float to complex
y = complex (b)
```

```
#conversion from complex to int
z = float (c)

#conversion from int to complex
x1 = int (a)

print (x)
print (y)
print (z)
print (x1)

print (type (x))
print (type (y))
print (type (z))
print (type (x1))
```

EXERCISE – View a random number between 10 and 20 by importing the random module.

USE YOUR DISCRETION HERE AND WRITE YOUR CODE FIRST

Now, check your code against the correct code below:

```
import random
print (random.randrange (10, 20))
```

Variable Casting with Constructor Functions

In the discussion and exercise above, you learned that variables could be declared by simply assigning desired data value to them and thereby the variables will assume the pertinent data type based on the data value. However, Python allows you to specify the data types for variables by using classes or "constructor functions" to define the data type for variables. This process is called "Casting."

Here are the 3 constructor functions used for "casting" numeric data type to a variable.

Constructor Functions	Data Type
int ()	Will construct an integer number from an integer literal, a string literal (provided the string is representing a whole number) or a float literal (by rounding down to the preceding whole number)
float ()	Will construct a float number from a string literal (provided the string is representing a float or an integer), a float literal or an integer literal

complex ()	Will construct a string from a large number of data types, such as integer literals, float literals, and strings

Here are some examples:

Integer:

a = int (5)   # a takes the value 5
b = int (3.6)   # b takes the value 3
c = int ('4')   # c takes the value 4

Float:

a = float (5)   # a takes the value 5.0
b = float (3.6)   # b takes the value 3.6
c = float ('4')   # c takes the value 4.0

String:

a = str ('serial')   # a takes the value 'serial'
b = str (3.6)   # b takes the value '3.6'
c = str ('4')   # c takes the value '4.0'

Python Strings

In Python, string data type for a variable is denoted by using single, double, or triple quotation marks. This implies that you can assign string data value to variable by quoting the string of characters. For example, "welcome" is the same as 'welcome' and "'welcome'".

EXERCISE – Create a variable "v" with a string data value as "sky is blue" and display it.

USE YOUR DISCRETION HERE AND WRITE YOUR CODE FIRST

Now, check your code against the correct code below:

v = 'sky is blue'
print (v)

OUTPUT – sky is blue

EXERCISE – Create a variable "A" with a multiple-line string data value as "Looking at the sky tonight, thinking of you by my side! Let the world go on and on, it will be alright if I stay strong!" and display it.

USE YOUR DISCRETION HERE AND WRITE YOUR CODE FIRST

Now, check your code against the correct code below:

a = "'Looking at the sky tonight,

thinking of you by my side!

Let the world go on and on,

it will be alright if I stay strong!'"

print (a)

OUTPUT – Looking at the sky tonight,

thinking of you by my side!

Let the world go on and on,

it will be alright if I stay strong!

Note – You must use triple quote to create multiline string data values.

String Arrays

In Python, string data values are arrays of bytes that represent Unicode characters as true for most programming languages. But unlike other programming languages, Python lacks data type for individual characters, which are denoted as string data type with length of 1.

The first character of every string is given the position of '0', and subsequently the subsequent characters will have the position as 1, 2, 3, and so on. In order to display desired characters from a string data value, you can use the position of the character enclosed in square brackets. For example, if you wanted to display the fifth character of the string data value "apple" of variable "x." You will use the command "print (x [4])"

EXERCISE – Create a variable "P" with a string data value as "awesome" and display the fourth character of this string.

USE YOUR DISCRETION HERE AND WRITE YOUR CODE FIRST

Now, check your code against the correct code below:

P = 'awesome'
print (P [3])

OUTPUT – s

Slicing

If you would like to view a range of characters, you can do so by specifying the start and the end index of the desired positions and separating the indexes by a colon. For example, to view characters of a string from position 1 to position 3, your code will be *"print (variable [1:3])"*.

You can even view the characters starting from the end of the string by using "negative indexes" and start slicing the string from the end of the string. For example, to view characters of a string from position 4 to position 1, your code will be *"print (variable [-4 : -2])"*.

In order to view the length of the string, you can use the "len ()" function. For example, to view the length of a string, your code will be *"print (len (variable))."*

EXERCISE – Create a variable "P" with a string data value as "roses are red!" and display characters from position 3 to 6 of this string.

USE YOUR DISCRETION HERE AND WRITE YOUR CODE FIRST

Now, check your code against the correct code below:

P = 'roses are red!'
print (P [3 : 6])

OUTPUT – esa

EXERCISE – Create a variable "x" with a string data value as "python is easy" and display characters from position 5 to 1, starting the count from the end of this string.

USE YOUR DISCRETION HERE AND WRITE YOUR CODE FIRST

Now, check your code against the correct code below:

x = 'python is easy'
print (x [-5 : -2])

OUTPUT - sea

EXERCISE – Create a variable "z" with a string data value as "coding beginner" and display the length of this string.

USE YOUR DISCRETION HERE AND WRITE YOUR CODE FIRST

Now, check your code against the correct code below:

z = 'coding beginner'
print (len (z))

OUTPUT - 14

String Methods

There are various built-in methods in Python that can be applied to string data values. Here are the Python codes for some of the most frequently used string methods, using variable *"P = 'roses are red!'"*.

"strip ()" method – To remove any blank spaces at the start and the end of the string.

P = " roses are red! "
print (P.strip ())

OUTPUT – roses are red!

"lower ()" method – To result in all the characters of a string in lower case.

P = "ROSES are RED!"
print (P.lower ())

OUTPUT – roses are red!

"upper ()" method – To result in all the characters of a string in upper case.

P = "Roses are Red!"
print (P.upper ())

OUTPUT – ROSES ARE RED!

"replace ()" method – To replace select characters of a string.

P = "roses are red!"
print (P.replace ("roses", "apples"))

OUTPUT – apples are red!

"split ()" method – To split a string into substrings using comma as the separator.

P = "Roses, Apples"
print (P.split (","))

OUTPUT – ['Roses', 'Apples']

String Concatenation

There might be instances when you need to collate different string variables. This can be accomplished with the use of the "+" logical operator. Here's the syntax for this Python code:

X = "string1"

Y = "string2"

Z = X + Y

print (Z)

Similarly, below is the syntax to insert a blank space between two different string variables.

X = "string1"

Y = "string2"

Z = X + " " + Y

print (Z)

However, Python does not permit the concatenation of string variables with numeric variables. But can be accomplished with the use of the *"format ()"* method, which will format the executed arguments and place them in the string where the placeholders "{ }" are used. Here's the syntax for this Python code:

X = numeric

Y = "String"

print (Y. format (X))

EXERCISE – Create two variables "A" and "B" with string data values as "I love" and "my country!" and display them as a concatenated string.

Now, check your code against the correct code below:

A = "I love"
B = "my country!"
C = A + B
print (C)

OUTPUT – I love my country!

EXERCISE – Create two variables "A" with string data values as "my lucky number is" and "B" with numeric data value as "333" and display them as a concatenated string.

Now, check your code against the correct code below:

A = "my lucky number is"
B = "333"
print (A. format (B))

OUTPUT – my lucky number is 333

Python Booleans

In the process of developing a software program, there is often a need to confirm and verify whether an expression is true or false. This is where Python Boolean data type and data values are used. In Python, comparison and evaluation of two data values will result in one of the two Boolean values: "True" or "False."

Here are some examples of comparison statement of numeric data leading to Boolean value:

print (100 > 90)

OUTPUT – True

print (100 == 90)

OUTPUT – False

print (100 < 90)

OUTPUT – False

Let's look at the *"bool ()"* function now, which allows for evaluation of numeric data as well as string data resulting in "True" or "False" Boolean values.

print (bool (99))

OUTPUT - True

print (bool ("Welcome"))

OUTPUT - True

Here are some key points to remember for Booleans:

1. If a statement has some kind of content, it would be evaluated as "True."
2. All string data values will be result ined as "True" unless the string is empty.
3. All numeric values will be result ined as "True" except "0"
4. Lists, Tuples, Set and Dictionaries will be result ined as "True", unless they are empty.
5. Mostly empty values like (), [], {}, "", False, None and 0 will be result ined as "False".
6. Any object created with the "_len_" function that result in the data value as "0" or "False" will be evaluated as "False".

In Python there are various built-in functions function that can be evaluated as Boolean, for example, the "isinstance()" function which allows you to determine the data type of an object. Therefore, in order to check if an object is integer, the code will be as below:

X = 10
print (isinstance (X, int))

EXERCISE – Create two variables "X" with string data values as "Yes I can!" and "Y" with numeric data value as "3.14" and evaluate them.

USE YOUR DISCRETION HERE AND WRITE YOUR CODE FIRST

Now, check your code against the correct code below:

X = "Yes I can!"
Y = 3.14
print (bool (X))
print (bool (Y)

OUTPUT –
True
True

Python Lists

In Python, lists are collections of data types that can be changed, organized and include duplicate values. Lists are written within square brackets, as shown in the syntax below.

X = ["string1", "string2", "string3"]
print (X)

The same concept of position applies to Lists as the string data type, which dictates that the first string is considered to be at position 0. Subsequently, the strings that will follow are given position 1, 2 and so on. You can selectively display desired string from a List by referencing the position of that string inside square bracket in the print command as shown below.

X = ["string1", "string2", "string3"]
print (X [2])

OUTPUT – [string3]

Similarly, the concept of **negative indexing** is also applied to Python List. Let's look at the example below:

X = ["string1", "string2", "string3"]
print (X [-2])

OUTPUT – [string2]

You will also be able to specify a **range of indexes** by indicating the start and end of a range. The result in values of such command on a Python List would be a new List containing only the indicated items. Here is an example for your reference.

X = ["string1", "string2", "string3", "string4", "string5", "string6"]
print (X [2 : 4])

OUTPUT – ["string3", "string4"]

* Remember the first item is at position 0, and the final position of the range (4) is not included.

Now, if you do not indicate the start of this range, it will default to the position 0 as shown in the example below:

X = ["string1", "string2", "string3", "string4", "string5", "string6"]
print (X [: 3])

OUTPUT – ["string1", "string2", "string3"]

Similarly, if you do not indicate the end of this range it will display all the items of the List from the indicated start range to the end of the List, as shown in the example below:

X = ["string1", "string2", "string3", "string4", "string5", "string6"]
print (X [3 :])

OUTPUT – ["string4", "string5", "string6"]

You can also specify a **range of negative indexes** to Python Lists, as shown in the example below:

X = ["string1", "string2", "string3", "string4", "string5", "string6"]
print (X [-3 : -1])

OUTPUT – ["string4", "string5"]

* Remember the last item is at position -1, and the final position of this range (-1) is not included in the Output.

There might be instances when you need to **change the data value** for a Python List. This can be accomplished by referring to the index number of that item and declaring the new value. Let's look at the example below:

X = ["string1", "string2", "string3", "string4", "string5",
"string6"]
X [3] = "newstring"
print (X)

OUTPUT – ["string1", "string2", "string3", "newstring,"
"string5", "string6"]

You can also determine the **length** of a Python List using the
"len()" function, as shown in the example below:

X = ["string1", "string2", "string3", "string4", "string5",
"string6"]
print (len (X))

OUTPUT – 6

Python Lists can also be changed by **adding new items** to an
existing list using the built-in "append ()" method, as shown in
the example below:

X = ["string1", "string2", "string3", "string4"]
X.append ("newstring")
print (X)

OUTPUT – ["string1", "string2", "string3", "string4", "newstring"]

You can also, add a new item to an exiting Python List at a specific position using the built-in "insert ()" method, as shown in the example below:

X = ["string1", "string2", "string3", "string4"]
X.insert (2, "newstring")
print (X)

OUTPUT – ["string1", "string2", "newstring", "string4"]

There might be instances when you need to **copy** an existing Python List. This can be accomplished by using the built-in "copy ( )" method or the "list ( )" method, as shown in the example below:
X = ["string1", "string2", "string3", "string4", "string5", "string6"]
Y = X.copy( )
print (Y)

OUTPUT – ["string1", "string2", "string3", "string4", "string5", "string6"]
X = ["string1", "string2", "string3", "string4", "string5", "string6"]

Y = list (X)

print (Y)

OUTPUT – ["string1", "string2", "string3", "string4", "string5", "string6"]

There are multiple built-in methods to **delete items** from a Python List.

- To selectively delete a specific item, the "remove ()" method can be used.

  X = ["string1", "string2", "string3", "string4"]

  X.remove ("string2")

  print (X)

  OUTPUT - ["string1", "string3", "string4"]

- To delete a specific item from the List, the "pop ()" method can be used with the position of the value. If no index has been indicated, the last item of the index will be removed.

  X = ["string1", "string2", "string3", "string4"]

  X.pop ( )

  print (X)

  OUTPUT - ["string1", "string2", "string3"]

- To delete a specific index from the List, the "del ()" method can be used, followed by the index within square brackets.

  X = ["string1", "string2", "string3", "string4"]

  del X [2]

print (X)

OUTPUT - ["string1", "string2", "string4"]

- To delete the entire List variable, the "del ()" method can be used, as shown below.
X = ["string1", "string2", "string3", "string4"]
del X

OUTPUT - .....

- To delete all the string values from the List without deleting the variable itself, the "clear ()" method can be used, as shown below.
X = ["string1", "string2", "string3", "string4"]
X.clear()
print (X)

OUTPUT – [ ]

Concatenation of Lists

You can join multiple lists with the use of the "+" logical operator or by adding all the items from one list to another using the "append ( )" method. The "extend ( )" method can be used to add a list at the end of another list. Let's look at the examples below to understand these commands.

```
X = ["string1", "string2", "string3", "string4"]
Y = [10, 20, 30, 40]


Z = X + Y
print (Z)
```

OUTPUT – ["string1", "string2", "string3", "string4", 10, 20, 30, 40]

```
X = ["string1", "string2", "string3", "string4"]
Y = [10, 20, 30, 40]


For x in Y:
    X.append (x)


print (X)
```

OUTPUT – ["string1", "string2", "string3", "string4", 10, 20, 30, 40]

```
X = ["string1", "string2", "string3"]
Y = [10, 20, 30]


X.extend (Y)
print (X)
```

OUTPUT – ["string1", "string2", "string3", 10, 20, 30]

EXERCISE – Create a list "A" with string data values as "red, green, blue, purple, yellow" and display the item at -2 position.

USE YOUR DISCRETION HERE AND WRITE YOUR CODE FIRST

Now, check your code against the correct code below:

A = ["red", "green", "blue", "purple", "yellow"]
print (A [-2])

OUTPUT – ["purple"]

EXERCISE – Create a list "A" with string data values as "red, green, blue, purple, yellow" and display the items ranging from the string on the second position to the end of the string.

USE YOUR DISCRETION HERE AND WRITE YOUR CODE FIRST

Now, check your code against the correct code below:

A = ["red", "green", "blue", "purple", "yellow"]
print (A [2 :])

OUTPUT – ["red", "teal", "blue", "purple", "yellow"]

EXERCISE – Create a list "A" with string data values as "red, green, blue, purple, yellow" and replace the string "green" to "teal."

USE YOUR DISCRETION HERE AND WRITE YOUR CODE FIRST

Now, check your code against the correct code below:

A = ["red", "green", "blue", "purple", "yellow"]
A [1] = ["teal"]

print (A)

OUTPUT – ["blue", "purple", "yellow"]

EXERCISE – Create a list "A" with string data values as "red, green, blue, purple, yellow" and copy the list "A" to create list "B."

USE YOUR DISCRETION HERE AND WRITE YOUR CODE FIRST

Now, check your code against the correct code below:

A = ["red", "green", "blue", "purple", "yellow"]

B = A.copy ( )

print (B)

OUTPUT – ["red", "green", "blue", "purple", "yellow"]

EXERCISE – Create a list "A" with string data values as "red, green, blue, purple, yellow" and delete the strings "red" and "purple."

USE YOUR DISCRETION HERE AND WRITE YOUR CODE FIRST

Now, check your code against the correct code below:

A = ["red", "green", "blue", "purple", "yellow"]
del.A [0, 2]
print (A)

OUTPUT – ["green", "blue", "yellow"]

Python Tuples

In Python, Tuples are collections of data types that cannot be changed but can be arranged in specific order. Tuples allow for duplicate items and are written within round brackets, as shown in the syntax below.

Tuple = ("string1", "string2", "string3")
print (Tuple)

Similar to the Python List, you can selectively display the desired string from a Tuple by referencing the position of that string inside square bracket in the print command as shown below.

Tuple = ("string1", "string2", "string3")
print (Tuple [1])

OUTPUT – ("string2")

The concept of **negative indexing** can also be applied to Python Tuple, as shown in the example below:
Tuple = ("string1", "string2", "string3", "string4", "string5")
print (Tuple [-2])

OUTPUT – ("string4")

You will also be able to specify a **range of indexes** by indicating the start and end of a range. The result in values of such command on a Python Tuple would be a new Tuple containing only the indicated items, as shown in the example below:

Tuple = ("string1", "string2", "string3", "string4", "string5", "string6")
print (Tuple [1:5])

OUTPUT – *("string2", "string3", "string4", "string5")*

* Remember the first item is at position 0 and the final position of the range, which is the fifth position in this example, is not included.

You can also specify a **range of negative indexes** to Python Tuples, as shown in the example below:

Tuple = ("string1", "string2", "string3", "string4", "string5", "string6")
print (Tuple [-4: -2])

OUTPUT – *("string4", "string5")*

* Remember the last item is at position -1 and the final position of this range, which is the negative fourth position in this example is not included in the Output.

Unlike Python lists, you cannot directly **change the data value of Python Tuples** after they have been created. However, conversion of a Tuple into a List and then modifying the data value of that List will allow you to subsequently create a Tuple from that updated List. Let's look at the example below:

Tuple1 = ("string1", "string2", "string3", "string4", "string5", "string6")
List1 = list (Tuple1)
List1 [2] = "update this list to create new tuple"
Tuple1 = tuple (List1)

print (Tuple1)

OUTPUT – ("string1", "string2", "update this list to create new tuple", "string4", "string5", "string6")

You can also determine the **length** of a Python Tuple using the "len()" function, as shown in the example below:

Tuple = ("string1", "string2", "string3", "string4", "string5", "string6")
print (len (Tuple))

OUTPUT – 6

You cannot selectively delete items from a Tuple, but you can use the "del" keyword to **delete the Tuple** in its entirety, as shown in the example below:

Tuple = ("string1", "string2", "string3", "string4")
del Tuple

print (Tuple)

OUTPUT – name 'Tuple' is not defined

You can **join multiple Tuples** with the use of the "+" logical operator.

Tuple1 = ("string1", "string2", "string3", "string4")
Tuple2 = (100, 200, 300)

Tuple3 = Tuple1 + Tuple2
print (Tuple3)

OUTPUT – ("string1", "string2", "string3", "string4", 100, 200, 300)

You can also use the "tuple ( )" constructor to create a Tuple, as shown in the example below:

Tuple1 = tuple (("string1", "string2", "string3", "string4"))
print (Tuple1)

EXERCISE – Create a Tuple "X" with string data values as "peas, carrots, broccoli, onion, potato" and display the item at -3 position.

USE YOUR DISCRETION HERE AND WRITE YOUR CODE FIRST

Now, check your code against the correct code below:

X = ("peas," "carrots," "broccoli," "onion," "potato")
print (X [-3])

OUTPUT – ("broccoli")

EXERCISE – Create a Tuple "X" with string data values as "peas, carrots, broccoli, onion, potato" and display items ranging from -2 to -4.

USE YOUR DISCRETION HERE AND WRITE YOUR CODE FIRST

Now, check your code against the correct code below:

X = ("peas," "carrots," "broccoli," "onion," "potato")
print (X [-4 : -2])

OUTPUT – ("carrots," "broccoli")

EXERCISE – Create a Tuple "X" with string data values as "peas, carrots, broccoli, onion, potato" and change it's item from "potato" to "tomato" using List function.

USE YOUR DISCRETION HERE AND WRITE YOUR CODE FIRST

Now, check your code against the correct code below:

X = ("peas", "carrots", "broccoli", "onion", "potato")
Y = list (X)
Y [4] = "tomato"
X = tuple (Y)

print (X)

OUTPUT – ("peas," "carrots," "broccoli," "onion," "tomato")

EXERCISE – Create a Tuple "X" with string data values as "peas, carrots, potato" and another Tuple "Y" with numeric data values as (2, 12, 22), then join them together.

***USE YOUR DISCRETION HERE AND WRITE YOUR CODE
FIRST***

Now, check your code against the correct code below:

X = ("peas," "carrots," "potato")
Y = (2, 12, 22)

Z = X + Y
print (Z)

OUTPUT – ("peas," "carrots," "potato," 2, 12, 22)

Python Sets

In Python, Sets are collections of data types that cannot be organized and indexed. Sets do not allow for duplicate items and must be written within curly brackets, as shown in the syntax below.

set = {"string1", "string2", "string3"}
print (set)

Unlike the Python List and Tuple, you cannot selectively display desired items from a Set by referencing the position of that item because the Python Set are not arranged in any order. Therefore, items do not have any indexing. However, the "for" loop can be used on Sets (more on this topic later in this chapter).

Unlike Python Lists, you cannot directly **change the data values of Python Sets** after they have been created. However, you can use the "add ()" method to add a single item to Set and use the "update ( )" method to one or more items to an already existing Set. Let's look at the example below:

set = {"string1", "string2", "string3"}
set. add ("newstring")
print (set)

OUTPUT – {"string1", "string2", "string3", "newstring"}

set = {"string1", "string2", "string3"}
set. update (["newstring1", "newstring2", "newstring3",)
print (set)

OUTPUT – {"string1", "string2", "string3", "newstring1", "newstring2", "newstring3"}

You can also determine the **length** of a Python Set using the "len()" function, as shown in the example below:

```
set = {"string1", "string2", "string3", "string4", "string5",
"string6", "string7"}
print (len(set))
```

OUTPUT – 7

To selectively **delete a specific item from a Set**, the "remove ()" method can be used as shown in the code below:

```
set = {"string1", "string2", "string3", "string4", "string5"}
set. remove ("string4")
print (set)
```

OUTPUT – {"string1", "string2", "string3", "string5"}

You can also use the "discard ( )" method to delete specific items from a Set, as shown in the example below:

```
set = {"string1", "string2", "string3", "string4", "string5"}
set. discard ("string3")
print (set)
```

OUTPUT – {"string1", "string2", "string4", "string5"}

The "pop ( )" method can be used to selectively delete only the last item of a Set. It must be noted here that since the Python Sets are unordered, any item that the system deems as the last item will be removed. As a result, the output of this method will be the item that has been removed.

set = {"string1", "string2", "string3", "string4", "string5"}
A = set.pop ( )
print (A)
print (set)

OUTPUT –
String2
{"string1", "string3", "string4", "string5"}

To delete the entire Set, the "del" keyword can be used, as shown below.

set = {"string1", "string2", "string3", "string4", "string5"}
delete set
print (set)

OUTPUT – name 'set' is not defined

To delete all the items from the Set without deleting the variable itself, the "clear ()" method can be used, as shown below.

set = {"string1", "string2", "string3", "string4", "string5"}
set.clear ( )

print (set)

OUTPUT – set ( )

You can **join multiple Sets** with the use of the "union ( )" method. The output of this method will be a new set that contains all items from both the sets. You can also use the "update ( )" method to insert all the items from one set into another without creating a new Set.

Set1 = {"string1", "string2", "string3", "string4", "string5"}
Set2 = {15, 25, 35, 45, 55}
Set3 = Set1.union (Set2)
print (Set3)

OUTPUT – {"string1", 15, "string2", 25, "string3", 35, "string4", 45, "string5", 55}

Set1 = {"string1", "string2", "string3", "string4", "string5"}
Set2 = {15, 25, 35, 45, 55}
Set1.update (Set2)
print (Set1)

OUTPUT – {25, "string1", 15, "string4",55, "string2", 35, "string3", 45, "string5"}

You can also use the "set ( )" constructor to create a Set, as shown in the example below:

Set1 = set (("string1", "string2", "string3", "string4", "string5"))
print (Set1)

OUTPUT – {"string3", "string5", "string2", "string4", "string1"}

EXERCISE – Create a Set "Veg" with string data values as "peas, carrots, broccoli, onion, potato" and add new items "tomato," "celery" and "avocado" to this Set.

***USE YOUR DISCRETION HERE AND WRITE YOUR CODE
FIRST***

Now, check your code against the correct code below:

Veg = {"peas," "carrots," "broccoli," "onion," "potato"}
Veg.update (["tomato," "celery," "avocado"])
print (Veg)

OUTPUT – {"peas," "celery," "onion," "carrots," "broccoli," "avocado," "potato," "tomato"}

EXERCISE – Create a Set "Veg" with string data values as "peas, carrots, broccoli, onion, potato," then delete the last item from this Set.

USE YOUR DISCRETION HERE AND WRITE YOUR CODE FIRST

Now, check your code against the correct code below:

Veg = {"peas", "carrots", "broccoli", "onion", "potato"}
X = Veg.pop ( )
print (X)
print (Veg)

OUTPUT –
broccoli
{"peas," "onion," "carrots," "potato"}

EXERCISE – Create a Set "Veg" with string data values as "peas, carrots, broccoli, onion, potato" and another Set "Veg2" with items as "tomato, eggplant, celery, avocado." Then combine both these Sets to create a third new Set.

USE YOUR DISCRETION HERE AND WRITE YOUR CODE FIRST

Now, check your code against the correct code below:

Veg = {"peas," "carrots," "broccoli," "onion," "potato"}
Veg2 = {"tomato", "eggplant", "celery", "avocado"}

AllVeg = Veg.union (Veg2)   #this Set name may vary as it
has not been defined in the exercise

print (AllVeg)

OUTPUT – {"peas", "celery", "onion", "carrots", "eggplant",
"broccoli", "avocado", "potato", "tomato"}

Python Dictionary

In Python, Dictionaries are collections of data types that can be
changed and indexed but are not arranged in any order. Each
item in a Python Dictionary will comprise a key and its value.
Dictionaries do not allow for duplicate items and must be
written within curly brackets, as shown in the syntax below.

dict = {
"key1": "value1",
"key2": "value2",
"key3": "value3",
}

print (dict)

You can selectively display desired item value from a Dictionary by referencing its key inside square brackets in the print command as shown below.

dict = {
"key1": "value1",
"key2": "value2",
"key3": "value3",
}

X = dict ["key2"]
print (X)

OUTPUT – value2

You can also use the "get ( )" method to view the value of a key, as shown in the example below:

dict = {
"key1": "value1",
"key2": "value2",
"key3": "value3",
}

X = dict.get ("key1")
print (X)

OUTPUT – value1

There might be instances when you need to **change the value** of a key in a Python Dictionary. This can be accomplished by referring to the key of that item and declaring the new value. Let's look at the example below:

dict = {
"key1": "value1",
"key2": "value2",
"key3": "value3",
}

dict ["key3"] = "NEWvalue"
print (dict)

OUTPUT – {"key1": "value1", "key2": "value2", "key3": "NEWvalue"}

You can also determine the **length** of a Python Dictionary using the "len()" function, as shown in the example below:

dict = {

"key1": "value1",
"key2": "value2",
"key3": "value3",
"key4": "value4",
"key5": "value5"
}

print (len (dict))

OUTPUT – 5

Python Dictionary can also be changed by **adding** new index key and assigning a new value to that key, as shown in the example below:

dict = {
"key1": "value1",
"key2": "value2",
"key3": "value3",
}

dict ["NEWkey"] = "NEWvalue"
print (dict)

OUTPUT – {"key1": "value1", "key2": "value2", "key3": "value3", "NEWkey": "NEWvalue"}

There are multiple built-in methods to **delete items** from a Python Dictionary.

- To selectively delete a specific item value, the "pop ()" method can be used with the indicated key name.

    dict = {
    "key1": "value1",
    "key2": "value2",
    "key3": "value3",
    }
    dict.pop ("key1")
    print (dict)

    OUTPUT – { "key2": "value2", "key3": "value3"}

- To selectively delete the item value that was last inserted, the "popitem ()" method can be used with the indicated key name.

    dict = {
    "key1": "value1",
    "key2": "value2",
    "key3": "value3",
    }
    dict.popitem ( )

print (dict)

OUTPUT – { "key1": "value1", "key2": "value2"}

- To selectively delete a specific item value, the "del" keyword can also be used with the indicated key name.

dict = {
"key1": "value1",
"key2": "value2",
"key3": "value3",
}
del dict ("key3")
print (dict)

OUTPUT – { "key1": "value1", "key2": "value2"}

- To delete a Python Dictionary in its entirety, the "del" keyword can also be used as shown in the example below:

dict = {
"key1": "value1",
"key2": "value2",
"key3": "value3",
}
del dict

print (dict)

OUTPUT – name 'dict' is not defined

- To delete all the items from the Dictionary without deleting the Dictionary itself, the "clear ()" method can be used as shown below.

dict = {
"key1": "value1",
"key2": "value2",
"key3": "value3",
}
dict.clear ( )
print (dict)

OUTPUT – { }

There might be instances when you need to **copy** an existing Python Dictionary. This can be accomplished by using the built-in "copy ( )" method or the "dict ( )" method, as shown in the examples below:

dict = {
"key1": "value1",
"key2": "value2",

"key3": "value3",

}

newdict = dict.copy ( )

print (newdict)

OUTPUT – {"key1": "value1", "key2": "value2", "key3": "value3"}

Olddict = {

"key1": "value1",

"key2": "value2",

"key3": "value3",

}

newdict = dict (Olddict)

print (newdict)

OUTPUT – {"key1": "value1", "key2": "value2", "key3": "value3"}

There is a unique feature that supports multiple Python Dictionaries to be **nested** within another Python Dictionary. You can either create a Dictionary containing child Dictionaries, as shown in the example below:

```
McDonaldFamilyDict = {
        "burger1" : {
                "name" : "McPuff",
                "price" : 2.99
```

```
        },
        "burger2" : {
                "name" : "BigMac",
                "price" : 5
        },
        "burger3" : {
                "name" : "McDouble",
                "price" : 1.99
        }
}
print (McDonaldFamilyDict)
```

OUTPUT - {"burger1" : { "name" : "McPuff", "price" : 2.99},
"burger2" : {"name" : "BigMac", "price" : 5}, "burger3" : {"name"
: "McDouble", "price" : 1.99}}

Or you can create a brand new Dictionary that contain other
Dictionaries already existing on the system; your code will look
like the one below:

```
burgerDict1 : {
        "name" : "McPuff,"
        "price" : 2.99
}

burgerDict2 : {
```

```
        "name" : "BigMac",
        "price" : 5
}


burgerDict3 : {
        "name" : "McDouble",
        "price" : 1.99
}


McDonaldFamilyDict = {
        "burgerDict1" : burgerDict1,
        "burgerDict2" : burgerDict2
        "burgerDict3" : burgerDict3
}
print (McDonaldFamilyDict)
```

OUTPUT - {"burger1" : { "name" : "McPuff", "price" : 2.99},
"burger2" : {"name" : "BigMac", "price" : 5}, "burger3" : {"name"
: "McDouble", "price" : 1.99}}

Lastly, you can use the "dict ( )" function to create a new Python
Dictionary. The key differences when you create items for the
Dictionary using this function are 1. Round brackets are used
instead of the curly brackets. 2. Equal to sign is used instead of
the semi-colon. Let's look at the example below:

*DictwithFunction = dict (key1 = "value1", key2 = "value2", key3
= "value3")*
print (DictwithFunction)

OUTPUT – {"key1": "value1", "key2": "value2", "key3": "value3"}

EXERCISE – Create a Dictionary "Starducks" with items
containing keys as "type," "size" and "price" with corresponding
values as "latte," "grande" and "4.99". Then add a new item with
key as "syrup" and value as "hazelnut."

****USE YOUR DISCRETION HERE AND WRITE YOUR CODE
FIRST****

Now, check your code against the correct code below:

Starducks = {
"type" : "latte",
"size" : "grande",
"price" : 4.99
}
Starducks ["syrup"] = "hazelnut"
print (Starducks)

OUTPUT – {"type" : "latte", "size" : "grande", "price" : 4.99,
"syrup" : "hazelnut"}

EXERCISE – Create a Dictionary "Starducks" with items containing keys as "type," "size," and "price" with corresponding values as "latte," "grande" and "4.99". Then use a function to remove the last added item.

USE YOUR DISCRETION HERE AND WRITE YOUR CODE FIRST

Now, check your code against the correct code below:

```
Starducks = {
"type" : "latte",
"size" : "grande",
"price" : 4.99
}
Starducks.popitem ( )
print (Starducks)
```

OUTPUT – {"type" : "latte", "size" : "grande"}

EXERCISE – Create a Dictionary "Starducks" with nested dictionary as listed below:

Dictionary Name	Key	Value
Coffee1	name	latte
	size	venti
Coffee2	name	espresso

	size	grande
Coffee3	name	mocha
	size	small

USE YOUR DISCRETION HERE AND WRITE YOUR CODE FIRST

Now, check your code against the correct code below:

```
Starducks = {
        "coffee1" : {
                "name" : "latte",
                "size" : "venti"
        },
        "coffee2" : {
                "name" : "espresso",
                "size" : "grande"
        },
        "coffee3" : {
                "name" : "mocha",
                "size" : "small"
        }
}
print (Starducks)
```

OUTPUT - {"coffee1" : { "name" : "latte", "size" : "venti"}, "coffee2" : {"name" : "espresso", "size" : "grande"}, "coffee3" : {"name" : "mocha", "size" : "small"}}

EXERCISE – Use the "dict ()" function to create a Dictionary "Starducks" with items containing keys as "type," "size" and "price" with corresponding values as "latte," "grande" and "4.99".

USE YOUR DISCRETION HERE AND WRITE YOUR CODE FIRST

Now, check your code against the correct code below:

Starducks = dict (type = "latte", size = "grande", price = 4.99}
print (Starducks)

OUTPUT – {"type" : "latte", "size" : "grande", "price" : 4.99, "syrup" : "hazelnut"}

Python Conditions and If statement

Python allows the usage of multiple mathematical, logical conditions as listed in the next page:

- Equal to – "x == y"

- Not equal – "x !=y"
- Less than – "x < y"
- Less than, equal to – "x <= y"
- Greater than – "x > y"
- Greater than, equal to – "x >=y"

If Statement

All these conditions can be used within loops and **"if statement"**. The "if" keyword must be used to write these statements, as shown in the syntax below:

```
X = numeric1
Y = numeric2
if X > Y:
        print ("X is greater than Y")
```

The most important thing to remember here is that the indentation or the blank space at the beginning of a line in the code above is critical. Unlike other programming languages that use curly brackets, Python programming is driven by indentation in the process of defining the scope of the code. Therefore, writing the Python code below will result in an error.

```
X = numeric1
Y = numeric2
```

```
if X > Y:
print ("X is greater than Y")        #leads to an error
```

Else-if Statement

You can use the "elif" keyword to evaluate if the preceding condition is not true, then execute the subsequent condition. Here is the syntax followed by an example to help you understand this concept further:

```
X = numeric1
Y = numeric2
if X > Y:
        print ("X is greater than Y")
elif X == Y:
        print ("X and Y are equal")
```

Example:

```
X = 58
Y = 58
if X > Y:
        print ("X is greater than Y")
elif X == Y:
        print ("X and Y are equal")
OUTPUT - X and Y are equal
```

Else Statement

You can use the "else" keyword to execute any condition if the preceding conditions are not true. Here is the syntax followed by an example to help you understand this concept further:

X = numeric1
Y = numeric2
if X > Y:
      print ("X is greater than Y")
elif X == Y:
      print ("X and Y are equal")
else:
      print ("Y is greater than X")

Example:

X = 58
Y = 59
if X > Y:
      print ("X is greater than Y")
elif X == Y:
      print ("X and Y are equal")
else:
      print ("Y is greater than X")

OUTPUT - Y is greater than X

Alternatively, you can use the "else" keyword without using the "elif" keyword, as shown in the example below:

X = 69
Y = 96
if X > Y:
        print ("X is greater than Y")
else:
        print ("X is not greater than Y")

OUTPUT - X is not greater than Y

Single Line If Statement

You could even execute single line statements with "If" clause, as shown in the syntax below:

If x > y: print ("y is greater than x")

Single Line If-Else Statement

You could even execute single line statements with "If - Else" clause, as shown in the syntax below:

x = 10

y = 15

print ("x") If x > y else print ("y")

Single Line If-Else Statement with multiple Else

You will also be able to execute single line statements with "If - Else" clause containing multiple "Else" statements in the same line, as shown in the syntax below:

x = 100

y = 100

print ("x") If x > y else print ("=") if a == b else print ("y")

"And" Keyword

If you are looking to combine multiple conditional statements, you can do so with the use of the "and" keyword, as shown in the example below:

x = 20

y = 18

z = 35

if x > y and z > x :

    print ("All conditions are True")

"Or" Keyword

If you are looking to combine multiple conditional statements, the other way you can do so is with the use of the "or" keyword, as shown in the example below:

x = 20
y = 18
z = 35
if x > y or x > z :
    print ("At least one of the conditions is True")

"Nested If" Statements

You can have multiple "if" statements within an "if" statement, as shown in the example below:

x = 110

if x > 50:
    print ("Greater than 50, ")
if x > 90:
    print ("and greater than 100")
else:
    print ("Not greater than 100")

"Pass" statements

In Python, if you ever need to execute "if" statements without any content, you must incorporate a "pass" statement to avoid triggering any error. Here is an example to further your understanding of this concept.

x = 20

y = 55

if y > x

    pass

EXERCISE – Write the code to check if X = 69 is greater than Y = 79, the output should read "X is greater than Y." If the first condition is not true, then check if X is equal to Y, the output should read "X and Y are equal" otherwise the output should read "Y is greater than X."

USE YOUR DISCRETION HERE AND WRITE YOUR CODE FIRST

Now, check your code against the correct code below:

X = 69

Y = 79

if X > Y:

print ("X is greater than Y")

elif X == Y:

    print ("X and Y are equal")

else:

    print ("Y is greater than X")

OUTPUT – "Y is greater than X"

EXERCISE – Write the code to check if x = 69 is greater '50', the output should read "Greater than 50". Then check if x is greater than '60', the output should read "And greater than 60", otherwise the output should read "Not greater than 60".

USE YOUR DISCRETION HERE AND WRITE YOUR CODE FIRST

Now, check your code against the correct code below:

x = 69

if x > 50:

    print ("Greater than 50")

if x > 60:

    print ("And greater than 60")

else:

    print ("Not greater than 60")

OUTPUT –

"Greater than 50"

"And greater than 60"

EXERCISE – Write the code to check if x = 9 is greater than y = 19 as well as if z = 25 is greater than x. The output should read if one or both the conditions are true.

USE YOUR DISCRETION HERE AND WRITE YOUR CODE FIRST

Now, check your code against the correct code below:

x = 9

y = 19

z = 25

if x > y and z > x :

　　　　print ("Both the conditions are True")

OUTPUT – "Both the conditions are True"

EXERCISE – Write the code to check if x = 45 is less than y = 459 or z = 1459 is less than x. The output should read if one or both the conditions are true.

Now, check your code against the correct code below:

```
x = 45
y = 459
z = 1459
if x < y and z < x :
        print ("At least one of the conditions is True")
```

OUTPUT – "At least one of the conditions is True"

Python "While" Loop

Python allows the usage of one of its standard loop commands i.e. "while" loop for execution of a block of statements, given that the initial condition holds true.

Here is the syntax for "while" loop statements:

```
p = num1
while p < num2:
        print (p)
        p += 1
```

In the syntax above, to prevent the loop from continuing with no end, the variable (p) was limited by setting to an increment. It is a pre-requisite for the "while" loop to index the variable in the statement.

"break" statements

These statements allow exiting from the "while" loop, even if the set condition holds true. In the example below, the variable will exit the loop when it reaches 4:

```
p = 2
while p < 7:
        print (p)
        if p == 4
            break
        p += 2
```

OUTPUT –

2

3

4

"continue" statements

These statements allow the system to stop the execution of the current condition and move to the next iteration of the loop. In the example below, system will continue the execution of the subsequent command if the variable equals 2:

```
p = 1
while p < 5:
        p += 1
        if p == 2:
            continue
        print (p)
```

OUTPUT –

1

3

4

5

(Note - The number 2 is missing from the result above)

"else" statement

The "else" statement allows you to execute a set of code after the "while" condition doesn't hold true any longer. The output in the example below will include a statement that the initial condition is no longer true:

```
p = 1
while p < 5:
        print (p)
        p += 1
else:
        print ("p is no longer less than 5")
```

OUTPUT –

1

2

3

4

p is no longer less than 5

EXERCISE – Write the code to print a series of number if x = 1 is smaller than 7.

USE YOUR DISCRETION HERE AND WRITE YOUR CODE FIRST

Now, check your code against the correct code below:

```
x = 1
while x < 7:
```

```
print (x)
x += 1
```

OUTPUT –

1

2

3

4

5

6

EXERCISE – Write the code to print a series of number if x = 1 is smaller than 6 and exit the loop when x is 3.

USE YOUR DISCRETION HERE AND WRITE YOUR CODE FIRST

Now, check your code against the correct code below:

```
x = 1
while x < 6:
        print (x)
        if x == 3
            break
        x += 1
```

OUTPUT –

1

2

3

EXERCISE – Write the code to print a series of number if x = 1 is smaller than 6 and continue to execute the initial condition if x is 3 in a new iteration.

USE YOUR DISCRETION HERE AND WRITE YOUR CODE FIRST

Now, check your code against the correct code below:

```
x = 1
while x < 6:
        x += 1
        if x == 3:
        continue
        print (x)
```

OUTPUT –

1

2

4

5

6

(Note – The number 3 is missing, but the initial condition is executed in a new iteration.)

EXERCISE – Write the code to print a series of number if x = 1 is smaller than 4. Once this condition turns false, print "x is no longer less than 4".

Now, check your code against the correct code below:

```
x = 1
while x < 4:
        print (x)
        x = 1
else:
        print ("x is no longer less than 4")
```

OUTPUT –

1

2

3

x is no longer less than 4

Python "For" Loop

Another one of the Python standard loops is "for" loop, which is used to execute iterations over a series such as string, tuple, set,

124

dictionary, list. The "for" keyword in Python functions like an iterator found in object-oriented programming languages. It allows the execution of a block of statements once for every single item of tuple, set, list, and other series.

Let's look at the example below:

veg = ["tomato," "onion," "potato"]
 for X in veg:
   print (X)

OUTPUT –
tomato
onion
potato

You will notice that in the code above that the variable was not defined. The "for" loop can be executed without setting an index for the variable in the code.

Loops for String

Python strings constitute a series of characters are iterative in nature. So if you wanted to loop through characters of a string, you could simply use the "for" loop as shown in the example below:

for X in "carrot":
print (X)

OUTPUT –

c

a

r

r

o

t

"break" statements

If you want to exit the loop prior to its completion, you can use the "break" statements as shown in the example below:

veg = ["tomato," "onion," "potato," "peas," "carrot"]
for X in veg:
print (X)
if X == "peas":
break
OUTPUT –
tomato

onion

potato

peas

In the example below, the print command was executed prior to the "break" statement and directly affected the output:

veg = ["tomato," "onion," "potato," "peas," "carrot"]
  for X in veg:
    if X == "peas":
      break
    print (X)

OUTPUT –
tomato

onion

potato

"continue" statement

Similar to the "while" loop, the "continue" statements in the "for" loop is used to stop the execution of the current condition and move to the next iteration of the loop. Let's looks at the example below to further understand this concept:

veg = ["tomato," "onion," "potato," "peas," "carrot"]
  for X in veg:

if X == "potato":
      continue
  print (X)

OUTPUT –
tomato
onion
peas
carrot

"range" function

The "range ( )" function can be used to loop through a block of code for a specific number of times. This function will result in a series of number beginning with "0" by default, with regular increments of 1 and ending at a specific number.

Here is an example of this function:

for X in range (5):
  print (X)

OUTPUT –
0
1
2

3

4

Note – The "range ( )" function defaulted to 0 as the first output, and the final value of the range, 5, is excluded from the output.

Let's look at another example with a start and end value of the "range ( )" function:

for X in range (1, 5):
    print (X)

OUTPUT –

1

2

3

4

In the example below, we will specify the increment value, which is set to 1 by default:

for X in range (3, 20, 5):
    print (X)

OUTPUT –

3

8

13

18

"Else" in "For" Loop

You can use the "else" keyword to specify a set of code that need to be executed upon the completion of the loop, as shown in the example below:

for X in range (5):

      print (X)

else:

      print ("The loop was completed")

OUTPUT –

0

1

2

3

4

The loop was completed

"Nested" Loops

When loops are defined within a loop, execution of the inner loop will occur once for each iteration of the outer loop. Let's look at the example below, where we want every single adjective must be printed for each listed vegetable:

adjective = ["green," "leafy," "healthy"]
veg = ["spinach," "kale," "asparagus"]

for X in adjective:
    for Y in veg:
        print (X, Y)

OUTPUT –

green spinach

green kale

green asparagus

leafy spinach

leafy kale

leafy asparagus

healthy spinach

healthy kale

healthy asparagus

"pass" statements

In Python, if you ever need to execute "for" loops without any content, you must incorporate a "pass" statement to avoid triggering any error. Here is an example to further your understanding of this concept.

```
for X in [ 1, 2, 3]
    pass
```

OUTPUT - ......
The empty "for" loop code above would have resulted in an error without the "pass" statement.

EXERCISE – Write the code to loop through a list of colors ("blue," "purple," "red") without defining a variable. Then loop through the characters of the string "blue."

USE YOUR DISCRETION HERE AND WRITE YOUR CODE FIRST

Now, check your code against the correct code below:

```
colors = ["blue," "purple," "red"]
for A in colors:
        print (A)
```

for B in "blue":

    print (B)

OUTPUT –

blue

purple

red

b

l

u

e

EXERCISE – Write the code to loop through a list of colors ("blue," "purple," "red," "white") without defining a variable. Then break the loop at "red," without printing it in the result.

***USE YOUR DISCRETION HERE AND WRITE YOUR CODE

FIRST***

Now, check your code against the correct code below:

colors = ["blue", "purple", "red", "white"]

    for A in colors:

        if A == "red":

        break

        print (A)

OUTPUT –

blue

purple

EXERCISE – Write the code to loop through a range of numbers starting with 5 and ending with 30. Make sure to define the increments at 6.

USE YOUR DISCRETION HERE AND WRITE YOUR CODE FIRST

Now, check your code against the correct code below:

for X in range (5, 30, 6):
        print (X)

OUTPUT –

5

11

16

22

28

EXERCISE – Write the code to loop phones ("iPhone," "Samsung," "Google"), and loop that with colors ("black," "white," "gold") using nested loops.

***USE YOUR DISCRETION HERE AND WRITE YOUR CODE
FIRST***

Now, check your code against the correct code below:

colors = ["black," "white," "gold"]
phones = ["iPhone," "Samsung," "Google"]

for X in colors:
    for Y in phones:
    print (X, Y)

OUTPUT –
black iPhone
black Samsung
black Google
white iPhone
white Samsung
white Google
gold iPhone
gold Samsung
gold Google

Chapter 3: Data Analysis and Machine Learning with Python

In 2001, Gartner defined Big data as "Data that contains greater variety arriving in increasing volumes and with ever-higher velocity." This led to the formulation of the "three V's." Big data refers to an avalanche of structured and unstructured data that is endlessly flooding and from a variety of endless data sources. These data sets are too large to be analyzed with traditional analytical tools and technologies but have a plethora of valuable insights hiding underneath.

The "Vs" of Big data

Volume – To be classified as big data, the volume of the given data set must be substantially larger than traditional data sets. These data sets are primarily composed of unstructured data with limited structured and semi structured data. The unstructured data or the data with unknown value can be collected from input sources such as webpages, search history, mobile applications, and social media platforms. The size and customer base of the company is usually proportional to the volume of the data acquired by the company.

Velocity – The speed at which data can be gathered and acted upon the first to the velocity of big data. Companies are increasingly using combination of on-premise and cloud-based servers to increase the speed of their data collection. The modern-day "Smart Products and Devices" require real-time access to consumer data, in order to be able to provide them a more engaging and enhanced user experience.

Variety – Traditionally a data set would contain majority of structured data with low volume of unstructured and semi-structured data, but the advent of big data has given rise to new unstructured data types such as video, text, audio that require sophisticated tools and technologies to clean and process these data types to extract meaningful insights from them.

Veracity – Another "V" that must be considered for big data analysis is veracity. This refers to the "trustworthiness or the quality" of the data. For example, social media platforms like Facebook and Twitter with blogs and posts containing hashtags, acronyms and all kinds of typing errors can significantly reduce the reliability and accuracy of the data sets.

Value – Data has evolved as a currency of its own with intrinsic value. Just like traditional monetary currencies, the ultimate value of the big data is directly proportional to the insight gathered from it.

History of Big Data

The origin of large volumes of data can be traced back to the 1960s and 1970s when the Third Industrial Revolution had just started to kick in, and the development of relational databases had begun along with construction of data centers. But the concept of big data has recently taken center stage primarily since the availability of free search engines like Google and Yahoo, free online entertainment services like YouTube and social media platforms like Facebook. In 2005, businesses started to recognize the incredible amount of user data being generated through these platforms and services, and in the same year and open-source framework called "Hadoop," was developed to gather and analyze these large data dumps available to the companies. During the same period non-relational or distributed database called "NoSQL," started to gain popularity due to its ability to store and extract unstructured data. "Hadoop" made it possible for the companies to work with big data with high ease and at a relatively low cost.

Today with the rise of cutting edge technology, not only humans but machines also generating data. The smart device technologies like "Internet of things" (IoT) and "Internet of systems" (IoS) have skyrocketed the volume of big data. Our everyday household objects and smart devices are connected to the Internet and able to track and record our usage patterns as well as our interactions with these products and feeds all this data directly into the big data. The advent of machine learning technology has further increased the volume of data generated on a daily basis. It is estimated that by 2020, "1.7 MB of data will be generated per second per person." As the big data will continue to grow, it usability still has many horizons to cross.

Importance of big data

To gain reliable and trustworthy information from a data set, it is very important to have a complete data set which has been made possible with the use of big data technology. The more data we have, the more information and details can be extracted out of it. To gain a 360 view of a problem and its underlying solutions, the future of big data is very promising. Here are some examples of the use of big data:

Product development – Large and small e-commerce businesses are increasingly relying upon big data to understand customer demands and expectations. Companies can develop predictive models to launch new products and services by using primary characteristics of their past and existing products and services and generating a model describing the relationship of those characteristics with commercial success of those products and services. For example, a leading fast manufacturing commercial goods company Procter & Gamble extensively uses big data gathered from the social media websites, test markets and focus groups in preparation for their new product launch.

Predictive maintenance – In order to besides leave project potential mechanical and equipment failures, a large volume of unstructured data such as error messages, log entries, and normal temperature of the machine must be analyzed along with available structured data such as make and model of the equipment and year of manufacturing. By analyzing this big data set using the required analytical tools, companies can extend the shelf life of their equipment by preparing for scheduled maintenance ahead of time and predicting future occurrences of potential mechanical failures.

Customer experience – The smart customer is aware of all of the technological advancements and is loyal only to the most engaging and enhanced user experience available. This has triggered a race among the companies to provide unique customer experiences analyzing the data gathered from customers' interactions with the company's products and services. Providing personalized recommendations and offers to reduce customer churn rate and effectively kind words prospective leads into paying customers.

Fraud and compliance – Big data helps in identifying the data patterns and assessing historical trends from previous fraudulent transactions to effectively detect and prevent potentially fraudulent transactions. Banks, financial institutions, and online payment services like PayPal are constantly monitoring and gathering customer transaction data in an effort to prevent fraud.

Operational efficiency – With the help of big data predictive analysis. companies can learn and anticipate future demand and product trends by analyzing production capacity, customer feedback, and data pertaining to top-selling items and product Will result in to improve decision-making and produce products that are in line with the current market trends.

Machine learning – For a machine to be able to learn and train on its own it requires humongous volume of data, i.e. big data. A solid training set containing structured, semi-structured and unstructured data will help the machine to develop a multidimensional view of the real world and the problem it is engineered to resolve. (Details on machine learning will be provided later in this book.)

Drive innovation – By studying and understanding the relationships between humans and their electronic devices as well as the manufacturers of these devices, companies can develop improved and innovative products by examining current product trends and meeting customer expectations.

"The importance of big data doesn't revolve around how much data you have, but what you do with it. You can take data from any source and analyze it to find answers that enable 1) cost reductions, 2) time reductions, 3) new product development and optimized offerings, and 4) smart decision making."

- SAS

The functioning of big data

There are three important actions required to gain insights from big data:

Integration – The traditional data integration methods such as ETL (Extract, Transform, Load) are incapable of collating data from a wide variety of unrelated sources and applications that are you at the heart of big data. Advanced tools and technologies are required to analyze big data sets that are exponentially larger than traditional data sets. By integrating big data from these disparate sources, companies are able to analyze and extract valuable insight to grow and maintain their businesses.

Management – Big data management can be defined as "the organization, administration, and governance of large volumes of both structured and unstructured data." Big data requires efficient and cheap storage, which can be accomplished using servers that are on-premise, cloud-based or a combination of both. Companies are able to seamlessly access required data from anywhere across the world and then processing this is data using required processing engines on as-needed basis. The goal is to make sure the quality of the data is high-level and can be accessed easily by required tools and applications. Big data gathered from all kinds of Dale sources including social media platforms, search engine history and call logs. The big data usually contains large sets of unstructured data and semi-structured data, which are stored in a variety of formats. To be able to process and store this complicated data, companies require more powerful and advanced data management software beyond the traditional relational databases and data warehouse platforms.

New platforms are available in the market that are capable of combining big data with the traditional data warehouse systems in a "logical data warehousing architecture." As part of this effort, companies are required to make decisions on what data must be secured for regulatory purposes and compliance, what data must be kept for future analytical purposes, and what data has no future use and can be disposed of. This process is called "data classification," which allows rapid and efficient analysis of subset of data to be included in immediate decision-making process of the company.

Analysis – Once the big data has been collected and is easily accessible, it can be analyzed using advanced analytical tools and technologies. This analysis will provide valuable insight and actionable information. Big data can be explored to make new discoveries and develop data models using artificial intelligence and machine learning algorithms.

Big Data Analytics

The terms of big data and big data analytics are often used interchangeably, going to the fact that the inherent purpose of big data is to be analyzed. "Big data analytics" can be defined as a set of qualitative and quantitative methods that can be employed to examine large amounts of unstructured, structured, and semi-structured data to discover data patterns and valuable hidden insights. Big data analytics is the science of analyzing big data to collect metrics, key performance indicators, and Data trends that can be easily lost in the flood of raw data, buy using machine learning algorithms and automated analytical techniques. The different steps involved in "big data analysis" are:

Gathering Data Requirements – It is important to understand what information or data needs to be gathered to meet the business objective and goals. Data organization is also very critical for efficient and accurate data analysis. Some of the categories in which the data can be organized are gender, age, demographics, location, ethnicity, and income. A decision must also be made on the required data types (qualitative and quantitative) and data values (can be numerical or alphanumerical) to be used for the analysis.

Gathering Data – Raw data can be collected from disparate sources such as social media platforms, computers, cameras, other software applications, company websites, and even third-party data providers. The big data analysis inherently requires large volumes of data, majority of which is unstructured with a limited amount of structured and semi structured data. Data organization and categorization – Depending on the company's infrastructure Data organization could be done on a simple Excel spreadsheet or using and man tools and applications that are capable of processing statistical data. Data must be organized and categorized based on data requirements collected in step one of the big data analysis process.

Cleaning the data – To perform the big data analysis sufficiently and rapidly it is very important to make sure the data set is void of any redundancy and errors. Only a complete data set fulfilling the Data requirements must be proceeded to the final analysis step. Preprocessing of data is required to make sure the only high-quality data is being analyzed, and company resources are being put to good use.

"Big data is high-volume, and high-velocity and/or high-variety information assets that demand cost-effective,

innovative forms of information processing that enable
enhanced insight, decision making, and process automation."
- Gartner

Analyzing the data – Depending on the insight that is expected to be achieved by the completion of the analysis, any of the following four different types of big data analytics approach can be adopted:

Predictive analysis – This type of analysis is done to generate forecasts and predictions for future plans of the company. By the completion of predictive analysis on the company's big data, the future state of the company can be more precisely predicted and derived from the current state of the company. The business executives are keenly interested in this analysis to make sure the company day-to-day operations are in line with the future vision of the company. For example, to deploy advanced analytical tools and applications in the sales division of a company, the first step is to analyze the leading source of data. Once believes source analysis has been completed, the type and number of communication channels for the sales team must be analyzed. This is followed by the use of machine learning algorithms on customer data to gain insight into how the existing customer base is interacting with company's products or services. This predictive analysis will conclude with deployment of artificial intelligence-based tools to skyrocket the company's sales.

Prescriptive analysis – Analysis that is carried out by primarily focusing on the business rules and recommendations to generate selective analytical path as prescribed by the industry standards to boost company performance. The goal of this analysis is to understand the intricacies of various departments of the organization and what measures should be taken by the company to be able to gain insights from its customer data by using prescribed analytical pathway. This allows the company to embrace domain specificity and conciseness by providing sharp focus on it's existing and future big data analytics process.

Descriptive analysis – All the incoming data received and stored by the company can be analyzed to produce insightful descriptions on the basis of the results obtained. The goal of this analysis is to identify data patterns and current market trends that can be adopted by the company to grow their business. For example, credit card companies often require risk assessment results on all prospective customers to be able to make predictions on the likelihood of the customer failing to make their credit payments and make a decision whether the customer should be approved for the credit or not. This risk assessment it's primarily based on the customer's credit history but also takes into account other influencing factors, including remarks from other financial institutions that the customer had approached for credit, customer income, and financial performance as well as their digital footprint and social media profile.

Diagnostic analysis – As the name suggests this type of analysis is done to diagnose or understand why a certain event unfolded and how that event can be prevented from occurring in future or replicated if needed. For example, web marketing strategies and campaigns often employ social media platforms to get publicity and increase their goodwill. Not all campaigns are as successful as expected; therefore, learning from failed campaigns is just as important, if not more. Companies can run diagnostic analysis on their campaign by collecting data pertaining to the mentions on the social media of the campaign, number of campaign page views, the average amount of time spent on the campaign page by an individual, number of social media fans and followers of the campaign, online reviews and other related metrics to understand why the campaign failed and how future campaigns can be made more effective.

The big data analysis can be conducted using one or more of the tools listed below:

- Hadoop – Open source data framework.
- Python – Programming language widely used for machine learning.
- SAS – Advanced analytical tool used primarily for big data analysis.

- Tableau – Artificial intelligence-based tool used primarily for data visualization.
- SQL – Programming language used to extract data from relational databases.
- Splunk – Analytical tool used to categorize machine-generated data
- R-programming – Programming language used primarily for statistical computing.

Machine Learning

Machine Learning can be defined as a subsidiary of Artificial Intelligence technology driven by the hypothesis that machines are capable of learning from data by identifying patterns and making decisions with little to no human assistance. The science of machine learning was birthed as a theory that computers have the potential to self learn specific tasks without needing to be programmed, using a pattern recognition technique. As the machines are exposed to new data the ability to adapt independently is the iterative aspect of machine learning. They can learn from and train themselves with prior computations to generate credible and reproducible decisions and results. Machine learning algorithms have been in use for much longer than one would think, but their enhanced capability to analyze "big data" by automatically applying highly complex and sophisticated mathematical calculations rapidly and repeatedly, has been developed recently.

Now the topic of machine learning is so "hot" that the academia, business world, and the scientific community have their own take on its definition. Here are some of the widely accepted definitions from select highly reputed sources:

- *"Machine learning is the science of getting computers to act without being explicitly programmed."* – Stanford University
- *"The field of Machine Learning seeks to answer the question, how can we build computer systems that automatically improve with experience, and what are the fundamental laws that govern all learning processes?"* – Carnegie Mellon University
- *"Machine learning algorithms can figure out how to perform important tasks by generalizing from examples."* – University of Washington
- *"Machine Learning, at its most basic, is the practice of using algorithms to parse data, learn from it, and then make a determination or prediction about something in the world."* – Nvidia
- *"Machine learning is based on algorithms that can learn from data without relying on rules-based programming."* – McKinsey.

Machine learning allows an analysis of large volumes of data and delivers faster and more accurate results. With proper training, this technology can allow organizations to identify profitable opportunities and business risks. Machine learning, in combination with cognitive technologies and artificial intelligence, tends to be even more effective and accurate in processing massive quantities of data. The machine learning algorithms can be categorized into four:

Supervised machine learning algorithms – These algorithms are capable of applying the lessons from the previous runs to new data set using labeled examples to successfully make predictions for future events. For example, a machine can be programmed with data points labeled as "F" (failed) or "S" (success). The learning algorithm will receive inputs with corresponding correct outputs and run a comparison of its own actual output against the expected or correct, in an attempt to identify errors that can be fixed to make the model more efficient and accurate. With sufficient training the algorithms are capable of providing 'targets' for any new data input through methods like regression, classification, prediction, and ingredient boosting. The analysis starts from a known training data set, and the machine learning algorithm then produces an "inferred function" to make future predictions pertaining to the output values. For example, supervised learning algorithm based system is smart enough to anticipate and detect the likelihood of fraudulent credit card transactions being processed.

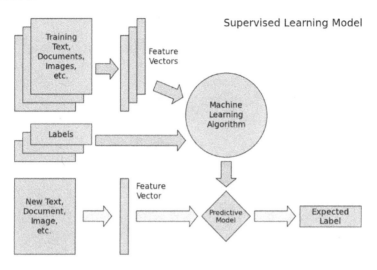

Unsupervised machine learning algorithms – These algorithms are used in the absence of classified and labeled training data sources. According to SAS, "Unsupervised Learning algorithms are used to study ways in which the system can infer a function to describe a hidden structure from unlabeled data, i.e. to explore the data and identify some structure within." Similar to the supervised learning algorithms, these algorithms are able to explore the data and draw inferences from data sets, but cannot figure out the right output. For example, identification of individuals with similar shopping attributes, who can be segmented together and targeted with similar marketing campaigns. These algorithms are widely used to identify data outliers, provide product recommendations, and segment text topics using techniques like "singular value decomposition," "self-organizing maps," and "k-means clustering."

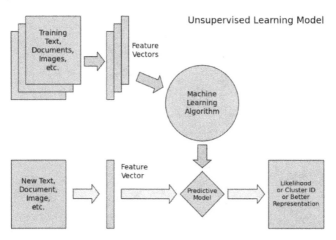

Semi-supervised machine learning algorithms – As the name indicates, these algorithms fall somewhere in between supervised and unsupervised learning and are capable of using labeled as well as unlabeled data as training sources. A typical training set would include a majority of the unlabeled data with a limited volume of the labeled data. The systems running on semi-supervised learning algorithms with methods such as prediction, regression, and classification are able to significantly improve their learning accuracy. In situations where the acquired labeled data requires relevant and skilled resources for the machine to be able to train or learn from it, the semi-supervised learning algorithms are best suited. For example, identification of individual faces on a web camera.

Reinforcement Machine learning algorithms – These algorithms are capable of interacting with their environment by producing actions and discovering errors or rewards. The primary characteristics of reinforcement learning are "trial and error research method and delayed reward." With the use of these algorithms machine can maximize its performance by automatically determining the ideal behavior within a specific context. The reinforcement signal is simply a reward feedback that is required by the machine or software agents to learn which actions yield fastest and accurate results. These algorithms are frequently used in robotics, gaming, and navigation.

Basic concepts of machine learning

The biggest draw of machine learning is the engineered capacity of the system to learn programs from the data automatically instead of manually constructing the program for the machine. Over the last decade the use of machine learning algorithms expanded from computer science to the industrial world. Machine learning algorithms are capable of generalizing tasks to execute them iteratively. The process of developing specific programs for specific tasks costs a lot of time and money, but occasionally it's just impossible to achieve. On the other hand, ML programming is often feasible and tends to be much more cost-effective. The use of machine learning in tackling ambitious issues of widespread importance, such as global warming and depleting underground water levels is promising with massive collection of relevant data.

"A breakthrough in machine learning would be worth ten Microsoft."
– Bill Gates

A number of types of machine learning exist today, but the concept of machine learning largely boils down to three components "representation," "evaluation" and "optimization." Here are some of the standard concepts that are applicable to all of them:

Representation

Machine learning models are incapable of directly hearing, seeing, or sensing input examples. Therefore, a data representation is required to supply the model with a useful vantage point into the key qualities of the data. To be able to successfully train a machine learning model selection of key features that best represent the data is very important. "Representation" simply refers to the act of "representing" data points to computer in a language that it understands using a set of classifiers. A classifier can be defined as "a system that inputs a vector of discrete and or continuous feature values and outputs a single discrete value called class." For a model to learn from the represented data the training data set or the "hypothesis space" must contain desired classifier that you want the models to be trained on. Any classifiers that are external to the hypothesis space cannot be learned by the model.

The data features used to represent the input are very critical to the machine learning process. The data features are so important to the development of desired machine learning model that it can easily be the difference between successful and failed machine learning projects. A training data set containing multiple independent features that are well correlated with the class can make the machine learning much smoother. On the other hand, class containing complex features may not be easy to learn from for the machine. This often requires the raw data to be processed so that desired features can be constructed from it, to be leveraged for the ML model. The process of deriving features from raw data tends to be the most time consuming and laborious part the ML project. It is also considered the most creative and interesting part of the project where intuition and trial and error play just as important role as the technical requirements.

The process of ML is not a one-shot process of developing a training data set and executing it instead it is an iterative process that requires analysis of the post-run output, followed by modification of the training data set and then repeating the whole process all over again. Another reason for the extensive time and effort required to engineer the training data set is domain specificity. Training data set for an e-commerce platform to generate predictions based on consumer behavior analysis will be very different from the training data set required to develop a self-driving car. However, the actual machine learning process remains largely the same across industrial domains. No wonder, a lot of research is being done to automate the feature engineering process.

Evaluation

Essentially the process of judging multiple hypotheses or models to choose one model over another is referred to as an evaluation. To be able to differentiate between useful classifiers from the vague ones an "evaluation function" is required. The evaluation function is also called as "objective," "utility" or "scoring" function. The machine-learning algorithm has its own internal evaluation function which tends to be different from the external evaluation function used by the researchers to optimize the classifier. Usually the evaluation function is defined prior to the selection of the data representation tool as the first step of the project. For example, the machine learning model for self-driving car has the feature for identification of pedestrians in its vicinity at near-zero false negatives and a low false-positive as an evaluation function and the pre-existing condition that needs to be "represented" using applicable data features.

Optimization

The process of searching the space of presented models to achieve better evaluations or highest-scoring classifier is called "optimization." For algorithms with more than one optimum classifier, the selection of optimization techniques is very critical in determination of the classifier produced and to achieve a more efficient learning model. A variety of off-the-shelf optimizers are available in the market to kick start new machine learning models before eventually replacing them with custom-designed optimizers.

Table 1. The three components of learning algorithms.

Representation	Evaluation	Optimization
Instances	Accuracy/Error rate	Combinatorial optimization
K-nearest neighbor	Precision and recall	Greedy search
Support vector machines	Squared error	Beam search
Hyperplanes	Likelihood	Branch-and-bound
Naïve Bayes	Posterior probability	Continuous optimization
Logistic regression	Information gain	Unconstrained
Decision trees	K-L divergence	Gradient descent
Sets of rules	Cost/Utility	Conjugate gradient
Propositional rules	Margin	Quasi-Newton methods
Logic programs		Constrained
Neural networks		Linear programming
Graphical models		Quadratic programming
Bayesian networks		
Conditional random fields		

Machine Learning in Practice

The complete process of machine learning is much more
extensive than just the development and application of machine
learning algorithms and can be divided into steps below:

1. Define the goals of the project, taking into careful
   consideration all the prior knowledge and domain
   expertise available. Goals can easily become ambiguous
   since there are always additional things you want to
   achieve than practically possible to implement.

2. The data pre-processing and cleaning must result in a
   high-quality data set. This is the most critical and time-
   consuming step of the whole project. The larger the
   volume of data, the more noise it brings to the training
   data set, which must be eradicated before feeding to the
   learner system.

3. Selection of appropriate learning model to meet the
   requirements of your project. This process tends to be
   rather simple, given the variety of types of data models
   available in the market.

4. Depending on the domain the machine learning model is
   applied to, the results may or may not require a clear
   understanding of the model by human experts as long as
   the model can successfully deliver desired results.

5. The final step is to consolidate and deploy the knowledge or information gathered from the model to be used on an industrial level.
6. The whole cycle from step 1 to 5 listed above is iteratively repeated until a result that can be used in practice is achieved.

Machine Learning Libraries

Machine learning libraries are sensitive routines and functions that are written in any given language. Software developers require a robust set of libraries to perform complex tasks without needing to rewrite multiple lines of code. Machine learning is largely based on mathematical optimization, probability, and statistics.

Python is the language of choice in the field of machine learning credited to consistent development time and flexibility. It is well suited to develop sophisticated models and production engines that can be directly plugged into production systems. One of its greatest assets being an extensive set of libraries that can help researchers who are less equipped with developer knowledge to easily execute machine learning.

"Scikit-Learn" has evolved as the gold standard for machine learning using Python, offering a wide variety of "supervised" and "unsupervised" ML algorithms. It is touted as one of the most user-friendly and cleanest machine learning libraries to date. For example, decision trees, clustering, linear and logistics regressions, and K-means. Scikit-learn uses couple of basic Python libraries: NumPy and SciPy and adds a set of algorithms for data mining tasks, including classification, regression, and clustering. It is also capable of implementing tasks like feature selection, transforming data and ensemble methods in only a few lines.

In 2007, David Cournapeau developed the foundational code of "Scikit-Learn" as part of a "Summer of code" project for "Google." Scikit-learn has become one of Python's most famous open-source machine learning libraries since its launch in 2007. But it wasn't until 2010 that Scikit-Learn was released for public use. Scikit-Learn is an open-sourced, and BSD licensed, data mining and data analysis tool used to develop supervise and unsupervised machine learning algorithms build on Python. Scikit-learn offers various ML algorithms such as "classification," "regression," "dimensionality reduction," and "clustering." It also offers modules for feature extraction, data processing, and model evaluation.

Designed as an extension to the "SciPy" library, Scikit-Learn is based on "NumPy" and "matplotlib," the most popular Python libraries. NumPy expands Python to support efficient operations on big arrays and multidimensional matrices. Matplotlib offers visualization tools and science computing modules are provided by SciPy. For scholarly studies, Scikit-Learn is popular because it has a well-documented, easy-to-use and flexible API. Developers are able to utilize Scikit-Learn for their experiments with various algorithms by only altering a few lines of the code. Scikit-Learn also provides a variety of training datasets, enabling developers to focus on algorithms instead of data collection and cleaning. Many of the algorithms of Scikit-Learn are quick and scalable to all but huge datasets. Scikit-learn is known for its reliability, and automated tests are available for much of the library. Scikit-learn is extremely popular with beginners in machine learning to start implementing simple algorithms.

Prerequisites for application of Scikit-Learn library

The Scikit-Learn library is based on the SciPy (Scientific Python), which needs to be installed before using SciKit-Learn. This stack involves the following:

NumPy (Base n-dimensional array package)
"NumPy" is the basic package with Python to perform scientific computations. It includes, among other things: "a powerful N-dimensional array object; sophisticated (broadcasting) functions; tools for integrating C/C++ and Fortran code; useful

linear algebra, Fourier transform, and random number capabilities." NumPy is widely reckoned as effective multi-dimensional container of generic data in addition to its apparent scientific uses. It is possible to define arbitrary data types. This enables NumPy to integrate with a wide variety of databases seamlessly and quickly. The primary objective of NumPy is the homogeneity of multidimensional array. It consists of an element table (generally numbers), all of which are of the same sort and are indicated by tuples of non-negative integers. The dimensions of NumPy are called "axes" and array class is called "ndarray."

Matplotlib (Comprehensive 2D/3D plotting)

"Matplotlib" is a 2-dimensional graphic generation library from Python that produces high-quality numbers across a range of hardcopy formats and interactive environments. The "Python script," the "Python," "IPython shells," the "Jupyter notebook," the web app servers, and select user interface toolkits can be used with matplottib. Matplotlib attempts to further simplify easy tasks and make difficult tasks feasible. With only a few lines of code, you can produce tracks, histograms, scatter plots, bar graphs, error graphs, etc.

A MATLAB-like interface is provided for easy plotting of the Pyplot Module, especially when coupled with IPython. As a power user, you can regulate the entire line styles, fonts properties, and axis properties through an object-oriented interface or through a collection of features similar to the one provided to MATLAB users.

SciPy (Fundamental library for scientific computing)
SciPy is a "collection of mathematical algorithms and convenience functions built on the NumPy extension of Python," capable of adding more impact to interactive Python sessions by offering high-level data manipulation and visualization commands and courses for the user. An interactive Python session with SciPy becomes an environment that rivals data processing and system prototyping technologies, including "MATLAB, IDL, Octave, R-Lab, and SciLab."

Another advantage of developing "SciPy" on Python, is the accessibility of a strong programming language in the development of advanced programs and specific apps. Scientific apps using SciPy benefit from developers around the globe, developing extra modules in countless software landscape niches. Everything produced has been made accessible to the Python programmer, from database subroutines and classes as well as "parallel programming to web." These powerful tools are provided along with the "SciPy" mathematical libraries.

IPython (Enhanced interactive console)

"IPython (Interactive Python)" is an interface or command shell for interactive computing using a variety of programming languages. "IPython" was initially created exclusively for Python, which supports introspection, rich media, shell syntax, tab completion, and history. Some of the functionalities provided by IPython include: "interactive shells (terminal and Qt-based); browser-based notebook interface with code, text, math, inline plots and other media support; support for interactive data visualization and use of GUI tool kits; flexible interpreters that can be embedded to load into your own projects; tools for parallel computing".

SymPy (Symbolic mathematics)

Developed by Ondřej Čertík and Aaron Meurer, SymPy is "an open-source Python library for symbolic computation." It offers algebra computing abilities to other apps, as a stand-alone app and/or as a library as well as live on the internet applications with "SymPy Live" or "SymPy Gamma." "SymPy" is easy to install and test, owing to the fact that it is completely developed in Python boasting limited dependencies. SymPy involves characteristics ranging from calculus, algebra, discrete mathematics, and quantum physics to fundamental symbolic arithmetic. The outcome of the computations can be formatted as "LaTeX" code. In combination with a straightforward, expandable codebase in a widespread programming language, the ease of access provided by SymPy makes it a computer algebra system with comparatively low entry barrier.

Pandas (Data structures and analysis)

Pandas provide highly intuitive and user-friendly high-level data structures. Pandas has achieved popularity in the machine learning algorithm developer community, with built-in techniques for data aggregation, grouping, and filtering as well as results of time series analysis. The Pandas library has two primary structures: one-dimensional "Series" and two-dimensional "Data Frames."

Seaborn (data visualization)

Seaborn is derived from the Matplotlib Library and an extremely popular visualization library. It is a high-level library that can generate specific kinds of graph including heat maps, time series, and violin plots.

Installing Scikit-Learn

The latest version of Scikit-Learn can be found on "Scikit-Learn.org" and requires "Python (version >= 3.5); NumPy (version >= 1.11.0); SciPy (version >= 0.17.0); joblib (version >= 0.11)". The plotting capabilities or functions of Scikit-learn start with "plot_" and require "Matplotlib (version >= 1.5.1)". Certain

Scikit-Learn examples may need additional applications: "Scikit-Image (version >= 0.12.3), Pandas (version >= 0.18.0)".

With the prior installation of "NumPy" and "SciPy," the best method of installing Scikit-Learn is using "pip: pip install -U scikit-learn" or "conda: conda install scikit-learn."

One must make sure that "binary wheels" are utilized when using pip and that "NumPy" and "SciPy" have not been recompiled from source, which may occur with the use of specific OS and hardware settings (for example, "Linux on a Raspberry Pi"). Developing "NumPy" and "SciPy" from source tends to be complicated (particularly on Windows). Therefore, they need to be set up carefully, making sure optimized execution of linear algebra routines is achievable.

Application of machine learning using Scikit-Learn library

To understand how Scikit-Learn library is used in the development of machine learning algorithm, let us use the "Sales_Win_Loss data set from IBM's Watson repository" containing data obtained from sales campaign of a wholesale supplier of automotive parts. We will build a machine learning model to predict which sales campaign will be a winner and which will incur loss.

The data set can be imported using Pandas and explored using Pandas techniques such as "head(), tail(), and dtypes()." The plotting techniques from "Seaborn" will be used to visualize the data. To process the data Scikit-Learn's "preprocessing.LabelEncoder()" will be used and "train_test_split()" to divide the data set into training subset and testing subset.

To generate predictions from our data set, three different algorithms will be used, namely, "Linear Support Vector Classification and K-nearest neighbors classifier." To compare the performances of these algorithms Scikit-Learn library technique "accuracy_score" will be used. The performance score of the models can be visualized using Scikit-Learn and "Yellowbrick" visualization.

Importing the data set

To import the "Sales_Win_Loss data set from IBM's Watson repository," first step is importing the "Pandas" module using *"import pandas as pd."*

Then we leverage a variable url as *"https://community.watsonanalytics.com/wp content/uploads/2015/04/WA_Fn-UseC_-Sales-Win-Loss.csv"* to store the URL from which the data set will be downloaded.

Now, *"read_csv() as sales_data = pd.read_csv(url)"* technique
will be used to read the above "csv or comma-separated values"
file, which is supplied by the Pandas module. The csv file will
then be converted into a Pandas data framework, with the result
in variable as *"sales_data,"* where the framework will be stored.

For new 'Pandas' users, the *"pd.read csv()"* technique in the
code mentioned above will generate a tabular data structure
called "data framework", where an index for each row is
contained in the first column, and the label / name for each
column in the first row are the initial column names acquired
from the data set. In the above code snippet, the *"sales data"*
variable results in a table depicted in the picture below.

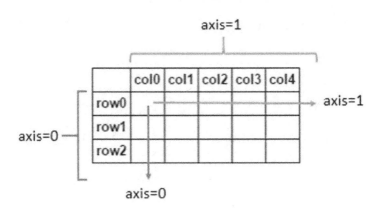

In the diagram above, the "row0, row1, row2" represents
individual record index, and the "col0, col1, col2" represent the
names for individual columns or features of the data set.

With this step, you have successfully stored a copy of the data set and transformed it into a "Pandas" framework!

Now, using the *"head() as Sales_data.head()"* technique, the records from the data framework can be displayed as shown below to get a "feel" of the information contained in the data set.

	opportunity number	supplies subgroup	supplies group	region	route to market	elapsed days in sales stage	opportunity result
0	1641984	Exterior Accessories	Car Accessories	Northwest	Fields Sales	76	Won
1	1658010	Exterior Accessories	Car Accessories	Pacific	Reseller	63	Loss
2	1674737	Motorcycle Parts	Performance & Non-auto	Pacific	Reseller	24	Won
3	1675224	Shelters & RV	Performance & Non-auto	Midwest	Reseller	16	Loss

Data Exploration

Now that we have our own copy of the data set, which has been transformed into a "Pandas" data frame, we can quickly explore the data to understand what information can tell can be gathered from it and accordingly to plan a course of action.

In any ML project, data exploration tends to be a very critical phase. Even a fast data set exploration can offer us significant information that could be easily missed otherwise, and this

171

information can propose significant questions that we can then attempt to answer using our project.

Some third-party Python libraries will be used here to assist us with the processing of the data so that we can efficiently use this data with the powerful algorithms of Scikit-Learn. The same *"head()"* technique that we used to see some initial records of the imported data set in the earlier section can be used here. As a matter of fact, *"(head)"* is effectively capable of doing much more than displaying data records and customize the "head()" technique to display only a selected records with commands like *"sales_data.head(n=2)"*. This command will selectively display the first 2 records of the data set. At a quick glance it's obvious that columns such as "Supplies Group" and "Region" contain string data, while columns such as "Opportunity Result," "Opportunity Number" etc. are comprised of integer values. It can also be seen that there are unique identifiers for each record in the' Opportunity Number' column.

Similarly, to display select records from the bottom of the table, the *"tail() as sales_data.tail()"* can be used.

To view the different data types available in the data set, the Pandas technique *"dtypes() as sales_data.dtypes"* can be used. With this information, the data columns available in the data framework can be listed with their respective data types. We can figure out, for example, that the column "Supplies Subgroup" is an "object" data type and that the column "Client Size By Revenue" is an "integer data type." So, we have an understanding of columns that either contain integer values or string data.

Data Visualization

At this point, we are through with basic data exploration steps, so we will not attempt to build some appealing plots to portray the information visually and discover other concealed narratives from our data set.

Of all the available Python libraries providing data visualization features, "Seaborn" is one of the best available options, so we will be using the same. Make sure that python plots module provided by "Seaborn" has been installed on your system and ready to be used. Now follow the steps below generate desired plot for the data set:

Step 1 - Import the "Seaborn" module with command *"import seaborn as sns"*.
Step 2 - Import the "Matplotlib" module with command *"import matplotlib.pyplot as plt"*.
Step 3 - To set the "background colour" of the plot as white, use command *"sns.set(style="whitegrid", color_codes=True)"*.

Step 4 - To set the "plot size" for all plots, use command *"sns.set(rc={'figure.figsize':(11.7,8.27)})"*.

Step 5 – To generate a "countplot", use command *"sns.countplot('Route To Market',data=sales_data,hue = 'Opportunity Result')"*.

Step 6 – To remove the top and bottom margins, use command *"sns.despine(offset=10, trim=True)"*.

Step 7 – To display the plot, , use command *"plotplt.show()"*.

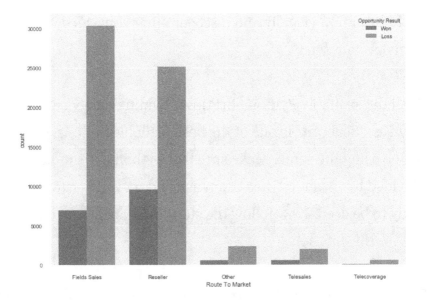

Quick recap - The "Seaborn" and "Matplotlib" modules were imported first. Then the *"set()"* technique was used to define the distinct characteristics for our plot, such as plot style and color. The background of the plot was defined to be white using the code snippet *"sns.set(style= "whitegrid," color codes= True)."*

Then the plot size was define using command *"sns.set(rc={'figure.figsize':(11.7,8.27)})"* that define the size of the plot as "11.7px and 8.27px".

Next the command *"sns.countplot('Route To Market',data= sales data, hue='Opportunity Result')"* was used to generate the plot. The "countplot()" technique enables creation of a count plot, which can expose multiple arguments to customize the count plot according to our requirements. As part of the first *"countplot()"* argument, the X-axis was defined as the column "Route To Market" from the data set. The next argument concerns the source of the data set, which would be "sales_data" data framework we imported earlier. The third argument is the color of the bar graphs that was defined as "blue" for the column labeled "won" and "green" for the column labeled "loss."

Data Pre-processing
By now you should have a clear understanding of what information is available in the data set. From the data exploration step, we established that majority of the columns in our data set are "string data," but "Scikit-Learn" can only process numerical data. Fortunately, the Scikit-Learn library offers us many ways to convert string data into numerical data, for example, *"LabelEncoder()"* technique. To transform categorical labels from the data set such as "won" and "loss" into numerical values, we will use the *"LabelEncoder()"* technique.

175

Let's look at the pictures below to see what we are attempting to accomplish with the *"LabelEncoder()"* technique. The first image contains one column labeled "color" with three records namely, "Red," "Green" and "Blue." Using the *"LabelEncoder()"* technique, the record in the same "color" column can be converted to numerical values, as shown in the second image.

	Color
0	Red
1	Green
2	Blue

	Color
0	1
1	2
2	3

Let's begin the real process of conversion now. Using the *"fit transform()"* technique given by *"LabelEncoder(),"* the labels in the categorical column like "Route To Market" can be encoded and converted to numerical labels comparable to those shown in the diagrams above. The function *"fit transform()"* requires input labels identified by the user and consequently Will result in encoded labels.

To know how the encoding is accomplished, let's go through an example quickly. The code instance below constitutes string data in the form of a list of cities such as ["paris," "paris," "tokyo," "amsterdam"] that will be encoded into something comparable to "[2, 2, 1,3]".

Step 1 - To import the required module, use command *"from sklearn import preprocessing."*

Step 2 – To create the Label encoder object, use command *"le = preprocessing.LabelEncoder()"*.

Step 3 – To convert the categorical columns into numerical values, use command:

"encoded_value = le.fit_transform(["paris", "paris", "tokyo", "amsterdam"])"

"print(encoded_value) [1 1 2 0]"

And there you have it! We just converted our string data labels into numerical values. The first step was importing the preprocessing module that offers the *"LabelEncoder()"* technique. Followed by development of an object representing the *"LabelEncoder()"* type. Then the *"fit_transform()"* function of the object was used to distinguish between distinct classes of the list ["paris," "paris," "tokyo," "amsterdam"] and output the encoded values of *"[1 1 20]"*.

Did you observe that the *"LabelEncoder()"* technique assigned the numerical values to the classes in alphabetical order according to the initial letter of the classes, for example "(a)msterdam" was assigned code "0", "(p)aris" was assigned code "1" and "(t)okyo" was assigned code "2".

Creating Training and Test subsets

To know the interactions between distinct characteristics and how these characteristics influence the target variable, a ML algorithm must be trained on a collection of information. We need to split the complete data set into two subsets to accomplish this. One subset will serve as the training data set, which will be used to train our algorithm to construct machine learning models. The other subset will serve as the test data set, which will be used to test the accuracy of the predictions generate by the machine learning model.

The first phase in this stage is the separation of feature and target variables using the steps below:

Step 1 – To select data excluding select columns, use command *"select columns other than 'Opportunity Number', 'Opportunity Result'cols = [col for col in sales_data.columns if col not in ['Opportunity Number','Opportunity Result']]"*.

Step 2 – To drop these select columns, use command *"dropping the 'Opportunity Number'and 'Opportunity Result' columns*
data = sales_data[cols]".

Step 3 – To assign the Opportunity Result column as "target", use command *"target = sales_data['Opportunity Result'] data.head(n=2)"*.

The "Opportunity Number" column was removed since it just acts as a unique identifier for each record. The "Opportunity Result" contains the predictions we want to generate, so it becomes our "target" variable and can be removed from the data set for this phase. The first line of the above code will select all the columns except "Opportunity Number" and "Opportunity Result" in and assign these columns to a variable "cols." Then using the columns in the "cols" variable a new data framework was developed. This is going to be the "feature set." Next, the column "Opportunity Result" from the *"sales_data"* data frame was used to develop a new data framework called "target."

The second phase in this stage is to separate the date frameworks into training and testing subsets using the steps below. Depending on the data set and desired predictions, it needs to be split into training and testing subset accordingly. For this exercise, we will use 75% of the data as training subset, and rest 25% will be used for the testing subset. We will leverage the *"train_test_split()"* technique in "Scikit-Learn" to separate the data using steps and code as below:

Step 1 – To import required module, use command *"from sklearn.model_selection import train_test_split"*.
Step 2 – To separate the data set, use command *"split data set into train and test setsdata_train, data_test, target_train,*

target_test = train_test_split (data,target, test_size = 0.30, random_state = 10)".

With the code above, the *"train_test_split"* module was first imported, followed by the use of *"train_test_split()"* technique to generate "training subset *(data_train, target_train)"* and "testing subset *(data_test, data_train)."* The *"train_test_split()"* technique's first argument pertains to the features that were divided in the preceding stage; the next argument relates to the target ("Opportunity Result"). The third "test size" argument is the proportion of the data we wish to divide and use as testing subset. We are using 30% for this example, although it can be any amount. The fourth 'random state' argument is used to make sure that the results can be reproduced every time.

Building the Machine Learning Model

The "machine_learning_map" provided by Scikit-Learn is widely used to choose the most appropriate ML algorithm for the data set. For this exercise, we will be using "K-nearest neighbors classifier" algorithms.

K-nearest Neighbors Classifier

The "k-nearest neighbors(k-NN)" algorithm is referred to as "a non-parametric method used for classification and regression in pattern recognition." In cases of classification and regression, "the input consists of the nearest k closest training examples in the feature space." K-NN is form of "instance-based learning" or "lazy learning," in which the function is only locally estimated, and all calculations are delayed until classification. The output is driven by the fact, whether the classification or regression method is used for k-NN:

- "k-nearest neighbors classification" - The "output" is a member of the class. An "object" is classified by its neighbors' plurality vote, assigning the object to the most prevalent class among its nearest "k-neighbors," where "k" denotes a small positive integer. If k= 1, the "object" is simply allocated to the closest neighbor's class.
- "k-nearest neighbors regression" - The output is the object's property value, which is computed as an average of the k-nearest neighbor's values.

A helpful method for both classification and regression can be assigning weights to the neighbors' contributions, to allow closer neighbors to make more contributions in the average, compared to the neighbors located far apart. For instance, a known "weighting scheme" is to assign each neighbor a weight of "$1/d$", where "d" denotes the distance from the neighbor. The neighbors are selected from a set of objects for which the "class" (for "k-NN classification") or the feature value of the "object" (for "k-NN regression") is known.

Here are the steps and code for this algorithm to build our next ML model:

Step 1 – To import required modules, use command *"from sklearn.neighbors import KNeighborsClassifier"* and *"from sklearn.metrics import accuracy_score"*.

Step 2 – To create object of the classifier, use command *"neigh = KNeighborsClassifier(n_neighbors=3)"*.

Step 3 – To train the algorithm, use command *"neigh.fit(data_train, target_train)."*

Step 4 – To generate predictions, use command *"pred = neigh.predict(data_test)"*.

Step 5 – To evaluate accuracy, use command *"print ('KNeighbors accuracy score:,' accuracy_score(target_test, pred))."*

With the code above, the required modules were imported in the first step. We then developed the object *"neigh"* of type "KNeighborsClassifier" with the volume of neighbors as *"n_neighbors=3"*. In the next step, the *"fit()"* technique was used to train the algorithm on the training data set. Next, the model was tested on the testing data set using *"predict()"* technique. Finally, the accuracy score was obtained, which could be *"KNeighbors accuracy score : 0.814550580998"*, for instance.

Now that our preferred algorithms have been introduced, the model with the highest accuracy score can be easily selected. But wouldn't it be great if we had a way to compare the distinct models' efficiency visually? In Scikit-Learn, we can use the "Yellowbrick library," which offers techniques for depicting various scoring techniques visually.

Python Tips and Tricks for Developers

Python was first implemented in 1989 and is regarded as highly user-friendly and simple to learn programming language for entry-level coders and amateurs. It is regarded ideal for individuals newly interested in programming or coding and need to comprehend programming fundamentals. This stems from the fact that Python reads almost the same as English language. Therefore, it requires less time to understand how the language works and focus can be directed in learning the basics of programming.

Python is an interpreted language that supports automatic memory management and object-oriented programming. This extremely intuitive and flexible programming language can be used for coding projects such as machine learning algorithms, web applications, data mining and visualization, game development.

Some of the tips and tricks you can leverage to sharpen up your Python programming skill set are:

In-place swapping of two numbers:

a, b = 101, 201

print (a, b)

a, b = b, a

print (a, b)"

Resulting Output =

101 201

201 101

Reversing a string:

a ="computer"

print ("Reverse is", a [::-1])

Resulting Output =

Reverse is retupmoc.

Creating a single string from multiple list elements:

a = ["this", "is", "learning","with", "passion"]

print (" ".join (a))

Resulting Output =

this is learning with passion

Stacking of comparison operators:

n = 101

result = 1 < n < 201

print (result)

result = 1 > n <= 91

print (result)

Resulting Output =

True

False

Print the file path of the imported modules:

import os;

import socket;

print(os)

print (socket

Resulting Output =

"<module 'os' from '/usr/lib/python3.5/os.py'>

<module 'socket' from '/usr/lib/python3.5/socket.py'>"

Use of enums in Python:

class MyName:

   Chic, For, Chic = range (3)

print (MyName.Chic)

print (MyName.For)

print (MyName.Chic)

Resulting Output =

2

1

2

Result in multiple values from functions:

def x ():

   result in 11, 21, 31, 41

a, b, c, d = x ()

print (a, b, c, d)

Resulting Output =

11 21 31 41

Identify the value with highest frequency:

test = [11, 21, 31, 41, 21, 21, 31, 11, 41, 41, 41]

print (max(set(test), key = test.count))

Resulting Output =

41

Check the memory usage of an object:

```
import sys
x = 1
print (sys.getsizeof (x))
```

Resulting Output =

28

Printing a string N times:

```
n = 2;
a = "ArtificialIntelligence";
print (a * n);
```

Resulting Output =

ArtificialIntelligenceArtificialIntelligenceArtificialIntelligence

Identify anagrams:

```
from collections import Counter
def is_anagram (str1, str2):
    result in Counter(str1) == Counter(str2)
print (is_anagram ('geek', 'eegk'))

print (is_anagram ('geek', 'reek'))
```

Resulting Output =

True

False

Transposing a matrix:

mat = [[11, 21, 31], [41, 51, 61]]

zip (*mat)

Resulting Output =

[(11, 41), (21, 51), (31, 61)]

Print a repeated string without using loops:

print "machine"*3+' '+"learning"*4

Resulting Output =

Machinemachinemachine learninglearninglearninglearning

Measure the code execution time:

import time

startTime = time.time()

"write your code or functions calls"

"write your code or functions calls"

endTime = time.time ()

totalTime = endTime – startTime

print ('Total time required to execute code is=' , totalTime)

Resulting Output =

Total time

Obtain the difference between two lists:

list1 = ['Brian', 'Pepper', 'Kyle', 'Leo', 'Sam']

```
list2 = ['Sam', 'Leo', 'Kyle']
set1 = set(list1)
set2 = set(list2)
list3 = list(set1.symmetric_difference(set2))
print(list3)
```
Resulting Output =

list3 = ['Brian', 'Pepper']

Calculate the memory being used by an object in Python:

```
import sys
list1 = ['Brian', 'Pepper', 'Kyle', 'Leo', 'Sam']
print ("size of list = ", sys.getsizeof(list1))
name = 'pynative.com'
print ('size of name =', sys.getsizeof(name))
```

Resulting Output =

('size of list = ', 112)

('size of name = ', 49)

Removing duplicate items from the list:

```
listNumbers = [20, 22, 24, 26, 28, 28, 20, 30, 24]
print ('Original=' , listNumbers)
listNumbers = list(set(listNumbers))
print ('After removing duplicate= ' , listNumbers)
```
Resulting Output =

'Original= ', [20, 22, 24, 26, 28, 28, 20, 30, 24]

'After removing duplicate= ', [20, 22, 24, 26, 28, 30]

Find if a list contains identical elements:

listOne = [20, 20, 20, 20]

print ('All elements are duplicate in listOne',

listOne.count(listOne[0]) == len(listOne))

listTwo = [20, 20, 20, 50]

print ('All elements are duplicate in listTwo',

listTwo.count(listTwo[0]) == len(listTwo))

Resulting Output =

"'All elements are duplicate in listOne', True"

"'All elements are duplicate in listTwo', False"

Efficiently compare two unordered lists:

from collections import Counter

one = [33, 22, 11, 44, 55]

two = [22, 11, 44, 55, 33]

print ('is two list are b equal', Counter(one) == Counter(two))

Resulting Output =

"'is two list are b equal', True"

Check if list contains all unique elements:

```python
def isUnique(item):
tempSet = set ()
result in not any (i in tempSet or tempSet.add(i) for i in item)
listOne = [123, 345, 456, 23, 567]
print ('All List elements are Unique' , isUnique(listOne))
listTwo = [123, 345, 567, 23, 567]
print ('All List elements are Unique' , isUnique(listTwo))
```

Resulting Output =

"All List elements are Unique True"

"All List elements are Unique False"

Convert Byte into String:

```python
byteVar = b"pynative"
str = str (byteVar.decode ('utf-8'))
print ('Byte to string is', str )
```

Resulting Output =

"Byte to string is pynative"

Merge two dictionaries into a single expression:

```python
currentEmployee = {1: 'Scott', 2: 'Eric', 3:'Kelly'}
 formerEmployee = {2: 'Eric', 4: 'Emma'}
def merge_dicts(dictOne, dictTwo):
dictThree = dictOne.copy()
dictThree.update(dictTwo)
```

result in dictThree

print (merge_dicts (currentEmployee, formerEmployee))

Conclusion

Thank you for making it through to the end of *Learn Python: A Crash Course On Python Programming And How To Start Coding With It. Learn The Basics Of Machine Learning And Data Analysis*, let's hope it was informative and able to provide you with all of the tools you need to achieve your goals whatever they may be.

The next step is to make the best use of your new-found wisdom of Python programming, data analysis, and machine learning that have resulted in the birth of the powerhouse, which is the "Silicon Valley." Companies across the industrial spectrum with an eye on the future are gradually turning into Technology companies under the façade of their intended business model. This book is filled with real-life examples to help you understand the nitty-gritty of the concepts and names and descriptions of multiple tools that you can further explore and selectively implement to make sound choices for development of a desired machine learning model. Now that you have finished reading this book and mastered the use of Scikit-Learn you are all set to start developing your own Python machine learning model using all the open sources readily available and explicitly mentioned in this book for that purpose. You can position yourself to use your deep knowledge and understanding of machine learning technologies obtained from this book to contribute to the growth of any company and land yourself a new high paying and rewarding job!

Finally, if you found this book useful in any way, a review on Amazon is always appreciated!

SQL PROGRAMMING

THE ULTIMATE GUIDE WITH EXERCISES, TIPS AND TRICKS TO LEARN SQL

By Damon Parker

Table of Contents

Introduction

Congratulations on downloading *SQL Programming: The Ultimate Guide with Exercises, Tips, and Tricks to Learn SQL,* and thank you for doing so.

The following chapters will discuss the foundational concepts of the Structured Query Language (SQL) to help you not only learn but master this data analysis language to extract information from the relational database management systems. This book is written to serve as your personal guide so you can efficiently and effectively use SQL to retrieve from and update information on SQL databases and servers, using the MySQL server for reference, which is one of the most widely used interface for relational database management.

The first chapter of this book titled *Introduction to SQL* will provide you an overview of the database management systems as well as different types of database management systems and their advantages. You will be introduced to the SQL language and the five fundamental types of SQL queries. In this chapter, you will learn the thumb rules for building SQL syntax or query. A variety of SQL data types that are a pre-requisite for learning SQL are provided in explicit detail.

In Chapter 2 titled, *Basic SQL Functions*, you will be introduced to the MySQL, which is a free and open-source relational database management system. A step by step walkthrough as well as installation of MySQL on your operating system(s) has been provided so you can easily download and install this free resource on your system. This will allow you to get hands-on practice utilizing all the practice exercises included in this book to master the SQL programming language. You will be learning how to generate a whole new database and subsequently create tables and insert data into those tables on the MySQL server. You will also learn the concept of temporary tables, derived tables and how you can generate a new table from a table already present in the database.

In Chapter 3 titled, *Advanced SQL Functions*, you will be learning about the SQL SELECT statements along with the various Data manipulation clauses such as ORDER BY and WHERE. The key concept of SQL Joins is provided in exquisite detail including different SQL JOIN functions such as INNER JOIN, LEFT JOIN and many more. The SQL Union function will also be explained along with the MySQL UNION and MySQL UNION ALL statements.

In Chapter 4 titled, *SQL Views and Transactions*, the concept of Database View in SQL has been explained, which is simply a virtual table defined using the SQL SELECT statements using the SQL JOIN clause(s). Some of the SQL view related statements explained in this chapter include CREATE VIEW, MERGE, TEMPTABLE, UNDEFINED, Updatable SQL Views, ALTER VIEW and CREATE OR REPLACE VIEW statements. The properties of SQL transactions as well as various SQL transaction statements with controlling clauses such as, START TRANSACTION, COMMIT, ROLLBACK among others are also explained in this chapter.

The last chapter titled, Database Security and Administration, mainly focuses on the user access privileges that are required to securely manage the data on a MySQL server. You will be walked through the entire process of creating new user accounts, updating the user password as well as granting and revoking access privileges to ensure that only permitted users have authorized and required access to the database.

There are plenty of books on this subject on the market, thanks again for choosing this one! Every effort was made to ensure it is full of as much useful information as possible; please enjoy!

Chapter 1: Introduction to SQL

A database could be defined as an organized collection of information or data, which can be stored electronically on a computer system and accessed as needed. A Database Management System (DBMS) can be defined as a program that allows end-user interactions with apps as well as the database for capturing and analyzing the data. It is an integrated computer software package enabling users to communicate with a number of databases and offering access to the information stored on the database. The DBMS offers multiple features that enable big volumes of data to be entered, stored and retrieved as well as offers methods for managing how the data can be organized. Considering this close association, the term database frequently refers to both databases as well as DBMS.

Existing DBMSs provide multiple features to manage and classify a database and its information into four primary functional groups as follows:

- **Data definition**–Definitions that represent the organization of data are created, modified and eliminated.
- **Update**–Inserting, modifying and deleting the actual data.
- **Retrieval**-Provision of data in a form that can be used directly or processed further by other applications. Data

collected may be accessed in the same format as existing in the database or in a different format that can be acquired through alteration or combination of data sets from various databases.

- **Management**–User registration and tracking, data security enforcement, performance tracking, data integrity, competence control, and the recovery of data damaged by a certain event, for example, an accidental glitch in the system.

A database and its DBMS are in accordance with a given model database. The database system can be defined as a collection of the database, DBMS, and database model.

Database servers are physically connected computers that only run DBMS and associated software, holding real databases. Multiprocessor machines with extensive memory and RAID disk arrays utilized for long term storage of the data are called as database servers. If one of the disks fails, RAID can be used to recover the data. In a heavy volume transaction processing setting, hardware DB accelerator linked withsingle or multipledatabases using the high-speed channels are being utilized. Most database applications have DBMS at their core. DBMS may be created with built-in network assistance around a custom multitasking kernel, but contemporary DBMSs typically use a normal operating system to offer the same functionalities.

As DBMS represents an important market, DBMS requirements are often taken into consideration by computers and storage providers for their production plans.

Databases and DBMSs may be grouped by on the basis of following parameters:

- The supported database models, for example, relational or XML databases.
- The variety of computers on they can operate on, for example, a cluster of servers linked to a wireless device.
- The programming language used to query the database, for example, SQL or XQuery.
- The internal engineering drives the efficiency, scalability, resiliency as well as safety of the system.

We will be primarily focusing on relational databases in this book, which pertains to the SQL language. In the beginning of the 1970s, IBM began to work on a prototype model based on the ideas of the computer scientist named EdgarCodd as System R. The first version was introduced in 1974 and 1975 and followed by work on multi-table systems that allowed splitting of the data so as to avoid storage of all the data as a single big slice for individual record. Customers tested subsequent multi-user versions in the late 1970s, after a standardized query language called SQL, was added to the database. Codd's concepts forced IBM to create a real version of "System R,"called as "SQL / DS" and subsequently "Database 2 (DB2)."

The "Oracle database" developed by Larry Ellison, began from a distinct chain on the basis of the work published by IBM on System R. Whilst the implementation of Oracle V1 was finished in 1978, but it was with the release of Oracle Version 2 in 1979 that Ellison succeeded over IBM in entering the market.

For the further development of a new database, Postgres, now referred to as PostgreSQL, Stonebraker had used the INGRES classes. PostgreSQL is widely utilized for worldwide critical apps. The registrations of '.org' and '.info' domain names are primarily using PostgreSQL for data storage and similarly done by various big businesses and financial institutions. The computer programmers at the Uppsala University in Sweden, were also inspired by Codd's work and developed Mimer SQL in the mid-1970s. In 1984, this project was transitioned into an independent company.

In 1976, the entity relationship model was developed and became highly popular for designing databasesas it produced a relatively better-known description compared to the preceding relational model. Subsequently, the structure of the entity-relationship was rebuilt into a data modeling construct, and their distinctions became insignificant.

Relational databases consist of a collection of tables that can be matched to one of the predetermined categories. Every table will have a minimum of one data category in a column and every row will contain some data instances for those categories that have been specifiedin the column. Relational databases have multiple names, such as Relational Database Management Systems (RDBMS) or SQL database. The Relational databases are mainly used in big corporate settings, with the exception of MySQL, which can also be used in web-based data storage.

All relation databases can be utilized for the management of transaction-oriented applications (OLTP). On the other hand, most non-relational databases in the classifications of Document Stores and Column Store, may also be used for OLTP, thus causing confusion between the two. OLTP databases can be considered operational databases, distinguished by regular quick transactions, including data updates, small volumes of data, and simultaneously processing hundreds and thousands of transactions, such as online reservations and banking apps.

Advantages of Database Management System

The DBMScan be described as a software system that is enabling its users in identification, development, maintenance, and regulated access to the data. It allows end customers to generate information in the database as well as to read, edit and delete desired data. It can be viewed as a layer between the information and the programs utilizing that data.

DBMS offers several benefits in comparison to the file-based data management system. Some of these advantages are listed below:

- **Reduction in the redundancy of data** - The file-based DBMScontains a number of files stored in a variety of location on a system and even across multiple systems. Due to this, several copies of the same file can often result in data redundancy. This can be easily avoided in a database since there is only a single database holding all the data and any modifications made to the database are immediately reflected across the entire system. Hence, there is no possibility that duplicate information will be found in the database.
- **Seamless data sharing** - Users can share all existing data with each other found within a database. Different levels of authorizations exist within the database for selective access to the information. Therefore, it is not possible to share the information without following the proper authorization protocols. Multiple remote users can concurrently access the database and share any desired information as needed.

- **Data integrity** - The integrity of data implies that the information in the database is reliable and accurate. The integrity of data is very crucial as a DBMS contains a variety of databases. The information contained in all of these databases is available to all the users across the board. It is therefore essential to make sure that all the databases and customers have correct and coherent data available to them at all times.

- **Data security** - Data security is vital in the creation and maintenance of a database. Only authorized users are allowed to access the database by authenticating their identity using a valid username and password. Unauthorized users cannot, under any conditions, be permitted to access the database, as it infringes upon the data integrity rules.

- **Privacy** - The privacy rule in a database dictates that only authorized users are allowed to access the database on the basis of the predefined privacy constraints of the database. There are multiple database access levels and only permitted data can be viewed by the user. For example, various access limitations on the social networking sites for accounts that a user may want to access.

- **Backup and Recovery** -DBMS is capable of generating automated backup and recovery of the database. As a result, the users are not required to backup data regularly since the DBMS can efficiently handle this. In addition, it restores the database to its preceding state in case of any technical errors or system failure.

- **Data Consistency** - In a database, the consistency of data is guaranteed due to the lack of any redundant data. The entire database contains all data consistently, and all the users accessing the database receive the same data. In addition, modifications to the database are instantly reported to all the users to avoid any inconsistency of the existing data.

Structured Query Language

In the context of relational databases, it is considered a standard user and application program interface. In 1986, SQL was incorporated into the "American National Standards Institute (ANSI)," and in 1987, it was added to the "International Organization for Standardization (ISO)." Since then, the standards are constantly being improved and are endorsed by all mainstream commercial relational DBMSs (with different extents of compliance).

For the relational model, SQL was one of the initial commercial languages, even though it is distinct from the relational structure in certain aspects, according to Codd. For instance, SQL allows an organization to create and update data rows and columns. The relational databases are highly extensible. After the initial database has been created, a new data category can be easily introduced without needing to alter any current apps.

Types of SQL Queries

Database languages are defined as special-purpose languages, that enable execution of one or more of the tasks listed below and often called as sublanguages:

Data definition language (DDL) – It is used to define the types of data including its creation, modification, or elimination as well as the relationships among them.

Data manipulation language (DML) –Only after the database is created and tables have been built using DDL commands, the DML commands can be used to manipulate the data within those tables and databases. The convenience of using DML commands is that they can readily be changed and rolled back if any incorrect modifications to the data or its values have been made. The DML commands used to perform specific tasks are:

- **Insert** – For insertion of new rows in the table.
- **Update**–For modification of the data values contained in the rows of the table.
- **Deletion** – For deletion of selected rows or complete table within the database.

215

- **Lock** – To define the user access to either read only or read and write privilege.
- **Merge** – To merge a couple of rows within a table.

Data control language (DCL) – As the name indicates, the DCL commands pertain to data control problems in a database. DCL commands provide users with unique database access permissions and are also used to define user roles as applicable. There are two DCL commands that are frequently used:

- **Grant** – To give access permissions to the users.
- **Revoke** – To remove the access permission given to the users.

Data query language (DQL) – DQL comprises of a single command that drives data selection in SQL. In conjunction with other SQL clauses, the SELECT command is used for the collection and retrieval of data from databases or tables based on select user-applied criteria. A"**SELECT**" statement is used to search for data and computing derived information from the table and/or database.

Transaction control language (TCL) – As indicated by its name, TCL administers transaction-related issues and problems in a database. They are used to restore modifications made to the original database or confirm them.

Roll back implies the modifications Undo, and Commit means the modifications Apply. The 3 main TCL commands available are:

- **Rollback** – Used to cancel or undo any updates made in the table or database.
- **Commit** – Used to deploy or apply or save any updates made in the table or database.
- **Save point** – Used to temporarily save the data in the table or database.

Database languages are limited to a specific data model as reflected in the examples below:

- **SQL** – It offers functions that allow you to define the data, manipulate the data as well as query the data as a unified language.
- **OQL**–This modeling language standard for objects was developed by the "Object Data Management Group."This language inspired the development of other modern query languages such as JDOQL and EJBQL.
- **XQuery** – This standard query language for XML was introduced by XML database technologies. The relational databases with these capabilities like Oracle and DB2, as well as XML processors.

SQL SYNATX

The picture below depicts the most common syntax (code structure that can be understood by the server) of a SQL query.

Before we jump into the actual SQL commands that you can execute for a hands-on learning experience. Here are some thumb rules that you must memorize first:

1. A semicolon must be used at the end of each command.
2. A keyword must be used at the beginning of the command. You will learn all the keywords as you progress through this book.
3. The case structure of the alphabets is irrelevant to the commands.
4. You must remember the name or title of the tables and databases, used at the time of creation and make sure you always use those specific names for all your commands.

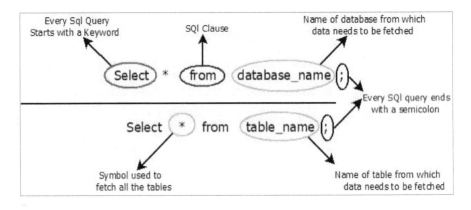

SQL Data Types

Another important concept in learning SQL, is the various data types that are required to define the types of data value to be inserted in specific columns. The commonly used data types are listed in the table below:

DATA TYPE	DESCRIPTION
char(size)	This is used to define a fixed length character string. The size of the data value can be specified using desired number in the parenthesis as shown. Maximum allowed size is 255 characters.
varchar(size)	This is used to define a variable length character string. The size of the data value can be specified using desired number in the parenthesis as shown. Maximum allowed size is 255 characters.
number(size)	This is used to define a numerical value with a specific number in parenthesis. The max number of digits in the column can be specified using desired number in the parenthesis as shown.
date	This is used to define a date value for pertinent column.
number(size,d)	This is used to define a numerical value with a specific number in parenthesis. The max number of digits in the column

	can be specified using desired number in the parenthesis, along with the no. of digits on the right of the decimal, as shown by the alphabet d.

Data Definition Language (DDL)

As the Codasyl database model was introduced, the term data definition language was coined. The concept of DDL required the database scheme to be developed in a syntax that described the record, field, and set of the user data models. Subsequently, DDL was considered a subset of SQL used to declare tables, columns, data types, and constraints. The third major revision of SQL, called SQL – 92, laid the foundation for manipulation languages and info tables to execute queries on schema. In SQL – 2003, the data tables were described as SQL/Schemata. DDL can be used to make or perform modifications to the physical structure of the desired table in a given database. All such commands can be inherently auto committed upon execution, and all modifications to the table are immediately reflected and stored across the database. Here are the most known and widely used DDL commands:

- **Create** – For creation of new table(s) or an entire database.

- **Alter** – To modify the data values of records that have been created for a table.
- **Rename** – To change the name of the table(s)or the database.
- **Drop** – To delete the table(s) from a database.
- **Truncate** – To delete an entire table from the database.

Now, we will explore various uses of these DDL commands to execute required operations. For ease of learning all the fixed codes or keywords will be written in CAPITAL LETTERS, so you can easily differentiate between the dummy data and command syntax.

SQL CREATECommand

Usage– As the name suggests, CREATE command is primarily used to build database(s) and table(s). This always tends to be the first step in learning SQL.

Syntax:

CREATE DATABASE db_name;

CREATE TABLE tab_name;

CREATE TABLE tab_name (col1 datatyp, col2 datatyp, col3 datatyp,.....);

Examples:

Let's assume you would like to create a database named as db_baseball, which contains one table that stores details of the teams called team_details and another table that stores details of the players called player_details.

The first step here would be to build the desired database, with the use of the command below:

CREATE DATABASE db_baseball;
Now, that you have your database in the system, use the command below to create desired tables:

CREATE TABLE team_details;

CREATE TABLE player_details;

If you wanted to create the table player_details with some columns like player_firstname with column size as 15, player_lastname with column size as 25 and player_age.

You will use the command below:
*CREATE TABLE player_details (*player_firstname varchar (15), player_lastname varchar (25), player_age int*);*

Remember the size of the varchar data type can be mentioned in the statement with the maximum size as255 characters and in case the column size has not been specified, the system will default you to the maximum size

Hands-on Exercise

For exercise purposes, imagine that you are a brand-new business owner and looking to hire some employees. Now, you would first have to create a database for your company, let's name your company Health Plus and create a database named database_HealthPlus. You can then add a table titled New_Employees with columns to StoreEmployees' FirstName, LastName, JobTitle, Age and Salary.

Use your discretion and write your SQL statements first!

Now you can verify your statement against the right command as given below:

CREATE DATABASE db_HealthPlus;

CREATE TABLE New_Employees (employee_firstname varchar, employee_lastname varchar,employee_jobtitle varchar, employee_age int, employee_salary int);

SQL ALTER command

Usage– This command is primarily used to add a column, remove a column, add different data constraints and remove predefined data constraints.

Data Constraints – In terms of SQL, constraints are nothing, but specific rules applied to the data in the table. They can be applied at a column level, which is only applicable to the selected column or at a table level, which is applicable to all table columns. They limit the types of data values that are allowed to be entered in the table, to ensure the accuracy and reliability of the data. Violating these constraints will abort the command that you are trying to execute.

The data constraints can be added while creating the table (with the CREATE command) or once the table has been generated (utilizing the ALTER command).

The most widely used SQL constraints are:

- **NOT NULL** –It is utilized to make sure that the column always contains a value and does not hold a NULL value. Meaning, a new record cannot be added or a record that already exists cannot be modified if there are no values added to this column.

- **UNIQUE** - This constraint is used to make sure that every single data value in a column is distinct from one another.

- **PRIMARY KEY** - This constraint is essentially a merge of the UNIQUE and NOT NULL constraints. It serves as a unique identifier for each record in the table, which is required to contain a data value. Only one primary key can be indicated for individual tables.

- **FOREIGN KEY** - This constraint serves as a unique identifier for a record existing in a different table that has been linked to the table you are working on. This helps in aborting commands that will break the link between the two tables i.e., invalid data cannot be added to the foreign key column as it has to be a value as contained in the table that is holding that specific column.

- **CHECK** - This constraint is used to make sure that all the data values in a column meet a specific condition and are limited to the predefined value range. Applying Check constraint on a column will allow only select values to be added to that column. However, applying Check constraint on a table will put restrictions on the values that are added in the specified column, as dictated by the values specified in other columns of a row.

- **DEFAULT** –It is utilized to designate a default data value for a specific column in case no other value has been specified for that column.

- **INDEX** - This constraint is utilized to create and retrieve data values at a quick pace, using indexes that are not visible to the users. This should only be used for columns that will be searched more frequently than the others.

Syntax:

Addition ofColumns

ALTER TABLE tab_name
ADD col_namedtype;

DroppingColumn

ALTER TABLE tab_name
DROP col_name;

Addition ofNot NullConstraint

ALTER TABLE tab_name
MODIFY col_namedtype NOT NULL;

Addition ofUniqueConstraint

ALTER TABLE tab_name
ADD UNIQUE col_name;

Addition ofPrimary KeyConstraint

ALTER TABLE tab_name
ADD PRIMARY KEY col_name;

Addition ofForeign KeyConstraint

ALTER TABLE tab_name
ADD FOREIGN KEY (col_name) REFERENCES tab_name
(col_name);

Addition ofCheckConstraint

ALTER TABLE tab_name
ADD CHECK(col_name<= 'numeric value');

Addition ofDefaultConstraint

ALTER TABLE tab_name
ADD CONSTRAINT (col_name) DEFAULT 'data_value' FOR
(col_name);

AddingIndexConstraint

CREATE INDEX index_name
ON tab_name (col1, col2, ...,);

DroppingNot NullConstraint

ALTER TABLE tab_name
DROP CONSTRAINT col_namedtype;

DroppingUniqueConstraint

ALTER TABLE tab_name
DROP CONSTRAINT col_namedtype;
DroppingPrimary KeyConstraint

ALTER TABLE tab_name
DROP PRIMARY KEY;

DroppingForeign KeyConstraint

ALTER TABLE tab_name
DROP FOREIGN KEY(col_name);

DroppingCheckConstraint

ALTER TABLE tab_name
DROP CHECK (col_name);

DroppingDefaultConstraint

ALTER TABLE tab_name
ALTER COLUMN (col_name)DROP DEFAULT;

DroppingIndexConstraint

DROP INDEX tab_name.indx_name;

Examples:

Now, assume that you would like to alter the player_details table, that was generated in the section above. To add a column titled player_ID and then drop the player_age column, you could execute the commands below:

ALTER TABLE player_details
ADD player_ID *number;*

ALTER TABLE player_details
DROP player_age;

Let's now look at how various constraints can be added with the player_details table!

You can specify that the column player_firstname has the Not Null constraint. The column player_lastname is unique. The primary key can be specified as column player_IDs, which will then become the foreign key in our other table titled team_details. We can define the check constraint on player_age to make sure all the values entered are above or equal to 20. We can also use the default value for player_age column as 20. Since, we will be frequently using the player_lastname column, let's add an index to it.

Step 1:
ALTER TABLE player_details
MODIFY player_firstname *varchar (15) NOT NULL;*

Step 2:
ALTER TABLE player_details
ADD UNIQUE player_lastname;

Step 3:
ALTER TABLE player_details
ADD PRIMARY KEY player_IDs;

Step 4:
ALTER TABLE team_details
ADD FOREIGN KEY (player_IDs) *REFERENCES* player_details (player_IDs);

Step 5:

ALTER TABLE player_details
ADD CHECK (player_age<= 20);

Step 6:

ALTER TABLE player_details
ADD CONSTRAINT (player_age) DEFAULT '20' FOR
(player_age);

Step 7:

CREATE INDEX idx_name
ON player_details(player_lastname,player_firstname);

Now, let's drop all these constraints we just defined above, in the same order.

Step 1:

ALTER TABLE player_details
DROP CONSTRAINT player_firstname *varchar (15) NOT*
NULL;

Step 2:

ALTER TABLE player_details
DROP CONSTRAINT player_lastname;

Step 3:

ALTER TABLE player_details

DROP PRIMARY KEY;

Step 4:

ALTER TABLE team_details

DROP FOREIGN KEY (player_IDs*);*

Step 5:

ALTER TABLE player_details

DROP CHECK (player_age);

Step 6:

ALTER TABLE player_details

ALTER COLUMN (player_age) DROP DEFAULT;

Step 7:

DROP INDEX player_details.*idx_name;*

Hands-on Exercise

For exercise purposes, we will continue to use the database_HealthPlus that we created in the previous section, which contains a table titled New_Employees with columns to store "Fst Name," "Lst Name," "Job Title," "Age" and "Salary" of the employee.

Now, let's add another table to this database titled Current_Employees. Then add a new column for employee ID which will be the primary key for table New_Employees and foreign key for Current_Employees. The salary column can be dropped for this exercise.

Make the column for the first name as Not Null and last name as Unique. Add a check constraint on the employee age column as equals or greater than 21. Then define its default value as 21. And lastly, indicate an index for the last name column to the New_Employees table.

Use your discretion and prep your SQL statements first!

Now you can verify your statement against the right command as given below:

Step 1:
CREATE TABLE Current_Employees (employee_fstname varchar, employee_lstname varchar, employee_jobtitl varchar, employee_age int, employee_salary int);

Step 2:
ALTER TABLE New_Employees
ADD employee_IDs number;

Step 3:

ALTER TABLE New_Employees

DROP employee_salary;

Step 4:

ALTER TABLE New_Employees

ADD PRIMARY KEY employee_IDs;

Step 5:

ALTER TABLE Current_Employees

*ADD FOREIGN KEY (*employee_ID*) REFERENCES*

New_Employees *(*employee_IDs*)*;

Step 6:

ALTER TABLE New_Employees

MODIFY employee_fstname *varchar NOT NULL;*

Step 7:

ALTER TABLE New_Employees

ADD UNIQUE employee _lstname;

Step 8:

ALTER TABLE New_Employees

*ADD CHECK (*employee _*age <= "21");*

Step 9:

ALTER TABLE New_Employees

ADD CONSTRAINT (employee _age) DEFAULT '21' FOR

(employee_age);

Step 10:

CREATE INDEX idx_name

ON New_Employees*(employee_lstname);*

Viola!Now you are tasked to drop all these constraints and then add the salary column back to the New_Employees table.

Use your discretion and write your SQL statements first!*

Now you can verify your statement against the right command as given below:

Step 1:

ALTER TABLE New_Employees

DROP PRIMARY KEY;

Step 2:

ALTER TABLE Current_Employees

DROP FOREIGN KEY (employee_IDs);

Step 3:

ALTER TABLE New_Employees

*DROP CONSTRAINT employee_*fstname *varchar NOT NULL;*

Step 4:

ALTER TABLE New_Employees

DROP CONSTRAINT employee_*lstname;*

Step 5:

ALTER TABLE New_Employees

DROP CHECK (employee _age);

Step 6:

ALTER TABLE New_Employees

ALTER COLUMN (employee_age) DROP DEFAULT;

Step 7:

DROP INDEX New_Employees.*idx_name;*

Step 8:

ALTER TABLE New_Employees

ADD employee_salary *number;*

SQL DROP DATABASECommand

***Usage*–** This command is primarily used to delete an already existing SQL database.

Syntax:

DROP DATABASE db_name;

Examples:

Let's assume you would like to delete the database database_baseball for any business reason like irrelevant data in the database or duplicate databases etc.

You can simply use the command below and the entire database will be wiped out from the system.

DROP DATABASE db_baseball;

Hands-on Exercise

For exercise purposes, imagine that your company Health Plus has gone under or renamed, and you want to discard all the data you have available related to the company. What would you do?

Use your discretion and write your SQL statements first!

Now you can verify your statement against the right command as given below:

DROP DATABASE db_HealthPlus;

SQL CREATE VIEWCommand

Usage– This command is primarily used to generate a virtual view of the tables on the basis of the result-set of a SQL command. The view resembles an actual database table, in that it also has columns and rows, but the data values are called from an individual or multiple table(s) using "WHERE" and "JOIN."SQL Views are used to enhance the structure of the data making it more user-friendly.

In SQL, the WHERE function is used to selectively filter the data or records on the basis of specific conditions. It is a highly versatile function and can also be used with other SQL statements including UPDATE and DELETE.

Only the latest and greatest data will be used for the generation of a view!

Syntax:

CREATE VIEW vw_name AS
SELECT col1, col2, ...
FROM tab_name
WHERE condtn;

Examples:

Let's go back to the database database_baseball and assume you would like to view details of the players who are 25 years old.

You can simply use the command below and view desired information.

CREATE VIEW young_playersAS
SELECT player_fstname, player_lstname
FROM player_details
WHERE player_age = '25';

Hands-on Exercise

For exercise purposes, imagine that your company Health Plus is undergoing an organizational change and you would like to view a list of all the employees with the job title as managers.

Use your discretion and write your SQL statements first!

Now you can verify your statement against the right command as given below:

CREATE VIEW employee_mgrsAS
SELECT employee_fstname, employee_lstname
FROM Current_Employees
WHERE employee_jobtitle= *'manager';*

Chapter 2: Basic SQL Functions

MySQL has always been a popular open source SQL based RDMS, which is available for free. In 1995, a Swedish company called MySQL AB originally developed, marketed and licensed the MySQL data management system, that was eventually acquired by Sun Microsystems (now called Oracle Co.). MySQL is a LAMP software stack web application component, an acronym for "Linux, Apache, MySQL, Perl / PHP / Python." Several database-controlled web apps, like "Drupal", "Joomla", "PhpBB", and "WordPress" are using "MySQL."It is one of the best applications for RDBMS to create various online software applications and has been used in development of multiple renowned websites including Facebook, YouTube, Twitter and Flickr.

MySQL has been used with both C and C++. MySQL can be operated on several systems, including "AIX, BSDi, FreeBSD, HP-Ux, eComStation, i5/OS, IRIX, Linux, macOS, Microsoft Windows, NetBSD, Novell NetWare, OpenSolaris, OS/2 Warp, QNX, Oracle Solaris, Symbian, SunOS, SCO OpenServer, SCO UnixWare, Sanos and Tru64." Its SQL parser is developed in "yacc" and it utilizes an in house developed lexical analyzer. A MySQL port for OpenVMS has also been developed. Dual-license distribution is utilized for the MySQL server and its client libraries, which are available under version 2 of the

GPL or a proprietary license. Additional free assistance is accessible on various IRC blogs and channels. With its MySQL Enterprise goods, Oracle is also providing paid support for their software. The range of services and prices vary. A number of third-party service providers, including MariaDB and Percona, offer assistance and facilities as well.

MySQL has been given highly favorable feedback from the developer community and reviewers have noticed that it does work exceptionally well in most cases. The developer interfaces exist and there's a plethora of excellent supporting documentation, as well as feedback from web locations in the real world. MySQL has also been successfully passed the test of a stable and fast SQL database server using multiple users and threads.

MySQL can be found in two editions: the "MySQL Community Server" (open source) and the "Enterprise Server," which is proprietary. "MySQL Enterprise Server" differentiates itself on the basis of a series of proprietary extensions that can be installed as server plug-ins, but nonetheless share the numbering scheme of versions and are developed using the same basic code.

Here are some of the key characteristics provided by MySQL v5.6:

- A largest subset of extensions and ANSI SQL-99 are supported by this version along with cross platforms.
- Stored procedures use procedural languages that are completely aligned with SQL/PSM.
- Cursors and triggers, views that can be updated, support for SSL; caching of queries; nested SELECT statements, integrated support for replication and info schema.
- Online Data Definition Language with the use of the InnoDB Storage Engine.
- Performance Schema that is capable of collecting and aggregating stats pertaining to monitor server executions and query performances.
- Aset of options pertaining to SQL Mode for controlling runtime behavior, includes restrictive mode for improved adherence to SQL standards.
- "X/Open XA distributed transaction processing (DTP)" supports 2 phases committed with the use of the default InnoDB engine.
- Any transaction with save points while using the default engine can be supported by the "NDB Cluster Storage Engine."

- The replication may not be synchronous: owner employee from an owner to multiple employees or multiple owners to one employee.
- The replication may be partially synchronous: owner to employee replication where the owner awaits replication.
- The replication may be completely synchronous: Multi-owner replication can be supplied in MySQL Cluster.
- The replication may be virtually synchronous: groups of MySQL servers that are managed on their own with multi owner support that could be done with the use of the "Galera Cluster" or the integrated plug-in for group replication.
- The index of the full text and search capability, integrated database library, support for Unicode.
- The tables can be sectioned with the pruning of sections in the optimizer.
- MySQL Cluster allows for clustering of data that has not been shared.
- A number of storage engines that allow selection of the most effective engine for every table.
- The groups can be committed, and various transactions can be gathered from a number of connections together to raise the number of commitments made every second.

User Interfaces for MySQL

A graphical user interface (GUI) is a kind of interface that enables user interactions with software programs and electronics utilizing graphics, icons, buttons, and other indicators including but not limited to features supporting notations in lieu of navigation driven by text and text-based interfaces. GUIs are considered very easy to learn in comparison to the "command-line interfaces (CLIs)," where command must be entered on your keypad. MySQL offers a variety of interfaces that you can leverage to best meet your need. Some of the widely popular MySQL interfaces are:

MySQL Workbench

It is considered as the built-in environment for MySQL database, created by "MySQL AB," and allows the user supervision of MySQL graphically as well as the designing of the databases visually. It has substituted MySQL GUI Tools, which was the preceding software suite. MySQL Workbench enables users to perform database designing& model creation, SQL implementation, which was replaced by the Query Browser and Database admin, which was replaced by the MySQL Admin. These functionalities are also available from other third-party applications, but MySQL Workbench is still regarded as the official MySQL front end. MySQL Workbench can be downloaded from the official MySQL website, in two separate versions: a regular free and open source community version, and a proprietary standard version, which continues to expand and enhance the community version feature set.

phpMyAdmin

It is another open source application which is available for free and developed in PHP programming language, that allows use of a web browser to manage MySQL administration. It allows undertaking of multiple functions such as generation, modification, or deletion of database, table, field, or row by running SQL queries as well as management of users and permissions. phpMyAdmin is easily accessible in whopping 78 different languages and managed by The phpMyAdmin Project. The data can be imported as CSV or SQL and used with a set of predefined features to convert stored data into a desirable format, such as representing BLOB data as pictures or download links.

Adminer

Adminer (previously referred to as phpMinAdmin) is another open and free source MySQL front end for maintaining information in the MySQL databases. The release of version 2, the Adminer can also be used on PostgreSQL, SQLite and Oracle databases. The Adminer can be used to manage several databases with multiple CSS skins that are easily accessible. It is supplied under the Apache License or GPL v2 as a single PHP file. Jakub Vrána, began developing Adminer, in July 2007, as a lightweight option to the original phpMyAdmin application.

ClusterControl

It is defined as a holistic MySQL management system or GUI for managing, monitoring, scaling and deploying versions of MySQL from an individual interface. It has been engineered by "Severalnines." Its community version can be accessed for free and allow deployment and tracking of the MySQL instances, directly by the user. Advanced characteristics such as load balance, backup and restoration, among other are additional features that can be paid for.

Database Workbench

Database Workbench application was created by UpScene Productions, for the creation and management of various relational databases that are interoperable within separate database systems, using SQL. Databases Workbench can support several database systems and offers a cross-database tool for computer programmers with a similar interface and production environment, for a variety of databases. The relational databases that can be supported by Database Workbench are: Oracle, SQL Anywhere, Firebird, Microsoft SQL Server, NexusDB and many more. The version 5 of Database Workbench can be operated on Windows systems that are either 32-bit or 64-bit as well as on Linux, FreeBSD, or MacOS operating systems by leveraging the Wine application.

DBeaver

DBeaver is an open source and free software application marketed under Apache License 2.0, used as a database administration tool and a SQL client with the source code hosted on GitHub. DBeaver incorporates extensive assistance for the following databases: "MySQL and MariaDB, PostgreSQL, Oracle, DB2 (LUW), Exasol, SQL Server, Sybase, Firebird, Teradata, Vertica, Apache Phoenix, Netezza, Informix, H2, SQLite and any other JDBC or ODBC driver database."

DBEdit

It is a database editor capable of connecting to MySQL, Oracle and other databases that supports a JDBC driver. It is importance that SourceForge hosts the source code of this software. It is also defined as open source software, which is available for free under the GNU license. It is available on Windows, Linux and Solaris.

HeidiSQL

HeidiSQL, used to be known as "MySQL Front," is another open source application which is available for free and serves as a front end for MySQL, operable with MariaDB, Percona Server,

Microsoft SQL Server and PostgreSQL. German computer scientist Ansgar Becker and several other contributors at Delphi, developed the HeidiSQL interface. To operate HeidiSQL databases, customers need to log in and create a session to a MySQL server locally or remotely with acceptable credentials. This session enables the users to develop a connection, in management of the database on the MySQL server and to disconnect from the server once they have completed their task. HeidiSQL function set is suitable for most popular and sophisticated activities pertaining to the database, table and data records, but it continues to actively grow towards the complete feature desired in a MySQL user interface.

LibreOffice Base

LibreOffice Base enables databases to be created and managed, forms to be prepared and reports providing simple access to information for the end-users. It also serves as an interface for different database systems like Microsoft Access, MySQL, OBDC info source, Access databases like JET and many more.

Navicat

It is a software that enables management of databases using graphics and coding programs for Oracle, MySQL, MariaDB, and other databases that have been manufactured by PremiumSoftCyberTech Ltd. It has a graphical user interface similar to the Microsoft Internet Explorer and supports various local and remote database connections. It has been designed to satisfy the demands of a range of customers, from database admins and developers to various corporations that are serving the public and share data with their partner companies. Navicat is a cross-platform software that can be operated on systems such as Microsoft Windows, OS X, and Linux. Once the software has been purchased, the user can select one of the available eight languages to work with their software, which are: Mandarin, Japanese, French, German, and many more.

Sequel Pro

It is another free and open source Macintosh operating system software that can be operated locally or remotely with MySQL databases and hosted on SourceForge. It utilizes the freemium model, which effectively provides Gratis users with most of the fundamental features. These applications need to be managed by a SQL Table itself. For newer unicode, it can manage the latest fun UTF-8 functions as well as having various GB tables with little to no difficulty.

SQLBuddy

SQLBuddy is a web-based open-source software published in PHP that manages MySQL and SQLite administration using a web browser. The objective of this design is easy software set-up and an enhanced and convenient interface for the users.

SQLyog

SQLyog is another MySQL GUI application which is available for free but also offers paid software versions of their platform. There is a spreadsheet resembling interface that allows data manipulation (e.g. insert, update and delete) to be accomplished easily.

Its editor offers multiple choices for automatic formatting such as syntax highlighting. A query can be used to manipulate both raw table data and outcome set. Its search function utilizes Google-like search syntax, which can be translated into SQL for users transparently. It is provided with a backup utility to execute unmonitored backups.

Toad

It was developed by Dell Software, as a computer application utilized by database programmers, database admins as well as data analysts, using SQL to operate on both relational and non-relational databases. Toad can be used with numerous databases and environments. It can be easily installed on all Windows operating systems such as Windows 7,Windows Vista, Server, XP and many more. A Toad Mac Edition has also been recently published by the Dell Software and is offered as a business version and trial / freeware version. The freeware version of Toad can be accessed from the ToadWorld.com community.

Webmin

Webmin was originally developed as an online system configuration software for Unix based systems, but the newer versions are available for installation and can be operated on Windows operating system as well. It allows customization of internal OS configurations such as disk quotas, utilities, users and open sourced applications such as MySQL, Apache HTTP Server among others that can be modified and controlled.

Webmin is primarily built on Perl, and one that runs as its own internet server and process. For communication, it would default to the TCP port 10000 and configured to utilize SSL (when OpenSSL has already been installed on the system with all Perl modules that are needed for execution). It is developed around modules that have an interface with the Webmin server and the configuration files. This makes adding latest features much more convenient. Because of the modular design of Webmin, custom plug-ins can be created for desktop setup for those who are keen. Webmin also enables control on many devices on the same subnet or LAN via one comprehensive user interface, or seamless connection to other Webmin hosts.

Installing MySQL on Linux/UNIX

MySQL should be installed using RPM on the Linux system. The following RPMs are accessible on the MySQL AB official site for download:

- **MySQL**–Its database server is used for management of the tables within a database, controlling the user access and processing the SQL statement.
- **MySQL bench** – These are the programs used to test and create a benchmark for the database servers.
- **MySQLshared**–These are the libraries that are shared with the MySQL client.
- **MySQL devel** – These are header files and libraries which are widely used during the compilation of other programs using MySQL.
- **MySQL client** – These programs allow development of a connection to the server and further interactions with it.

In order to continue with your setup, you must follow the instructions below:

1. Use the root user to log into the system.
2. Change to the RPM-containing directory.
3. Execute the command below to install the MySQL database server. Keep in mind to substitute "the filename in italics with a desired file name of your RPM."

[root@host] # rpm -i MySQL-6.0.12-0.i395.rpm

This function is responsible for the installation of the MySQL server and for creation of its user, the required setup and automated startup of the MySQL server.

All MySQL associated binaries can be easily located in the /usr / bin as well as the /usr / sbin directories. Every database and table would be generated in the /var / lib / mysql directory.

The commands below are optional and can be used to install the other RPMs using the same approach, but it is highly recommended to install all these RPMs on your system:

[root@host]# rpm -i MySQL-client-6.0.12-0.i395.rpm
[root@host]# rpm -i MySQL-devel-6.0.12-0.i395.rpm
[root@host]# rpm -i MySQL-shared-6.0.12-0.i395.rpm
[root@host]# rpm -i MySQL-bench-6.0.12-0.i395.rpm

Installation of MySQL on Windows Operating System

To install MySQL on any version of Windows is much easier now than in the past, as MySQL is now offered as an installation package. All you have to do is save the installer package on your system, open the zipped file then execute the setup.

Installation processes in the default setup.exe file is insignificant and all of them are installed under C:\mysql by default.

To test the server for the first time simply open user interface using the command prompt. Go to the MySQL server location that is likely going to be C:\mysql\bin then enter these keywords: mysqldexe console.

After successful installation some startup and InnoDB messages will be displayed on your screen. A failed installation may be related to system permissions issue. It is important to ensure that the directory holding the data is available to every user (likely MySQL) under which the procedures of the database are run.

MySQL cannot be added to the start menu with installation and no user-friendly way is offered to exit the server. So, you should consider stopping the process manually with the use of mysql admin, task manager and list, or other methods specified for Windows, instead of double-clicking on the mysqld executable to launch the server.

Installing MySQL on Macintosh Operating System

Follow the instruction below for installation of MySQL on Mac OS X:

- Download the disk image file (.dmg) containing the MySQL package installer. For mounting the disk image and viewingthe contents, click twice on the .dmg file.
- Now, click twice on the MySQL installer package. The name of the OS X MySQL installer package version would be in accordance with the MySQL as well as your computer's current OS X version. For instance, if you could download the package for MySQL 6.1.46 and OS X 11.2, then double click on the mysql 6.1.22-osx-11.2-x90 64.pkg.
- The opening installer message will be displayed on the screen. To start installation, click Continue.
- The accompanying GNU General Public License will be displayed for all downloads of the MySQL community version. Click Continue and then Agree to proceed.
- You can select Install to run the installation wizard from the Installation Type page with all default settings. Then click Customize to select the components you desire to install Launchd Support or Preference Pane and MySQL server all of which will be activated by default.
- To start the installation process, click Install.
- After successful installation has been done, an Install Succeeded message with a brief overview will be displayed on the screen. You can exit the

installation assistant at this point and start using the MySQL server.

MySQL has been configured now but cannot be launched automatically. You can either select launchctlor, click on Start on the Preference Pane to fire up the MySQL server.

Installations done using the package installer will configure the files within /usr / local directory, that matches the name of the installation version and operating system being used. For instance, the installer file mysql 6.1.22-osx-11.2-x90 64.dmg installs MySQL into /usr/local/mysql 6.1.22-osx-11.2-x90 64/. A symbolic connection to a particular directory depending on the version or platform will be generated during the setup phase from /usr / local / mysql, which is automatically updated while you are installing the package. The table below illustrates the installation directory layouts.

Directory	Contents of Directory
bin, scripts	Includes server and programs for utility and client
data	Includes log file and database
docs	Includes help documents such as Release Notes
include	Includes header file
lib	Library

Directory	Contents of Directory
man	Includes manual page for Unix
mysql-test	Includes test cases for MySQL
share	Includes various support files such as errors, file samples for configuration used to install the database
sql-bench	Includes various benchmark
support-files	Includes file samples for configuration and scripts
/tmp/mysql.sock	Includes the location of the MySQL Unix socket

Creating a New Database Using MySQL Server

In MySQL server, databases are implemented as directories that contain all the files corresponding to the tables in a particular database.

Now that you have installed the MySQL Server, you can follow the instructions below to generate new databases with the CREATE command, using the syntax below:

CREATE DATABASE [IF NOT EXISTS] db_title
[CHARACTER SET chrst_title]
[COLLATE collatn_title]

In the syntax above, the first step is specifying the database_name right after the CREATE DATABASE command. In the MySQL server instance, the title of any database being created must be unique. When you're trying to build a database with an existing name, the server will abort the action. Next you can indicate the choice IF NOT EXISTS to prevent an infringement, if you erroneously generate a new database that shares its name with a database that already exists on the server. In this scenario, MySQL will not generate an issue but will instead terminate the CREATE DATABASE statement. Lastly, when the new database is created, you are able to indicate the character set and combination requirements. If the clauses CHARACTER SET and COLLATE are omitted, then MySQL utilizes the default settings for the new database.

Alternatively, you can build a new database using **MySQL Workbench** and following the steps below:

1. Open MySQL Workbench then select the set up new Connection icon on the screen.
2. Enter desired title for your connection and click on the Test Connection icon. A windowpane requiring the root user password would be displayed in MySQL Workbench. You are required to enter the root user password, click on the checkbox for the save password option and select OK.

3. For connecting with the MySQL server, click twice on the connection name Local. MySQL Workbench opens the window containing four different components namely: Query, Navigator, Info and O/P.

4. Select the icon to create a new schema on the screen. The database is also known as schema in MySQL. Therefore, developing a new schema just implies that you are generating a new database.

5. In the subsequent window you are required to provide the schema name and modify the collation and character set as required then select the Apply icon.

6. The software will open up in a new window displaying the SQL script that needs to be executed. Keep in mind that the CREATE SCHEMA query will lead to the same result as the CREATE DATABASE query. If all goes well, the new database will be generated and displayed in the "schemas tab of the Navigator section."

7. For selection of the testdb database, simply right click on its name and select Set as Default Schema.

8. The testdb node would be open so you can run queries on testdb using the MySQL Workbench.

Managing a Database Using MySQL Server

Once all the databases containing your desired data have been created, you can selectively display and use the content needed using the instructions below.

Display Databases

The SHOW DATABASES statement is utilized to list all the databases currently existing on the MySQL server. You can inspect only your database or every database on the server through the use of a SHOW DATABASES statement before building a new database. For example, if you assume that the databases, we have created so far are all on the MySQL Server and the *SHOW DATABASES;* statement is executed, you will see the result as information_schema; *database_baseball; database_HealthPlus; mysql.*

Now you know that there are four different databases on your MySQL server. The information_schema and mysql are default databases that are created upon installation of the MySQL server and the other two databases, namely *database_baseball* and *database_HealthPlus* were created by us.

Selection of a Database

Before operating with a specific database, you are required to first inform MySQL, which database you would like to operate by utilizing the USE command as below:

USE db_nam;

To select the *database_HealthPlus, you can write the command as below:*

USE database_HealthPlus;

Creating a NewDatabaseTableUsing MySQL Server

You will be using the CREATE TABLE statement to build new tables. The CREATE TABLE command is considered as one of the most complicated statements in SQL. A simple CREATE TABLE syntax can be written as in the next page:

CREATE TABLE [IF NOT EXISTS] tbl_nam(

colum_lst

) ENGINE = storag_engin

Start by indicating the table name after the CREATE TABLE clause, that you would like to create. The name of the new table must be unique. The IF NOT EXISTS is one of the auxiliary clauses that allow for verification of whether the table being build has previously been created in that database. If there is a duplication in the table name, the entire statement will be ignored by MySQL and the new table will not be generated. You are advised to use this clause in every statement for creating tables, in order to prevent an accidental creation of any new table name that can be found on the server.

Next, in the column list section, a list of table columns can be specified, and each column name can be distinguished with the use of commas.

Lastly, in the ENGINE clause, you have the option to indicate the table storage engine. Any storage engine like InnoDB and MyISAM could be used. If the storage engine is not specifically declared, MySQL will be using the default InnoDB engine.

The following syntax can be utilized to describe a table column in the CREATE TABLE statement:
column_namdata_typ(length) [NOT NULL] [DEFAULT val] [AUTO_INCREMENT]

In the syntax above, the column name has been specified by the column_name clause. Each column contains a particular type and the desired length of the data, for example, VARCHAR(255). The NOT NULL clause indicates that NULL value will not be permitted by this column.

The value DEFAULT can be utilized to indicate the default value for specific columns. The AUTO_INCREMENT shows that when adding any new rows, the column value would be automatically created by the column. The AUTO_INCREMENT columns in each table are unique. For instance, you will be able to build a new table to store data pertaining to tasks called "tsks", with the command below:

```
CREATE TABLE IF NOT EXISTS tsks (
    tsk_id INT AUTO_INCREMENT,
    titl VARCHAR(255) NOT NULL,
    strt_dte DATE,
    due_dte DATE,
    stats TINYINT NOT NULL,
    prity TINYINT NOT NULL,
    desc TEXT,
    PRIMARY KEY (tsk_id)
) ENGINE=INNODB;
```

In the syntax above, the tsk Id is an auto increment column. In case the INSERT query is used for adding a new record to the table, with the tsk Id column value not being specified, the tsk Id column will be given an auto-generated integer value starting with '1'. The tsk Id column has been specified as the primary key.

The title column has been given a variable character string data type with max allowed length of 255 characters. This implies that a string of characters larger than 255 characters in length cannot be inserted in this column. The NOT NULL suggests that a value is required for the column i.e. when inserting or updating this column, a value must be provided.

The strtdte and due dte are date columns that will allow NULL values.

The stats and prity are the "TINYINT" columns and will not permit NULL values.

The desc column is a TEXT column that will allow NULL values.

Inserting Data into a Table on the MySQL Server

To add single or multiple records into the table, the "INSERT" statement is used, as shown in the syntax below:

INSERT INTO tbl(p1,p2,...)
VALUES (q1,q2,...);

In the statement above, the table name must be specified next to a list of desired columns separated by "commas" written within "parentheses," following the INSERT INTO clause. After which, all the values separated by commas pertaining to the columns within the parentheses must be written, following the VALUES function. Make sure there is same quantity of columns and corresponding column values. Furthermore, the column positions must correspond with the position of the column values.

Execute the code below to add one or more records to the table, using only one INSERT statement:

INSERT INTO tbl (p1, p2,...)
VALUES
  (q11, q12,...),
  (q21, q22,...),

  ...
  (qmm, qm2,...);"

The example below will generate three rows or records in the table "tutorials tbl" and display the confirmation that the "row has been affected":

root@host# mysql -u root -p password;
Entrpswd: *****
msql> using BOOK;
Db changes

msql> INSERT INTO book_tble
  ->(book_titl, bookl_athr, submsn_dat)
  ->VALUES
  ->('Master the Code', 'Pam Podds', NOW());
Qry OK, 1 rwaffctd (0.02 secs)

msql> INSERT INTO book_tble

->(book_titl, bookl_athr, submsn_dat)

->VALUES

->('Master the Code', 'Bob Suddds, NOW());

Qry OK, 1 rwaffctd (0.02 secs)

mysql> INSERT INTO book_tble

->(book_titl, bookl_athr, submsn_dat)

->VALUES

->('Skills of a Programmer', 'Samuel Jack', '2017-15-09');

Qry OK, 1 rwaffctd (0.02 secs)

msql>"

Here is another example, the query below can be utilized for inserting a new record to the tsks table that was created earlier:

"INSERT INTO

tsks(titl,prity)

VALUES

('Learning all the coding languages, 2);

1 row(s) affected;"

The output should look like the sample image below with the column and row values used in the code above:

task_id	title	start_date	due_date	priority	description
1	Learn MySQL INSERT Statement	NULL	NULL	1	NULL

We indicated the values, in the example above, only for the title and priority columns. MySQL will use the default values for the other non-specified columns.

The tsk_id column has been specified as an auto increment column. This implies that upon insertion of a new record to the table, MySQL will generate a subsequent integer.

The strt_dte, due_dte and desc columns have been specified to hold NULL as the default value, so if no values are specified in the INSERT statement, MySQL will insert NULL into those columns.

To add default values into desired columns, either simply disregard the column name and its corresponding values or indicate the name of the columns in the INSERT INTO function and type DEFAULT in the VALUES clause. For example, in the syntax below the prity column has been specified with the DEFAULT keyword.

INSERT INTO
tsks(titl,prity)
VALUES
('Learning how to use various functions for coding',
DEFAULT);

You can insert dates into the table using the YYYY-MM-DD format, which represents year, month and date in the mentioned order. For example, you can add the strtdte and due date values to the tsks table using the command below:

INSERT INTO tsks (titl, strt_dte, due_dte)

VALUES ('Learning how to use date function for coding','2019-02-19','2019-12-18'):

The VALUES clause also supports expressions as shown in the example below, where the syntax will add a new task utilizing the current date for strtdte and due dte columns using the CURRENT_DATE() function. Remember the CURRENT_DATE() function will always return the current date in the system.

"INSERT INTO tsks(titl,strt_dte,due_dte)

VALUES

('Learning how to use variousfunctions for coding',CURRENT_DATE(),CURRENT_DATE());

To insert multiple rows or records in the, take a look at the example below of the tsks table, where each record is indicated as values listed in the VALUES clause:

INSERT INTO tsks (titl, prity)

VALUES

('This is how we start', 2),

('Moving to the next task', 3),

('Moving to the next task', 4),

('Moving to the final task before the weekend', 5);

The resulting output should be:*4 row(s) affected Records:4 Dupes: 0 Warning: 0*, which implies that the records were added to the table and there are no duplicates or warnings in the table.

Creating a Temporary table in the database using MySQL server

A temp table in MySQL is a peculiar kind of table that enables the storage of a temporary outcome set for reuse over multiple times over the same session.

A temp table is extremely useful when querying information that needs only one SELECT statement containing the JOIN clause, which is not feasible or costly. In such a scenario, the temporary table can be used as a storage for the immediate result which can be processed further using a different query.

A temp table in MySQL may have the characteristics listed below:

- A temp table is generated by executing the CREATE TEMPORARY TABLE statement. Note that between

CREATE and TABLE functions, the
TEMPORARY keyword must be added.

- When the session is completed or the connection is ended, MySQL server will automatically remove the temporary table from its memory. Another thing to remember is that once you are done with the temporary table, it can be explicitly deleted utilizing the DROP TABLE command.

- Only the user that generates the temp table is able to access it. Other users can potentially generate multiple temporary tables with the same name and still not cause any error since they can only be seen by the user who produced that specific temporary table. Two or more temporary tables cannot, however, share the same name over the same session.

- In a database, a temporary table may be given the same name as a standard table. The existing employee table, for instance, cannot be accessed by creating a temporary table called employees, within the sample database. All queries you execute on the employees table will now be referred to the temporary employees table. When the employees temporary table is deleted, the permanent employees table would still be in the system and can be accessed again.

While it can be given the same title as a standard table without triggering any error, it is advised to have a different name for the temp table. As the same name can lead to confusion and may result in an unexpected loss of information. For example, you cannot distinguish between these two types of tables, if the connection to the database server is dismissed for some reason and then automatically reconnected to the server. Then, rather than the temp table, you could enter a DROP TABLE statement to delete the standard table unexpectedly.

Now, a temp table can be created in MySQL by using the "TEMPORARY" keyword within statements used to generate new tables. For instance, the command below will generate a temp table containing only the top ten clients by profit with the given table name as "top10clients":

CREATE TEMPORARY TABLE top10clients
SELECT x.clientNbr,
y.clientNam,
*   ROUND(SUM(z.amt), 2) sale*
FROM pay a
INNER JOIN clients y ON y.clientNbr = a.clientNbr
GROUP BY a.clientNbr
ORDER BY sale DESC
LIMIT 10;

Using this temp table, you can further run queries on this table like you would on a standard or permanent table in the database.

SELECT
clientNbr,
clientNam,
  sale
FROM
  top10clients
ORDER BY sale;

Creating a NewTable from an Existing Table in the DatabaseUsing MySQL Server

You may also generate a copy of a table that can be found in the table with the use of the CREATE TABLE command, as shown in the syntax below:

CREATE TABLE nw_tbl_nam AS
  SELECT col1, col2,...
  FROM existin_tbl_nam
  WHERE ....;"

The new table will have the same specifications for the columns as the parent table. It is possible to select all columns or a particular column. If a new table is generated using a table that already exists in the database, then the current values from the parent table will be automatically loaded into the new table. For example, in the syntax below a table called TstTbl will be created as a replica of the parent Clients table:

CREATE TABLE TstTbl AS
SELECT clientnam, contctnam
FROM clients;

You might encounter a scenario, when you require a precise copy or clone of a table and the standard statement for creation of new tables does not meet the requirement, since you would like the clone to contain the identical indexes, default values, etc as the parent table.

This scenario can be addressed by executing the measures provided below:

- The "SHOW CREATE TABLE" can be used to execute a CREATE TABLE query specifying the structures, index and other feature of the source or parent table.
- Adjust the query to alter the table name to be same as the clone table and run the query. You would be able to get the precise clone of the table with this method.

- Optionally, if you would also like to copy the table contents, you can execute an INSERT INTO... SELECT statement.

For example, you can generate a clone table for tution_tab using the syntax below:

FIRST, copy the entire schema of the table:

msql> SHOW CREATE TABLE tution_tab \G;

*********************** 2. row ***********************

   Table: tution_tab

Creating Tab: CREATE TABLE 'tution_tab' (

   `tution_id` *int (15) NOT NULL auto_increment,*

   `tution_titl` *varchar (100) NOT NULL default',*

   `tution_author' varchar (40) NOT NULL default',*

   `submsn_dte' dte default NULL,*

   PRIMARY KEY (`tution_id`),

   UNIQUE KEY 'AUTHOR_INDEX' (`tution_author')

) TYPE = MyISAM

2 rows in set (0.02 secs)

ERROR:

"No query specified"

SECOND, change the name of the parent table to generate a new clone table:

msql> CREATE TABLE clone_tbl (

-> `tution_id` int (15) NOT NULL auto_increment,

-> `tution_titl` varchar (100) NOT NULL default',

-> `tution_author' varchar (40) NOT NULL default',

-> `submsn_dte' dte default NULL,

-> PRIMARY KEY (`tution_id`),

->UNIQUE KEY 'AUTHOR_INDEX' (`tution_author')

) TYPE = MyISAM

Query OK, 1 row affected (0.02 secs)

LASTLY, if you need to replicate the source table to the clone tables, you can use the command below:

msql> INSERT INTO clone_tbl (tutorial_id,

  ->tutorial_title,

  ->tutorial_author,

  ->submission_date)

  -> SELECT tutorial_id,tutorial_title,

  ->tutorial_author,submission_date

  -> FROM tutorials_tbl;

Query OK, 3 rows affected (0.07 sec)

Records: 3 Duplicates: 0 Warnings: 0"

DERVIVED TABLES in MySQL Server

A derived table can be defined as virtual table obtained upon execution of a SELECT statements. It is comparable to temp tables, however, in the SELECT statement it is much easier and quicker to use a derived table than a temp table as it would not entail additional steps to create the temp table.

There is often interchangeable use of the term derived table and subquery. When the FROM clause of a SELECT query uses a stand-alone subquery, it is called as a derived table. For example, the syntax below can be used to create a derived table:

SELECT
col_list
FROM
(SELECT
col_list
FROM
tab_1) dervd_tab_nam;
WHERE dervd_tab_nam.d1 > 1;

A derived table is required to have an alias, which can be referenced in future queries, however, there is no such requirement for a subquery. If there is no alias defined for a derived table, the error message below will be displayed by MySQL:

"Every derived table must have its own alias"

Review the example below of a query that will generate Top six products by sales in 2013 from the order and order detail tables in the MySQL server "sample database":

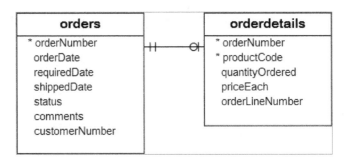

SELECT
pdctCode,
   ROUND(SUM(qtyOrdrd * pricEch)) sale
FROM
orderdetail
      INNER JOIN
   order USING (orderNo)
WHERE
YEAR(shippdDte) = 2013
GROUP BY pdctCode
ORDER BY sale DESC
LIMIT 6;

The resulting table would be similar to the picture shown in the next page:

productCode	sales
S18_3232	103480
S10_1949	67985
S12_1108	59852
S12_3891	57403
S12_1099	56462

The resulting derived table shown in the picture above can be joined with the product table using the syntax below:

products

* productCode
productName
productLine
productScale
productVendor
productDescription
quantityInStock
buyPrice
MSRP

SELECT
pdctNam, sale
FROM
  (SELECT
pdctCode,
  ROUND(SUM(qtyOrdrd * pricEch)) sale
  FROM

orderdetail

   INNER JOIN order USING (orderNo)

   WHERE

YEAR(shippdDte) = 2013

   GROUP BY pdctCode

   ORDER BY sale DESC

   LIMIT 6) top6products2013

INNER JOIN

   product USING (pdctCode);"

The query above will result in the output similar to the one shown in the picture below:

	productName	sales
▶	1992 Ferrari 360 Spider red	103480
	1952 Alpine Renault 1300	67985
	2001 Ferrari Enzo	59852
	1969 Ford Falcon	57403
	1968 Ford Mustang	56462

To drive this concept home, review a relatively complicated example of derived tables below:

Assume that the clients from the year 2019 have to be classified into three groups: platinum, gold and silver. Moreover, taking into consideration the criteria below, you would like to calculate the number of clients within each group:

- Platinum clients with orders larger than 99K in quantity.
- Gold clients with quantity orders ranging from 9K to 99K.
- Silver clients with orders less than 9K in quantity.

To generate a query for this analysis, you must first classify each client into appropriate group using CASE clause and GROUP BY function as shown in the syntax below:

```
SELECT
clientNo,
    ROUND(SUM(qtyOrdrd * pricEch)) sale,
    (CASE
        WHEN SUM(qtyOrdrd * pricEch) < 9000 THEN 'Silver'
        WHEN SUM(qtyOrdrd * pricEch) BETWEEN 9000 AND
99000 THEN 'Gold'
        WHEN SUM(qtyOrdrd * pricEch) >99000 THEN
'Platinum'
    END) clientGroup
FROM
orderdetail
    INNER JOIN
    orders USING (orderNo)
WHERE
```

YEAR(shippdDte) = 2019

GROUP BY clientNo;

The query output will be similar to the one shown in the picture below:

customerNumber	sales	customerGroup
103	14571	Gold
112	32642	Gold
114	53429	Gold
121	51710	Gold
124	167783	Platinum
128	34651	Gold
129	40462	Gold
131	22293	Gold
141	189840	Platinum

Now, you can execute the code below to generate a derived table and group the clients as needed:

SELECT

clientGroup,

COUNT(cg.clientGroup) AS grpCount

FROM

  (SELECT

clientNo,

    ROUND(SUM(qtyOrdrd * pricEch)) sales,

    (CASE

WHEN SUM(qtyOrdrd * pricEch) <9000 THEN 'Silver'

WHEN SUM(qtyOrdrd * pricEch) BETWEEN 9000 AND 99000 THEN 'Gold'

WHEN SUM(qtyOrdrd * pricEch) >99000 THEN 'Platinum'

END) clientGroup

FROM

orderdetail

INNER JOIN orders USING (orderNo)

WHERE

YEAR(shippdDte) = 2019

GROUP BY clientNo) cg

GROUP BY cg.clientGroup; "

The query output will be similar to the one shown in the picture below:

customerGroup	groupCount
Gold	61
Silver	8
Platinum	4

Chapter 3: Advanced SQL Functions

The most common command used in SQL is the SELECT command, which we have already used in the exercises mentioned earlier in this book. So, now let me give you a deep dive into the SQL SELECT command and various clauses that can be used with it.

MySQL SELECT

You can selectively fetch desired data from tables or views, using the SELECT statement. As you already know, similar to a spreadsheet, a table comprises rows and columns. You are highly likely to view a subset of columns, a subset of rows, or a combo of them both. The outcome of this query is known as a "result set," which are lists of records comprising the same number of columns per record.

In the picture shown below of the employee table from the "MySQL sample database", the table has 8 different columns and several records, as shown in the picture in the next page:

employeeNumb	lastName	firstName	extension	email	officeCode	reportsTo	jobTitle
1002	Murphy	Diane	x5800	dmurphy@classicmodelcars.com	1	NULL	President
1056	Patterson	Mary	x4611	mpatterso@classicmodelcars.com	1	1002	VP Sales
1076	Firrelli	Jeff	x9273	jfirrelli@classicmodelcars.com	1	1002	VP Marketing
1088	Patterson	William	x4871	wpatterson@classicmodelcars.com	6	1056	Sales Manager (APAC)
1102	Bondur	Gerard	x5408	gbondur@classicmodelcars.com	4	1056	Sale Manager (EMEA)
1143	Bow	Anthony	x5428	abow@classicmodelcars.com	1	1056	Sales Manager (NA)
1165	Jennings	Leslie	x3291	ljennings@classicmodelcars.com	1	1143	Sales Rep
1166	Thompson	Leslie	x4065	lthompson@classicmodelcars.com	1	1143	Sales Rep
1188	Firrelli	Julie	x2173	jfirrelli@classicmodelcars.com	2	1143	Sales Rep
1216	Patterson	Steve	x4334	spatterson@classicmodelcars.com	2	1143	Sales Rep
1286	Tseng	Foon Yue	x2248	ftseng@classicmodelcars.com	3	1143	Sales Rep
1323	Vanauf	George	x4102	gvanauf@classicmodelcars.com	3	1143	Sales Rep
1337	Bondur	Loui	x6493	lbondur@classicmodelcars.com	4	1102	Sales Rep
1370	Hernandez	Gerard	x2028	ghernande@classicmodelcars.com	4	1102	Sales Rep
1401	Castillo	Pamela	x2759	pcastillo@classicmodelcars.com	4	1102	Sales Rep
1501	Bott	Larry	x2311	lbott@classicmodelcars.com	7	1102	Sales Rep

The SELECT query dictates the columns and records that can be fetched from the table. For instance, if you would like to display just the fstnam, lstnam, and job titl of all the employees or you selectively desire to see the info pertaining to employees with job titl as sales reps, then you will be able to utilize the SELECT query to achieve this.

Here is a standard syntax for SELECT statement:

SELECT
  col_1, col_2, ...
FROM
  tab_1
[INNER | LEFT |RIGHT] JOIN tab_2 ON condition
WHERE
  condition
GROUP BY col_1

HAVING grp_condition
ORDER BY col_1
LIMIT offst, len;

The SELECT query above contains various provisions, as described below:

- The SELECT clause after a list of columns isolated by asterisks or commas suggests that all columns are to be returned.
- The FROM clause defines the table or view from which the data should be queried.
- The JOIN clause receives associated data from other tables as dictated by the specified join criteria.
- In the output, the WHERE clause will be utilized for selectively filtering the rows or records.
- The GROUP BY clause will be utilized to selectively group a set of records and apply aggregate functions to each group.
- The HAVING clause will be utilized to sift through a group on the basis of the GROUP BY clause specified groups.
- The ORDER BY clause can be utilized for specifying a list of columns to be sorted.
- The LIMIT clause is utilized for restricting the number of records displayed upon execution of the command.

Note that only SELECT and FROM clauses are necessary to execute the command and all other clauses can be used on ad-hoc basis.

For example, in case you would like to selectively display certain records of all employees, you can utilize the syntax below:

SELECT
lstnam, fstnam, jobtitl
FROM
  employee;

But if you would like to view all the columns in this table, use the syntax below:

SELECT * FROM employee;

In practice, it is recommended to list the columns you would like to view instead of using the asterisk (*) command, as the asterisk (*) will return all column data, some of which you may not be allowed to use. It will create network traffic and non-essential input output disk between the server and the app. If the columns are defined explicitly, then the result set becomes simpler to predict and handle. Suppose you are using the asterisk(*) and some other user modified the table and generated additional columns, you would receive a result set containing different columns than needed. Moreover, the use of asterisk(*) can potentially reveal sensitive data to unauthorized users.

MySQL SELECT DISTINCT

You can receive duplicate rows when searching for information from a table. You could utilize the DISTINCT clause in the SELECT query to get rid of these redundant rows.

The DISTINCT clause syntax is given below:

SELECT DISTINCT
  cols
FROM
tab_nam
WHERE
whr_condtns;

EXAMPLE

The syntax below presents an example for the DISTINCT clause, used to selectively view unique records of the column lstnam from the employee table.

First, all the records from the column lstnam from the employee tables must be displayed using the syntax below:

SELECT
lstnam

FROM

   employee

ORDER BY lstnam;

Now to get rid of the repeated last names, use the syntax below:

SELECT DISTINCT

lstnam

FROM

   employee

ORDER BY lstnam;

Please note, if a column has been indicated to hold NULL values and the DISTINCT clause is used. Only one NULL value will be retained by the sever since the DISTINCT clause will consider all NULL values as identical.

Using DISTINCTClause on MultipleColumns

To accomplish this MySQL server will use a combination of all values in selected columns to identify unique records in the result set. For example, you can view singular combinations of cty and stat columns from the clients table using the syntax below:

SELECT DISTINCT

   stat, cty

FROM

clients

WHERE

  stat IS NOT NULL

ORDER BY stat, cty;

MySQL ORDER BY

When using SELECT statements, the output will not be organized in a particular format. That is where the ORDER BY clause can be utilized to organize the output as desired. The ORDER BY clause would allow sifting through the output on the basis of one or more columns as well as sorting a number of columns in increasing or decreasing order.

Here is the ORDER BY clause syntax:

SELECT col01, col02,...

FROM tbl

ORDER BY col01 [ASC|DESC], col02 [ASC|DESC], ...;

As you would expect the ASC means ascending and the DESC means descending. By default, if ASC or DESC has not been specified explicitly, the ORDER BY clause can sort the output in ascending order.

EXAMPLE

The syntax below presents an example for the ORDER
BY clause, used to selectively view contacts from the clients table
and sort them in ascending order of the column lstnam.

SELECT

contctlstnam,

contctfstnam

FROM

clients

ORDER BY

contctlstnam;

A sample of the ascending result set is shown in the picture
below:

contactLastname	contactFirstname
Accorti	Paolo
Altagar,G M	Raanan
Andersen	Mel
Anton	Carmen
Ashworth	Rachel
Barajas	Miguel
Benitez	Violeta
Bennett	Helen
Berglund	Christina

Now, if you wanted to view the last name in descending order, you will use the syntax below:

SELECT
contctlstnam,
contctfstnam
FROM
clients
ORDER BY
contctlstnam DESC;"

A sample of the descending result set is shown in the picture below:

contactLastname	contactFirstname
Young	Jeff
Young	Julie
Young	Mary
Young	Dorothy
Yoshido	Juri
Walker	Brydey
Victorino	Wendy
Urs	Braun
Tseng	Jerry

Or, if you would like to arrange the column lstnamin decreasing order and the fstnam in the increasing order, you can utilize the ASC and DESC clause in the same query but with the relevant column as shown in the syntax below:

SELECT

Contctlstnam,

contctfstnam

FROM

clients

ORDER BY

contctlstnam DESC,

contctfstnam ASC;

A sample of the result set is shown in the picture in the next page, where the ORDER BY clause will first sort the lst name in decreasing order and then subsequently sort the fstnam in the increasing order:

contactLastname	contactFirstname
Young	Dorothy
Young	Jeff
Young	Julie
Young	Mary
Yoshido	Juri
Walker	Brydey
Victorino	Wendy
Urs	Braun
Tseng	Jerry

MySQL WHERE

The WHERE clause enables the search criteria to be specified for the records displayed after running the query. The WHERE clause syntax is given below:

SELECT
slct_lst
FROM
tab_nam
WHERE
srch_cndtn;"

The "search_condition" is a composite of single or multiple predicate utilizing the logical operators, as shown in the table below. A "predicate" in SQL, can be defined as a query that assesses unknown, false or true.

Operators	Descriptions
=	Equals. Can be used with any type of data
<>or !=	Not equals
<	Less than. Mostly used with numeric and date data type
>	Greater than
<=	Less than or equals
>=	Greater than or equals

The final result set includes any record from the tab_nam that makes the "search_condition" to be evaluated as valid.

In addition to the SELECT statement, you may indicate the rows that need to be updated and deleted, utilizing the WHERE clause in the DELETE and UPDATE query.

EXAMPLE

The syntax below presents an example for the WHERE clause, used to selectively view employees with job title as Sales Reps from the employee table:

```
SELECT
lstnam,
fstnam,
jobtitl
FROM
    employee
WHERE
jobtitl = 'Sales Reps';
```

Although the WHERE clause is usually defined at the very end, MySQL query first selects the corresponding rows after evaluating the phrase in the WHERE clause. It selects the rows with a job title as Sales Reps followed by the selection of the column in the SELECT clause from the select list. The highlighted rows in the picture below, include the final result set columns and rows.

employeeNumber	lastName	firstName	extension	email	officeCode	reportsTo	jobTitle
1002	Murphy	Diane	x5800	dmurphy@classicmodelcars.com	1	NULL	President
1056	Patterson	Mary	x4611	mpatterso@classicmodelcars.com	1	1002	VP Sales
1076	Firrelli	Jeff	x9273	jfirrelli@classicmodelcars.com	1	1002	VP Marketing
1088	Patterson	William	x4871	wpatterson@classicmodelcars.com	6	1056	Sales Manager (APAC)
1102	Bondur	Gerard	x5408	gbondur@classicmodelcars.com	4	1056	Sale Manager (EMEA)
1143	Bow	Anthony	x5428	abow@classicmodelcars.com	1	1056	Sales Manager (NA)
1165	Jennings	Leslie	x3291	ljennings@classicmodelcars.com	1	1143	Sales Rep
1166	Thompson	Leslie	x4065	lthompson@classicmodelcars.com	1	1143	Sales Rep
1188	Firrelli	Julie	x2173	jfirrelli@classicmodelcars.com	2	1143	Sales Rep
1216	Patterson	Steve	x4334	spatterson@classicmodelcars.com	2	1143	Sales Rep
1286	Tseng	Foon Yue	x2248	ftseng@classicmodelcars.com	3	1143	Sales Rep
1323	Vanauf	George	x4102	gvanauf@classicmodelcars.com	3	1143	Sales Rep
1337	Bondur	Lou	x6493	lbondur@classicmodelcars.com	4	1102	Sales Rep
1370	Hernandez	Gerard	x2028	ghernande@classicmodelcars.com	4	1102	Sales Rep

MySQL JOIN Statements

The MySQL JOIN function is a way to link information between one or more tables on the basis of common attributes or column values between the selected tables. A relational database comprises of various tables that have been linked by a shared or common column, known as foreign key. As a result, information in each individual table can be deemed incomplete from the business perspective.for instance, there are two separate tables in the MySQL sample database called order and order detail that have been connected to each other using a column called orderNo. You will have to search for information in both the order and the order detail table to obtain complete order information.

There are 6 different SQL JOINS functions, namely, "INNER JOIN,""LEFT JOIN," "RIGHT JOIN,""CROSS JOIN" and "SELF JOIN."

We will be using tables named t01 and t02 as described in the syntax below, in order to facilitate your understanding of each type of JOIN. The pattern column in both t01 and t02 tables serves as the common column between them.

```
CREATE TABLE t01 (
  id INT PRIMARY KEY,
ptrn VARCHAR(45) NOT NULL
);
```

```
CREATE TABLE t02 (
  id VARCHAR(45) PRIMARY KEY,
ptrn VARCHAR(45) NOT NULL
);
```

We can insert some data into the two tables using INSERT function as shown in the syntax below:

```
INSERT INTO t01(id, ptrn)
VALUES(01,'Pivots'),
    (02,'Bricks'),
    (03,'Grids');
```

INSERT INTO to2(id, ptrn)
VALUES('X','Bricks'),
  ('Y','Grids'),
  ('Z','Diamonds');"

The result of the syntax above will be similar to the one shown in the picture in the next page:

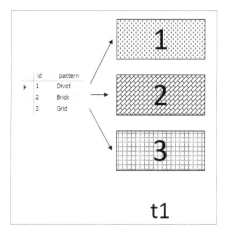

Now, let us look at every type of "JOIN" clause in detail!

"INNER JOIN"

The MySQL INNER JOIN is used to align records of a table with another, so that rows containing columns from the two tables can be queried.

The SELECT statement is not required to contain the INNER JOIN clause for execution, which appears right next to the FROM clause.

You must indicate the following requirements before using the INNER JOIN clause:

- Start with the primary table to be included in the FROM clause.
- Then, choose the table that needs to be connected to the primary table included in the INNER JOIN clause, in step 1. Remember theoretically you can join one table to multiple tables at the same time. However, it is recommended to restrict the number of tables to be joined, to achieve higher performance and efficiency.
- Lastly, the join condition or join predicate must be defined. Following the initial "ON" keyword the join condition can be indicated. The join condition is the rule that dictates the matching of a record in the main table with the rows from another.

The INNER JOIN syntax is given below:

SELECT col_lst
FROM to1
INNER JOIN to2 ON join_cndtn1
INNER JOIN to3 ON join_cndtn2
...
WHERE whr_cndtns;

Now, for further simplification of the query above, just assume that you are interested in linking only tables to1 and to2 using the syntax below:

SELECT col_lst
FROM to1
INNER JOIN to2 ON jn_cndtn;

This clause will compare every row of to1 with every single row of to2 to determine whether the two tables fulfill the defined condition. Once the condition has been satisfied, a new record will be returned, consisting of columns from both to1 and to2.

Note that the records in both to1 and to2 need to be merged according to the conditions. If none of the records from the two tables are identified meeting the join condition, an empty result set is returned by the query. The same logic applies when more than two tables are joined.

The Venn diagram below shows the working of the "INNER JOIN" clause. The records in the output are required to be present in both to1 and to2 as represented by the section overlapping the 2 circles, depicting each table respectively.

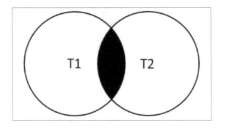

EXAMPLE

Consider the two tables from the "sample database," shown in the picture below. The second table is connected to the first table by referencing the productline column. Therefore, the productline column serves as foreign key in the products table. Conventionally, tables that have foreign key relationships are queried using the JOIN clause.

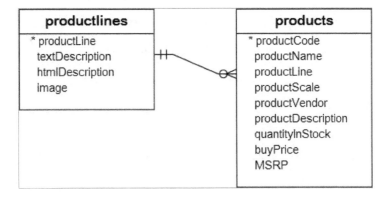

Let's assume that you would like to view the pdctCod and pdctNam columns from the second table as well as txtDesc of the product lined from the first table. You can accomplish this by using the syntax below and matching the rows of both the tables on the basis of productline columns in the two tables.

SELECT
pdctCod,
pdctNam,
txtDesc
FROM
pdcts to1
    INNER JOIN
pdctlines to2 ON to1.pductlin = to2.pductlin;

A sample of the result set is shown in the picture below:

productCode	productName	textDescription
S10_1949	1952 Alpine Renault 1300	Attention car enthusiasts: Make your wildest car ownership dreams come true.
S10_4757	1972 Alfa Romeo GTA	Attention car enthusiasts: Make your wildest car ownership dreams come true.
S10_4962	1962 LanciaA Delta 16V	Attention car enthusiasts: Make your wildest car ownership dreams come true.
S12_1099	1968 Ford Mustang	Attention car enthusiasts: Make your wildest car ownership dreams come true.
S12_1108	2001 Ferrari Enzo	Attention car enthusiasts: Make your wildest car ownership dreams come true.

Here's a tip!

Since both the tables contain identical column called "productline", you could use the simpler query below (without the need of using the table aliases) and obtain the same "result set" as shown in the picture above:

SELECT
pdctCod,
pdctNam,

303

txtDes

FROM

pdct

    INNER JOIN

pdctlines USING (pductlin);"

INNER JOIN with GROUP BY

The picture below contains two sample tables:

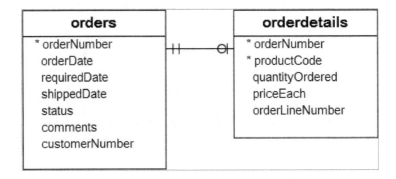

You could utilize this clause to obtain desired information from the two tables as shown in the two syntax below:

SELECT

    To1.orderNo,

    stats,

    *SUM(qtyOrdrd * pricEch) total*

FROM

    order AS To1

INNER JOIN

orderdetail AS To2 ON To1.orderNo = To2.orderNo

GROUP BY orderNo;

SELECT

orderNo,

  stats,

*SUM(qtyOrdrd * pricEch) total*

FROM

  order

  INNER JOIN

orderdetail USING (orderNo)

GROUP BY orderNo;"

A sample of the result set is shown in the picture below:

orderNumber	status	total
10100	Shipped	10223.83
10101	Shipped	10549.01
10102	Shipped	5494.78
10103	Shipped	50218.95
10104	Shipped	40206.20

MySQL INNER JOIN with Different Operators

We have only explored the join condition using the equal operator (=) to match the rows. But we can also use other operators with the join predicate including greater than (>), less than (<), and not-equal (<>) operators.

The syntax below utilizes a less than (<) operator to identify the sales price for the item with the code S11 1789, which are lower than the marked price.

SELECT

orderNo,

prdctNam,

mrp,

pricEch

FROM

  product x

    INNER JOIN

orderdetail y ON x.pdctcod = y.pdctcod

    AND x.mrp>y.pricEch

WHER

x.pdctcode = 'S11_1789';

A sample of the result set is shown in the picture below:

orderNumber	productName	msrp	priceEach
10107	1969 Harley Davidson Ultimate Chopper	95.70	81.35
10121	1969 Harley Davidson Ultimate Chopper	95.70	86.13
10134	1969 Harley Davidson Ultimate Chopper	95.70	90.92
10145	1969 Harley Davidson Ultimate Chopper	95.70	76.56
10159	1969 Harley Davidson Ultimate Chopper	95.70	81.35
10168	1969 Harley Davidson Ultimate Chopper	95.70	94.74
10180	1969 Harley Davidson Ultimate Chopper	95.70	76.56
10201	1969 Harley Davidson Ultimate Chopper	95.70	82.30

LEFT JOIN

The MySQL LEFT JOIN enables querying of data from 2 or multiple tables on a database. The SELECT statement is not required to contain the LEFT JOIN clause for execution, which appears right next to the FROM clause. The principles of left table and right table are implemented when the 2 tables are linked, using the LEFT JOIN clause.

Unlike an INNER JOIN, these will return all rows in the left table, the rows meeting the condition and even the records not meeting the condition. The NULL value appears in the result set of the columns from the table on the right for records not meeting the condition.

Now, to further simplify this query we will assume that we are interested in linking only tables to1 and to2with the LEFT JOIN per the syntax below:

SELECT
to1.co1, to1.co2, to2.co1, to2.co2
FROM
to1
   LEFT JOIN
to2 ON to1.co1 = to2.co1;

In the syntax above, you are using the LEFT JOIN clause to connect the to1 to the to2, on the basis of a record from the table to1 on the left, aligning a record from the to2 on the right as defined by the join predicate (to1.co1= to2.co1), which are then included in the output.

If the record in the table on the left has no matching record that aligns with it in the table on the right, then the record in the table on the left will still be chosen and
joined with a virtual record containing NULL values from the table on the right.

To put it simply, the LEFT JOIN clause enables selection of matching records from both the left and right tables, as well as all records from the left table (t01), even without aligning records from the right table (t02).

The Venn diagram shown in the picture below will help you understand how the working of the LEFT JOIN. The overlapping section of the two circles includes records that matched from the two tables, and the rest of the portion of the left circle includes rows in the t01 table with no corresponding record in the t02 table. Therefore, the output will include all records in the next table.

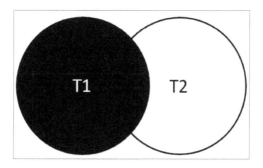

EXAMPLE

Consider the two tables, shown in the picture below, wherein every order value in the second table corresponds to a customer value in the first table but every customer value in the first table may not have a corresponding order value in the second table.

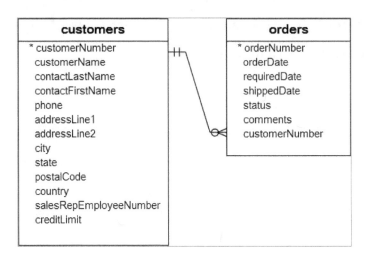

All the orders corresponding to a client can be queried using the LEFT JOIN clause using the syntax in the next page:

SELECT
x.clientNo,
x.clientNam,
orderNo,
y.stats
FROM
clients x
LEFT JOIN order y ON x.clientNo = y.clientNo;"

The sample output is shown in the picture below, where the left table refers to the clients table, so all the rows with value in the clients table will beadded to the output; although it contains rows with client data that have no order data such as

168 and 169. For such rows, the order data value is reflected as NULL implying that there is no order in the order table for those clients.

customerNumber	customerName	orderNumber	status
166	Handji Gifts& Co	10288	Shipped
166	Handji Gifts& Co	10409	Shipped
167	Herkku Gifts	10181	Shipped
167	Herkku Gifts	10188	Shipped
167	Herkku Gifts	10289	Shipped
168	American Souvenirs Inc	NULL	NULL
169	Porto Imports Co.	NULL	NULL
171	Daedalus Designs Imports	10180	Shipped
171	Daedalus Designs Imports	10224	Shipped
172	La Corne D'abondance, ...	10114	Shipped

Here's a tip!

Since both the tables share the column nameclientsNo, you could utilize the simpler query below (without the need of using the table aliases) and obtain the same output as shown in the picture above:

SELECT
x.clientNo,
x.clientNam,
orderNo,
stats
FROM

clients x

LEFT JOINorder USING (clientNo);

MySQL LEFT JOIN with WHEREClause

Consider the syntax below with WHERE clause is used after the "LEFT JOIN" to retrieve desired information from the two tables.

SELECT

y.orderNo,

clientNo,

pdctCod

FROM

  Order y

    LEFT JOIN

orderDetail USING (orderNo)

WHERE

orderNo = 10125;

A sample of the "result set" is shown in the picture below for all the order number listed as 10123:

orderNumber	customerNumber	productCode
10123	103	S18_1589
10123	103	S18_2870
10123	103	S18_3685
10123	103	S24_1628

Note that if the join condition was changed from WHERE clause to the ON clause as shown in the syntax below, then the query will produce a different result set containing all orders but only the details associated with the order number 10125 will be displayed, similar to the picture below for 10123:

SELECT
y.orderNo,
clientNo,
pdctCod
FROM
  orders y
    LEFT JOIN
orderDetailz ON y.orderNo = y.orderNo
  AND y.orderNo = 10125;

orderNumber	customerNumber	productCode
10123	103	S18_1589
10123	103	S18_2870
10123	103	S18_3685
10123	103	S24_1628
10298	103	NULL
10345	103	NULL
10124	112	NULL
10278	112	NULL
10346	112	NULL
10120	114	NULL

RIGHT JOIN

The RIGHT JOIN or RIGHT OUTER JOIN is similar to the LEFT JOIN with the only difference being the treatment of the tables, which has been reversed from left to right. Each record from the table (to2) on the right appears in the output with a RIGHT JOIN. The NULL value will be displayed for columns in the table (to1) on the left for the records in the right table without any corresponding rows in the table (to1).

You could utilize the RIGHT JOIN clause to link tables to1 and to2 as illustrated in the syntax below:

SELECT
   *

FROM to1
  RIGHT JOIN to2 ON jn_predict;

In the syntax above, the right table is to2 and the left table is to1 and join_predicate indicated the matching criteria with which records from to1 will be aligned with records from to2.

With the execution of the query above, all the rows from the to2 will be displayed in the output and on the basis of the join condition, if no match are found for to2 with the rows of to1 then NULL value will be added to those columns from to1 table.

EXAMPLE

Let's consider the tables to1 and to2 as described in the syntax below:

CREATE TABLE to1 (
id INT PRIMARY KEY,
ptrn VARCHAR(45) NOT NULL
);

CREATE TABLE to2 (
id VARCHAR(45) PRIMARY KEY,
ptrnVARCHAR(45) NOT NULL
);

INSERT INTO to1(id, ptrn)
VALUES(o1,'Pivot'),
(o2,'Bricks'),
(o3,'Grids');

INSERT INTO to2(id, pattern)
VALUES('A','Bricks'),
('B','Grids'),
('C','Diamonds');

The tables to1 and to2 can be joined with the pattern columns, as illustrated in the query below:

SELECT

to1.id, to2.id

FROM

to1

    RIGHT JOIN to2 USING (ptrn)

ORDER BY to2.id;

The result set is shown in the picture below:

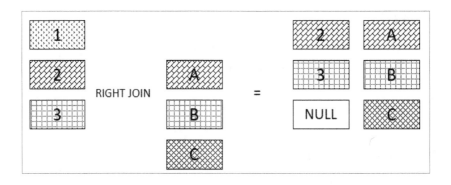

Or look at the syntax below to view the sales reps and their clients from the employee and client table:

SELECT

Cncat (h.fstNam,' ', h.lstNam) salesmn,

h.jobTitl,

clientNam

FROM

  employee h

RIGHT JOIN

clients x ON h.employeeNo = x.salesRepEmployeeNo

AND h.jobTitl = 'Sales Reps'

ORDER BY clientNam;

A sample of the result set is shown in the picture below:

salesman	jobTitle	customerName
Gerard Hernandez	Sales Rep	Alpha Cognac
Foon Yue Tseng	Sales Rep	American Souvenirs Inc
Pamela Castillo	Sales Rep	Amica Models & Co.
NULL	NULL	ANG Resellers
Andy Fixter	Sales Rep	Anna's Decorations, Ltd
NULL	NULL	Anton Designs, Ltd.
NULL	NULL	Asian Shopping Network, Co
NULL	NULL	Asian Treasures, Inc.

CROSS JOIN

The CROSS JOIN clause is used to obtain a Cartesian product, which is defined as joining of each record of a table to each record of another. When this clause is utilized, the output contains all records from the two tables, which are a composite of the record from the 1st table and record from the 2nd table. This case exists only when a common link or column between the two tables that are joined cannot be found.

The biggest drawback is sheer volume of data, assume each table contains 1,000 rows, then the result set will contain 1,000x 1,000= 1,000,000 rows.

You could utilize the CROSS JOIN to join to1 and to2 as displayed in the syntax below:

SELECT

   *

FROM

To1

   CROSS JOIN

To2;

Unlike the RIGHT JOIN and LEFT JOIN, the CROSS JOIN can be operated without using a join predicate. Moreover, if the WHERE clause is added to the CROSS JOIN and the two tables to1 and to2 have a connection then it will operate as INNER JOIN, as displayed in the syntax below:

SELECT

   *

FROM

To1

   CROSS JOIN

To2

WHERE

To1.id = To2.id;

EXAMPLE

Let's use testdb database as described in the syntax below to better understand how the CROSS JOIN operates:

CREATE DATABASE IF NOT EXISTS testdb3;

USE testdb3;

CREATE TABLE pdct (
  id INT PRIMARY KEY AUTO_INCREMENT,
pdct_nam VARCHAR(110),
pric DECIMAL(12, 3)
);

CREATE TABLE stre (
  id INT PRIMARY KEY AUTO_INCREMENT,
stre_nam VARCHAR(110)
);

CREATE TABLE sale (
pdct_id INT,
stre_id INT,
  qty DECIMAL(12 , 3) NOT NULL,
sale_dat DATE NOT NULL,

PRIMARY KEY (pdct_id ,stre_id),
FOREIGN KEY (pdct_id)
  REFERENCES pdcts (id)
  ON DELETE CASCADE ON UPDATE CASCADE,
FOREIGN KEY (stre_id)
  REFERENCES stres (id)
  ON DELETE CASCADE ON UPDATE CASCADE
);

In the syntax above, we have 3 tables:
- The pdct table, which holds the fundamental data of the pdct including pdct id, pdct name, and sales pric.
- The stre table, which holds the data pertaining to the stores where the products are available for purchase.
- The sale table, which holds the data pertaining to the products sold in specific stores by date and quantity.

Let's assume there are 3 itemsMyPhone, Tablet and Comp available for selling 2 stores named North's and South's. We can populate the tables to hold this data using the syntax below:

INSERT INTO product(pdct_name, price)
VALUES('MyPhone', 899),
  ('Tablet', 499),
  ('Comp', 1599);

INSERT INTO stres(stre_name)

VALUES('North's'),

    ('South's');

INSERT INTO sale (stre_id,pdct_id, qty,sale_dat)

VALUES(10,10,200,'2018-02-03'),

    (10,20, 35, '2018-01-05'),

    (10, 30, 35,'2018-01-05'),

    (20 ,10 ,40,'2018-02-03'),

    (20, 20, 45,'2018-01-06');"

Now, to view the total sales for every product and store, the sales must be calculated first and then grouped by the store and product using the syntax below:

SELECT

stre_name,

pdct_name,

    *SUM(qty * pric) AS rev*

FROM

    sale

      INNER JOIN

pdct ON pdct.id = sale.pdct_id

      INNER JOIN

stres ON stres.id = sale.stre_id

GROUP BY stre_name ,pdct_name;

A sample of the result set is shown in the picture below:

store_name	product_name	revenue
North	iPad	8985.0000
North	iPhone	13980.0000
North	Macbook Pro	32475.0000
South	iPad	20965.0000
South	iPhone	20970.0000

Now, if you wanted to view the stores that had zero sale for a particular product, the syntax above will not provide you that information. This is where you can utilize the CROSS JOIN to first view a composite of all products and stores, as displayed in the query below:

SELECT
stre_name, pdct_name
FROM
stres AS p
*   CROSS JOIN*
pdct AS q;

A sample of the result set is shown in the picture below:

store_name	product_name
North	iPhone
South	iPhone
North	iPad
South	iPad
North	Macbook Pro
South	Macbook Pro

And then, you can join the query result received earlier with this query that will result in the total sales by products and stores, using the syntax below:

SELECT

y.stre_name,

x.pdct_name,

  IFNULL(z.rev, a) AS rev

FROM

pdcts AS x

  CROSS JOIN

stres AS y

  LEFT JOIN

  (SELECT

stres.id AS stre_id,

pdcts.id AS pdct_id,

stre_name,

pdct_name,

*ROUND(SUM (quantity * price), a) AS rev*

FROM

  sale

INNER JOIN pdcts ON pdcts.id = sales.pdct_id

INNER JOIN stres ON stres.id = sales.stre_id

GROUP BY stre_name ,pdct_name) AS c ON z.stre_id = y.id

  AND z.pdct_id= x.id

ORDER BY y.stre_name;

A sample of the result set is shown in the picture below:

store_name	product_name	revenue
North	Macbook Pro	32475
North	iPad	8985
North	iPhone	13980
South	iPhone	20970
South	Macbook Pro	0
South	iPad	20965

The IFNULL function was used in the syntax above to return 0 in case the revenue was reported as NULL.

SELF JOIN

As the name indicates, the SELF JOIN statements are utilized to link records of one table to records within the same table instead of another table. This requires you to use a table alias to aid the server in differentiating between the table on the left from the right within the same query. For instance, take the employees table in the "MySQL sample database" where structural data for the organization is stored along with the employee data, as shown in the picture below. The "reportsTo" column can be utilized to view the manager Id of any employee.

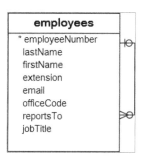

If you would like to view the complete org structure, you could self-join the employee table using employeeNo and reports to column, using the syntax below. The 2 roles in the employees table are Manager and Direct Reports.

SELECT

    CONCAT(n.lstname, ', ', n.fstname) AS 'Mgr',

    CONCAT(a.lstname, ', ', a.fstname) AS 'Drct rprt'

FROM

    Employee a

      INNER JOIN

    employee n ON n.employeeNo = a.reportsto

ORDER BY mgr;

A sample of the output is shown in the picture below:

Manager	Direct report
Bondur, Gerard	Jones, Barry
Bondur, Gerard	Bott, Larry
Bondur, Gerard	Castillo, Pamela
Bondur, Gerard	Hernandez, Gerard
Bondur, Gerard	Bondur, Loui
Bondur, Gerard	Gerard, Martin
Bow, Anthony	Tseng, Foon Yue
Bow, Anthony	Patterson, Steve
Bow, Anthony	Firrelli, Julie
Bow, Anthony	Thompson, Leslie
Bow, Anthony	Jennings, Leslie
Bow, Anthony	Vanauf, George

Only employees who are reporting to a manager can be seen in the result set above. But the lead manager is not visible as his name has been filtered out with the INNER JOIN clause. The lead manager is the manager who is not reporting to anyone or their manager no is holding a NULL value.

We can alter the INNER JOIN clause in the syntax above to the LEFT JOIN clause so it would include the lead manager in the output. If the name of the manager is holding a NULL value, you can utilize the "IFNULL" clause to include the lead manager in the output, as shown in the query below:

SELECT
  IFNULL(CONCAT(n.lstname, ', ', n.fstname),
    'Lead Mgr') AS 'Mgr',

CONCAT(a.lstname, ', ', a.fstname) AS 'Drct rprt'

FROM

   Employee a

     LEFT JOIN

   employee n ON n.employeeNo = a.reportsto

ORDER BY mgr DESC;

A sample of the output is shown in the picture below:

Manager	Direct report
Top Manager	Murphy, Diane
Patterson, William	King, Tom
Patterson, William	Marsh, Peter
Patterson, William	Fixter, Andy
Patterson, Mary	Bondur, Gerard
Patterson, Mary	Nishi, Mami
Patterson, Mary	Patterson, William
Patterson, Mary	Bow, Anthony
Nishi, Mami	Kato, Yoshimi
Murphy, Diane	Firrelli, Jeff
Murphy, Diane	Patterson, Mary

You will be able to show a list of clients at a selected location by linking the clients table to itself with the use of the MySQL self join, as shown in the query below:

SELECT

   j1.cty, j1.clientName, j2.clientName

FROM

   clients j1

INNER JOIN

clients j2 ON j1.cty = j2.cty

    AND j1.clientname> j2.clientName

ORDER BY j1.cty;"

A sample of the output is shown in the picture below:

city	customerName	customerName
Auckland	Kelly's Gift Shop	Down Under Souveniers, Inc
Auckland	GiftsForHim.com	Down Under Souveniers, Inc
Auckland	Kelly's Gift Shop	GiftsForHim.com
Boston	Gifts4AllAges.com	Diecast Collectables
Brickhaven	Online Mini Collectables	Auto-Moto Classics Inc.
Brickhaven	Collectables For Less Inc.	Auto-Moto Classics Inc.
Brickhaven	Online Mini Collectables	Collectables For Less Inc.
Cambridge	Marta's Replicas Co.	Cambridge Collectables Co.
Frankfurt	Messner Shopping Network	Blauer See Auto, Co.
Glendale	Gift Ideas Corp.	Boards & Toys Co.
Lisboa	Porto Imports Co.	Lisboa Souveniers, Inc
London	Stylish Desk Decors, Co.	Double Decker Gift Stores, Ltd

MySQL UNION

The UNION function in MySQL is used to merge multiple result sets to obtain one comprehensive output. The syntax for the UNION operator is given below:

SELECT col_list

UNION [DISTINCT | ALL]

SELECT col_list

UNION [DISTINCT | ALL]

SELECT col_list

.....

The fundamental rules to follow with the use of the UNION
operator are:

- It is very critical that the number and the sequence of
  columns included in the SELECT statement is the same.
- The data types of the columns are required to be identical
  or convertible to the same.
- The redundant or duplicate rows will be removed without
  explicitly using the DISTINT function in the query.

EXAMPLE

Consider the sample tables to1 and to2 as described in the
syntax below:

DROP TABLE IF EXISTS to1;
DROP TABLE IF EXISTS to2;

CREATE TABLE to1 (
  identity INT PRIMARY KEY
);

CREATE TABLE to2 (
identity INT PRIMARY KEY
);

INSERT INTO to1 VALUES (10),(20),(30);

INSERT INTO to2 VALUES (20),(30),(40);

The query below can be used to combine the result sets from to1 and to2 tables using the UNION operator:

SELECT identity
FROM to1
UNION
SELECT identity
FROM to2;

The combined output generated will contain varying values from both the result sets, as shown below:

```
+------+
| identity |
+------+
| 10 |
| 20 |
| 30 |
| 40 |
| 50 |
+------+
```
5 rows in set (0.3 sec)

One can notice that the rows containing values 2 and 3 are redundant, so the UNION function dropped the duplicate and retain the distinct values only. The picture below of the Venn diagram, represents the combination of the output from t01 and t02 tables:

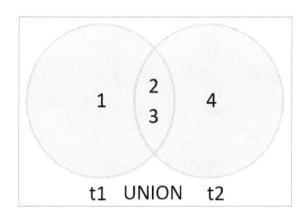

t1 UNION t2

MySQL UNION ALL

The UNION ALL operator is utilized when you want to retain the duplicate rows (if any) in the output. The speed with which the query is executed is much higher for the UNION ALL operator than the UNION or UNION DISTINCT operator, as it does not need to deal with the redundancy of the data. The syntax for the UNION ALL operator is shown in the query below:

SELECT identity
FROM t01

UNION ALL

SELECT identity

FROM to2;

The result set is given below, which contains duplicate rows:

```
+------+
| identity |
+------+
| 10 |
| 20 |
| 50 |
| 30 |
| 20 |
| 30 |
| 40 |
+----+
```

7 rows in set (0.02 sec)

MySQL JOIN vs UNION

The JOIN clause is utilized to merge the result sets horizontally or on the basis of the rows or records. On the other hand, the UNION clause is utilized to merge the result sets vertically or on the basis of the columns of the tables. The picture below will help you understand the distinction between UNION and JOIN operators:

id		id		id		
1		2		1		Append result sets vertically
2	UNION	3	⟹	2		
3		4		3		
				4		

id		id		id	id	Append result sets horizontally
1		2		2	2	
2	INNER	3	⟹	3	3	
3	JOIN	4				

MySQL UNION and ORDER BY

This clause can be utilized to sort the results of a UNION operator as shown the query below:

SELECT
conct(fstName,' ',lstName) fulname
FROM
   employee
UNION SELECT
conct(cntctFstName,' ',cntctLstName)
FROM
clients
ORDER BY fulname;

A sample of the output is shown in the picture below:

fullname
▶ Adrian Huxley
Akiko Shimamura
Alejandra Camino
Alexander Feuer
Alexander Semenov
Allen Nelson
Andy Fixter
Ann Brown
Anna O'Hara
Annette Roulet

If you would like to sort the result on the basis of a column position, you could utilize the ORDER BY by executing the syntax below:

SELECT
conct (fstName,' ',lstName) fulname
FROM
  employee
UNION SELECT
conct (cntctFstName,' ',cntctLstName)

FROM
clients
ORDER BY 2;

Chapter 4: SQL Views and Transactions

A Database View in SQL is defined as a "virtual or logical table" described as the SELECT statements containing join function. As a Database View is like a table in the database consisting of rows and columns, you will be able to easily run queries on it. Many DBMSs, including MySQL, enable users to modify information in the existing tables using Database View by meeting certain prerequisites, as shown in the picture below.

A SQL database View can be deemed dynamic since there is no connection between the SQL View to the physical system. The database system will store SQL Views in the form on SELECT statements using JOIN clause. When the information in the table is modified, the SQL View will also reflect that modification.

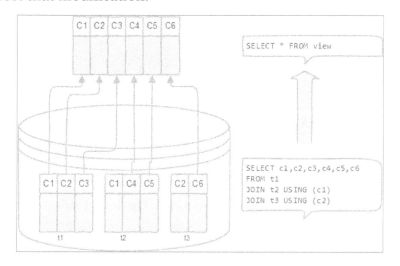

Pros of Using SQL View

- A SQL View enables simplification of complicated queries: a SQL View is characterized by a SQL statement which is associated with multiple tables. To conceal the complexity of the underlying tables from the end-users and external apps, SQL View is extremely helpful. You only need to use straightforward SQL statements instead of complicated ones with multiple JOIN clauses using the SQL View.

- A SQL View enables restricted access to information depending on the user requirements. Perhaps you would not like all users to be able to query a subset of confidential information. In such cases SQL View can be used to selectively expose non-sensitive information to a targeted set of users.

- The SQL View offers an additional layer of safety. Data security is a key component of every DBMS. It ensures additional security for the DBMS. It enables generation of a read only view to display read only information for targeted users. In read only view, users are able to only retrieve data and are not allowed to update any information.

- The SQL View is used to enable computed columns. The table in the database is not capable of containing computed columns but a SQL View can easily contain computed column. Assume in the

OrderDetails table there is the quantity Order column for the amount of products ordered and priceEach column for the price of each item. But the OrderDetails table cannot contain a calculated column storing total sales for every product from the order. If it could, the database schema may have never been a good design. In such a situation, to display the calculated outcome, you could generate a computed column called total, which would be a product of quantityOrder and priceEach columns. When querying information from the SQL View, the calculated column information will be calculated on the fly.

- A SQL View allows for backward compatibility. Assume that we have a central database that is being used by multiple applications. Out of the blue you have been tasked to redesign the database accommodating the new business needs. As you delete some tables and create new ones, you would not want other applications to be affected by these modifications. You could generate SQL Views in such situations, using the identical schematic of the legacy tables that you are planning to delete.

Cons of Using SQL View

In addition to the pros listed above, the use of SQL View may have certain disadvantages such as:

- Performance: Executing queries against SQL View could be slow, particularly if it is generated from another SQL View.
- Table dependencies: Since a SQL View is created from the underlying tables of the database. Anytime the tables structure connected with SQL View is modified, you also need to modify the SQL View.

Views in MySQLServer

As of the release of MySQL version 5+, it has been supporting database views. In MySQL, nearly all characteristics of a View conform to the standard SQL: 2003.

MySQL can run queries against the views in couple of ways:
1. MySQL can produce a temp table based on the "view definition statement" and then execute all following queries on this temp table.
2. MySQL can combine the new queries with the query that specifies the SQL View into a single comprehensive query and then this merged query can be executed.

MySQL offers versioning capability for all SQL Views. Whenever a SQL View is modified or substituted, its clone is backed up in the arc (archive) directory residing in a particular folder, which is named view name.frm-0001. If the view is modified in future,

338

then MySQL would generate a new backup file called view name.frm-0002.

You can also generate a view based on other views through MySQL, by creating references for other views in the SELECT statement defining the target SQL View.

CREATE VIEW in MySQL

The CREATE VIEW query can be utilized to generate new SQL Views in MySQL, as shown in the syntax below:

CREATE
[ALGRTHM = {MRG | TEMPTAB | UNDEFND}]
VIEW view_nam [(col_lst)]
AS
select statmnt;
"View Processing Algorithms"

The attribute of the algorithm enables you to regulate which mechanism is utilized by MySQL to create the SQL View. Three algorithms are provided by MySQL, namely: MERGE, TEMPTABLE and UNDEFINED.

- To use the MERGE algorithm, server will start by combining the incoming queries with the SELECT statement, that will define the view into a merged query. Subsequently, the merged query is executed by MySQL to retrieve the output. This algorithm cannot be used if the SELECT statements consist of aggregate functions like "MIN, MAX, SUM, COUNT, AVG or DISTINCT, GROUP BY, HAVING, LIMIT, UNION, UNION ALL, subquery." If these statements do not refer to a table, then this algorithm cannot be utilized. In the cases, where the MERGE algorithm is not permitted, server will instead use the UNDEFINED algorithm. Please remember that the view resolution is defined as a combo of input queries and the view definition queries into one.

- Using the TEMPTABLE algorithm, server will start with production of a temporary table that describes the SQL View on the basis of the SELECT statement. Subsequently any incoming query will be executed against this temp table. This algorithm has lower efficiency than the "MERGE" algorithm because MySQL requires generation of a temp table to save the output and will transfer the data from the standard table to the temp. Moreover, a SQL View using the TEMPTABLE algorithm cannot be updated.

- If you generate a view without explicitly stating an algorithm that needs to be used, then the UNDEFINED algorithm will be used by default. The UNDEFINED algorithm allows MySQL to choose from the MERGE or TEMPTABLE algorithm to be used. Since the MERGE algorithm is much more effective,

MySQL prefers MERGE algorithm
over TEMPTABLE algorithm.

View Name

Views and tables are stored in the same space within
the database, so it is not possible to give the same name to a
view and a table. Furthermore, the name of a view has to be in
accordance with the naming conventions of the table.

SELECT statements

It is easy to retrieve desired data from tables or views contained
within a database by utilizing these statements.
These statements are required to meet various guidelines, such
as:

- It may comprise of sub-queries in the "WHERE" clause
  but cannot have any in the "FROM" clause.
- No variables, including session variables, local variables,
  user variables, and, can be referred to in these
  statements.
- These statements can also not have a reference to the
  parameters of prepared statements and is not required to
  refer to any other table.

EXAMPLE

To generate a view of the orderDetail table that contains the total sales per order, you can use the query below:

CREATE VIEW SalePrordr AS
  SELECT
*orderNo, SUM(qtyOrdrd * pricEch) total*
  FROM
orderDetail
  GROUP by orderNo
  ORDER BY totl DESC;

By using the "SHOW TABLE" command you can check all the tables in the classic model database, it is easily visible that the SalesPrOrdr view is on the displayed list (shown in the picture below):

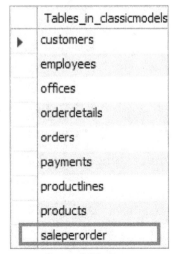

This proves that the view names and table names are stored in the same space within the database. So, now if you would like to know which object in the picture above is view or table, use the "SHOW FULL TABLE" query and the output will be displayed as shown in the picture below:

Tables_in_classicmodels	Table_type
customers	BASE TABLE
employees	BASE TABLE
offices	BASE TABLE
orderdetails	BASE TABLE
orders	BASE TABLE
payments	BASE TABLE
productlines	BASE TABLE
products	BASE TABLE
saleperorder	VIEW

You can check the table_type column in the picture above to confirm objects that may be views or tables.

Now, you can simply utilize these statements below to view total sales for each sales order:

SELECT
   *

FROM
salePrOrdr;

The output is displayed in the picture below:

orderNumber	total
▶ 10165	67392.84
10287	61402
10310	61234.66
10212	59830.54
10207	59265.14
10127	58841.35
10204	58793.53
10126	57131.92

Creating a SQL View from Another SQL View

The MySQL server permits creation of a new view on the basis of another view. For instance, you could produce a view named BigSalesOrdr based on the SalesPrOrdr view that we created earlier to show every sales order for which the total adds up to more than 61,000 using the syntax below:

CREATE VIEW BigSalesOrdr AS
   SELECT
orderNo, ROUND (totl, 3) as total
   FROM

saleprordr

   WHERE

totl> 61000;

You could easily retrieve desired data from the BigSalesOrdr view as shown below:

SELECT

orderNo, totl

FROM

BigSalesOrdr;

	orderNumber	total
▶	10165	67392.85
	10287	61402.00
	10310	61234.67

Create SQL View with JOIN Clause

The MySQL database allows you to create SQL View using JOIN clause. For instance, the query below with the INNER JOIN clause can be used to create a view containing order no, client name, and totl sale per ordr:

CREATE VIEW clientOrdrs AS

   SELECT

x.orderNo,

clientName,

   SUM(qtyOrdrd * pricEch) total

   FROM

orderDetail d

     INNER JOIN

     order r ON r.orderNo = x.orderNo

     INNER JOIN

     clients y ON y.clientNo = y.clientNo

   GROUP BY x.orderNo

   ORDER BY totl DESC;

By executing the syntax below, the desired data can be retrieved from the client order view:

SELECT *FROM

clientOrder;

The result set is displayed in the picture below:

orderNumber	customerName	total
10165	Dragon Souveniers, Ltd.	67392.84
10287	Vida Sport, Ltd	61402
10310	Toms Spezialitäten, Ltd	61234.66
10212	Euro+ Shopping Channel	59830.54
10207	Diecast Collectables	59265.14
10127	Muscle Machine Inc	58841.35
10204	Muscle Machine Inc	58793.53
10126	Comida Auto Replicas, Ltd	57131.92

Create SQL View with a Subquery

The query below can be used to generate a SQL View with a subquery, containing products with purchase prices greater than the average product prices.

CREATE VIEW abvAvgPdcts AS
  SELECT
pdctCode, pdctName, buyPric
  FROM
pdcts
  WHERE
buyPric>
(SELECT
AVG(buyPric)
  FROM
pdcts)
  ORDER BY buyPric DESC;

The query to extract data from the aboveAvgPdcts view is even more straightforward, as shown in the picture below:

SELECT
  *
FROM
abvAvgPdcts;

The result set is displayed in the picture below:

productCode	productName	buyPrice
S10_4962	1962 LanciaA Delta 16V	103.42
S18_2238	1998 Chrysler Plymouth Prowler	101.51
S10_1949	1952 Alpine Renault 1300	98.58
S24_3856	1956 Porsche 356A Coupe	98.3
S12_1108	2001 Ferrari Enzo	95.59
S12_1099	1968 Ford Mustang	95.34
S18_1984	1995 Honda Civic	93.89
S18_4027	1970 Triumph Spitfire	91.92

Updatable SQL Views

The MySQL server offers the capability to not only query the view but also to update them. The INSERT or UPDATE statements can be used add and edit the records of the underlying table through the updatable MySQL View. Moreover, the DELETE statement can be used to drop records from the underlying table through the updatable MySQL View.

Furthermore, the SELECT statement used to generate and define an updatable view can not include any of the functions listed below:

- "Aggregate functions" such as "MIN, MAX, SUM, AVG, and COUNT."
- "DISTINCT, GROUP BY, HAVING, UNION or UNION ALL, LEFT JOIN or OUTER JOIN."

348

- Subquery in the WHERE clauses or SELECT statements referring to the table indicated in the FROM clauses.
- References to non-updatable views in the FROM clause.
- References only to literal values.

Remember, the TEMPTABLE algorithm cannot be used to generate an updatable MySQL View.

EXAMPLE

You can use the syntax below to generate a view called ofcInfo on the basis of the ofc table. This updatable view will refer to 3 columns of the ofcs table: ofcCode, phne, and cty.

CREATE VIEW ofcInfo

AS

SELECT ofcCode, phne, cty

FROM ofcs;

Now, if you would like to query the data from the ofcInfo view, you can easily do that by using the syntax below:

SELECT

*

FROM

ofcInfo;

The result set is displayed in the picture below:

officeCode	phone	city
1	+1 650 219 4782	San Francisco
2	+1 215 837 0825	Boston
3	+1 212 555 3000	NYC
4	+33 14 723 4404	Paris
5	+81 33 224 5000	Tokyo
6	+61 2 9264 2451	Sydney
7	+44 20 7877 2041	London

You could also update the office contact number with ofcCode 4 using the UPDATE statement as given below, on the ofcInfo view:

UPDATE ofcInfo
SET
phne = '+1 24 763 5345'
WHERE
ofcCode = 3;

Lastly, you can confirm this modification, using the syntax below to retrieve desired data from the ofcInfo view:

SELECT
 *
FROM
ofcInfo
WHERE
ofcCode = 2;

A sample of the output for code = 4, is displayed in the picture below:

	officeCode	phone	city
▶	4	+33 14 723 5555	Paris

Check if an Existing View is Updatable

By running a query against the is_updtble column from the view in the info_schema database, you should verify whether a view in the database is updatable or not.

You can use the query below to display all the views from the classicmodeldb and check which for views that can be updated:

SELECT
tab_name,
is_updtble
FROM
info_schema.view
WHERE
tab_schema = 'classicmodel';

The result set is displayed in the picture below:

table_name	is_updatable
aboveavgproducts	YES
customerorders	NO
officeinfo	YES
saleperorder	NO

Dropping Rows Using SQL View

To understand this concept, execute the syntax below to first create a table called itms, use the INSERT statements to add records into this table and then use the CREATE clause to generate a view containing items with prices higher than 701.

--- *creating new tbl called itms*

CREATE TABLE itms (

  identity INT AUTO_INCREMENT PRIMARY KEY,

nam VARCHAR (110) NOT NULL,

pric DECIMAL (10 , 1) NOT NULL

)

-- *addingrecords into itmstbl*

INSERT INTO itms (nam,pric)

VALUES ('Comp', 600.54), ('Laptop', 799.99),('Tablet', 699.50)

;

--- *creating views based on itmstbl*

CREATE VIEW LxryItms AS

   SELECT

     *

   FROM

itms

   WHERE

pric> 899;

--- *retrieve records from the LxryItms view*

SELECT

   *

FROM

LxryItms;

The result set is displayed in the picture below:

	id	name	price
▶	1	Laptop	700.56
	3	iPad	700.50

Now, using the DELETE clause record with identity value 3 can be dropped.

DELETE FROM LxryItms

WHERE

  id = 3;

After you run the query above, you will receive a message stating 1 row(s) affected.

Now, to verify the data with the view use the query below:

SELECT

    *

FROM

LxryItms;

The result set is displayed in the picture below:

	id	name	price
▶	1	Laptop	700.56

Finally, use the syntax below to retrieve desired records from the underlying table to confirm that the "DELETE" statement in fact removed the record:

SELECT

    *

FROM

itms;

The result set is displayed in the picture below, which confirms that the record with identity value 3 has been deleted from the items table:

id	name	price
1	Laptop	700.56
2	Desktop	699.99

Modification of SQL View

In MySQL, you can use ALTER VIEW and CREATE OR REPLACE VIEW statements to make changes to views that have already been created.

Using ALTER VIEWStatement

The syntax for ALTER VIEW works a lot like the CREATE VIEW statement that you learned earlier, the only difference being that the ALTER keyword is used instead of the CREATE keyword, as shown below:

ALTER
[ALGRTHM = {MERG | TEMPTBL | UNDEFND}]
VIEW [db_nam]. [vw_nam]
AS
[SELECT statemnt]

The query below will change the organization view by incorporating the email column in the table:

```
ALTER VIEW org
 AS
 SELECT CONCAT (x.lastname,x.firstname) AS Emplye,
x.emailAS emplyeEmail,
CONCAT(y.lstname, y.fstname) AS Mgr
 FROM emplyes AS x
 INNER JOIN emplyes AS y
  ON y.emplyeNo = x.ReprtsTo
 ORDER BY Mgr;
```

You may run the code below against the org view to verify the modification:

```
SELECT
  *
FROM
  Org;
```

The result set is displayed in the picture below:

Employee	employeeEmail	Manager
JonesBarry	bjones@classicmodelcars.com	BondurGerard
HernandezGerard	ghernande@classicmodelcars.com	BondurGerard
BottLarry	lbott@classicmodelcars.com	BondurGerard
GerardMartin	mgerard@classicmodelcars.com	BondurGerard
BondurLoui	lbondur@classicmodelcars.com	BondurGerard
CastilloPamela	pcastillo@classicmodelcars.com	BondurGerard
VanaufGeorge	gvanauf@classicmodelcars.com	BowAnthony

Using CREATE OR REPLACE VIEW Statement

These statements can be used to replace or generate a SQL View that already exists in the database. For all existing views, MySQL will easily modify the view but if the view is non-existent, it will create a new view based on the query.

The syntax below can be used to generate the contacts view on the basis of the employees table:

CREATE OR REPLACE VIEW cntcts AS
SELECT
fstName, lstName, extnsn, eml
FROM
emplyes;

The result set is displayed in the picture below:

	firstName	lastName	extension	email
▶	Diane	Murphy	x5800	dmurphy@classicmodelcars.com
	Mary	Patterson	x4611	mpatterso@classicmodelcars.com
	Jeff	Firrelli	x9273	jfirrelli@classicmodelcars.com
	William	Patterson	x4871	wpatterson@classicmodelcars.com
	Gerard	Bondur	x5408	gbondur@classicmodelcars.com
	Anthony	Bow	x5428	abow@classicmodelcars.com
	Leslie	Jennings	x3291	ljennings@classicmodelcars.com

Now, assume that you would like to insert the jobtitl column to the cntcts view. You can accomplish this with the syntax below:

CREATE OR REPLACE VIEW cntcts AS
   SELECT
fstName, lstName, extnsn, eml, jobtitl
   FROM
emplyes;

The result set is displayed in the picture below:

	firstName	lastName	extension	email	jobtitle
▶	Diane	Murphy	x5800	dmurphy@classicmodelcars.com	President
	Mary	Patterson	x4611	mpatterso@classicmodelcars.com	VP Sales
	Jeff	Firrelli	x9273	jfirrelli@classicmodelcars.com	VP Marketing
	William	Patterson	x4871	wpatterson@classicmodelcars.com	Sales Manager (APAC)
	Gerard	Bondur	x5408	gbondur@classicmodelcars.com	Sale Manager (EMEA)
	Anthony	Bow	x5428	abow@classicmodelcars.com	Sales Manager (NA)
	Leslie	Jennings	x3291	ljennings@classicmodelcars.com	Sales Rep

Dropping a SQL View

The DROP VIEW statement can be utilized to delete an existing view from the database, using the syntax below:

DROP VIEW [IF EXISTS] [db_name]. [vw_name]

The "IF EXISTS" clause is not mandatory in the statement above and is used to determine if the view already exists in the database. It prevents you from mistakenly removing a view that does not exists in the database.

You may, for instance, use the DROP VIEW statement as shown in the syntax below to delete the organization view:

DROP VIEW IF EXISTS org;

SQL TRANSACTIONS

Any actions that are executed on a database are called as transactions. These are actions that are executed logically, either manually by a user or automatically using by the database program.

Or simply put, they are the spread of one or more database modifications. For instance, every time you create a row, update a row, or delete a row a transaction is being executed on that table. To maintain data integrity and address database errors, it is essential to regulate these transactions.

Basically, to execute a transaction, you must group several SQL queries and run them at the same time.

Properties of Transactions

The fundamental properties of a transaction can be defined using the acronym **ACID** for the properties listed below:

- **Atomicity** – guarantees successful completion of all operations grouped in the work unit. Or else, at the point of failure, the transaction will be aborted, and all prior operations will be rolled back to their original state.

- **Consistency** – makes sure that when a transaction is properly committed, the database states are also correctly updated.

- **Isolation** – allows independent and transparent execution of the transactions.

- **Durability** – makes sure that in case of a system malfunction, the outcome or impact of a committed transaction continues to exist.

To explain this concept in greater detail, consider the steps below for addition of new sales orders:

- Start by querying the most recent sales ordr no from the ordrs table and utilize the subsequent ordr no as the new ordr no.
- Then use the INSERT clause to add a new sales ordr into the ordrs table.
- Next, retrieve the sales ordr no that was inserted in the previous step.
- Now, INSERT the new ordritms into the order detail table containing the order no.
- At last, to verify the modifications, select data from the ordrs table as well as the order detail table.

Imagine how would the sales order data be modified, if even a single step listed here were to fail, for whatever reason. For instance, if the step for inserting items of an order to the order detail table failed, it will result in a blank sales ordr.

This is where the "transaction processing" is used as a safety measure. You can perform MySQL transactions to run a set of operations making sure that the database will not be able to contain any partial operations. When working with multiple operations concurrently, if even one of the operations fails, a rollback can be triggered. If there is no failure, all the statements will be committed to the db.

MySQL Transaction Statements

MySQL offers statements listed below for controlling the transactions:

- For initiating a transaction, utilize the START/ BEGIN/ BEGIN WORK TRANSACTION statements.
- For committing the latest transactions and making the modifications permanent, utilize the COMMIT declaration.
- By using the ROLLBACK declaration, you can simply undo the current transaction and void its modifications.
- By using the SET autocommit statement, you can deactivate or activate the auto commit mode for the current transaction.

By default, MySQL is designed to commit the modifications to the database permanently. By using the statement below, you can force MySQL not to commit the modifications by default:

SET auto commit = 1;
Or
SET autocommit = OFF;
To reactivate the default mode for auto-commit, you can use the syntax below:

SET autocommit = ON;

EXAMPLE

Let's utilize the orders and orderDetails tables, shown in the picture below, from the MySQL sample database to understand this concept further.

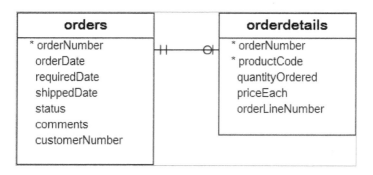

COMMIT Transaction

You must first split the SQL statement into logical parts to effectively use a transaction and assess when the transaction needs to be committed or rolled back.

The steps below show how to generate a new sales order:

1. Utilize the START TRANSACTION statement to begin a transaction.
2. Select the most recent sales ordr no from the ordrs table and utilize the subsequent ordr no as the new ordr no.
3. Add a new record in the ordrs table.
4. Add sales order items into the orderdetail table.

363

5. Lastly, commit the transaction.

You could potentially use data from ordrs and order detail table to verify the new ordr, as shown in the syntax below:

initiate new transactions
START TRANSACTION;

Retrieve the most recent ordr no
SELECT
  @ordrNo:=MAX (ordrNo)+2
FROM
ordrs;

add a new record for customer 140
INSERT INTO ordrs(ordrNo,
ordrDat,
reqrdDat,
shipdDat,
sttus,
clientNo)
VALUES(@ordrNo,
   '2015-05-31',
   '2015-06-10',
   '2015-06-11',
   'In Process',

140);

Add ordr line itms
INSERT INTO ordrdetail(ordrNo,
pdctCode,
qtyOrdrd,
pricEch,
ordrLineNo)
VALUES(@ordrNo, 'S19_1748', 20, '135', 2),
*   (@ordrNo, 'S19_2349', 40, '45', 2);*

commitingupdates
COMMIT;

The result set is displayed in the picture:

@orderNumber:=IFNULL(MAX(orderNUmber),0)+1
▶ 10426

Using the query below, you can retrieve the new sales order that you just created:

SELECT
x.ordrNumber,
ordrDate,
rqrdDate,

shipdDate,

sttus,

cmnts,

clientNo,

ordrLineNo,

pdctCode,

qtyOrdrd,

pricEch

FROM

ordrs x

    INNER JOIN

ordrdetail y USING (ordrNumber)

WHERE

x.ordrno = 10426;

The result set is displayed in the picture below:

orderNumber	orderDate	requiredDate	shippedDate	status	comments	customerNumber	orderLineNumber	productCode	quantityOrdered	priceEach
10426	2005-05-31	2005-06-10	2005-06-11	In Process	NULL	145	1	S18_1749	30	136.00
10426	2005-05-31	2005-06-10	2005-06-11	In Process	NULL	145	2	S18_2248	50	55.09

ROLLBACK Transaction

The first step here is deletion of the data in the ordrs table, using the statement below:

START TRANSACTION;
Query OK, 0 record affctd (0.01 sec)

DELETE FROM ordrs;

Query OK, 310 record affcted (0.02 sec)

It's obvious from from the output of the queries above that all records from the "orders" table have been removed.

Now, you need to login to the MySQL in a distinct session and run the statement below against the ordrstable.

SELECT COUNT (*) FROM ordrs;

+-------+

| COUNT (*)

+-------+

| 311 |

+-------+

2 rows in set (0.02 secs)

The data from the ordrs table can still be viewed from the second session.

The updates made in the first session are not permanent, so you need to either commit them or roll them back. Let's assume you would like to undo the changes from the first session, utilize the query below:

ROLLBACK;

Query OK, 2 rows affected (0.07 secs)"

The data in the ordrs table from the first session can be verified, using the syntax below:

SELECT COUNT (*) FROM ordrs;
```
+--------+
```
| COUNT(*) |
```
+--------+
```
| 311 |
```
+--------+
```
2 rows in set (0.10 secs)

It can be seen in the result set above that the modifications have been rolled back.

SAVEPOINT Transaction

The SAVEPOINT is defined as transaction points when the transaction can be rolled back to a predefined point without rolling it back completely, as shown in the syntax below:

SAVEPOINT SVEPNT_NAME;

The query above is only used to create a SAVEPOINT within all the transaction statements and then the ROLLBACK query can be utilized to retract desired transactions, as shown in the query below:

ROLLBACK TO SVPNT_NAME;

For example, assume you have a client's table as shown in the picture below and want to delete 3 rows and create a SAVEPOINT prior to every deletion and then subsequent ROLLBACK the change to the preceding state as needed.

```
+------+-----------+------+-------------+-------------+
|  ID  |  NAME     | AGE  |  ADDRESS    |  SALARY     |
+------+-----------+------+-------------+-------------+
|   1  |  Ramesh   |  32  |  Ahmedabad  |   2000.00   |
|   2  |  Khilan   |  25  |  Delhi      |   1500.00   |
|   3  |  kaushik  |  23  |  Kota       |   2000.00   |
|   4  |  Chaitali |  25  |  Mumbai     |   6500.00   |
|   5  |  Hardik   |  27  |  Bhopal     |   8500.00   |
|   6  |  Komal    |  22  |  MP         |   4500.00   |
|   7  |  Muffy    |  24  |  Indore     |  10000.00   |
+------+-----------+------+-------------+-------------+
```

You can accomplish this by running the queries below:

SQL> SAVEPOINT SP001;
Save point generated

SQL> DELETE FROM CLIENTS WHERE ID= 001;
2 rows deleted.

SQL> SAVEPOINT SP002;
Save point generated

SQL> DELETE FROM CLIENTS WHERE ID= 002;

0 row deleted.

SQL> SAVEPOINT SP3;
Save point generated

SQL> DELETE FROM CLIENTS WHERE ID= 003;
2 rows deleted.

With the query above, you have successfully deleted 3 records and are now ready to use the query below to ROLLBACK the change to the SAVEPOINT named SP002, which was generated post first deletion so the last 2 deletions will be rolled back:

SQL> ROLLBACK TO SP002;
Rolling back has been completed.

The result set is displayed in the picture below:

```
ID | NAME     | AGE | ADDRESS    | SALARY
---+----------+-----+------------+----------
 2 | Khilan   |  25 | Delhi      |   1500.00
 3 | kaushik  |  23 | Kota       |   2000.00
 4 | Chaitali |  25 | Mumbai     |   6500.00
 5 | Hardik   |  27 | Bhopal     |   8500.00
 6 | Komal    |  22 | MP         |   4500.00
 7 | Muffy    |  24 | Indore     |  10000.00
```

RELEASE SAVEPOINT Transaction

It can be utilized to delete a save point that might have been generated earlier, as shown in the syntax below:

RELEASE SAVEPOINT SVPNT_NAME;

Remember, once you run the query above there is no function to undo the transactions that might have been executed after the last save point.

SET TRANSACTION

It can be utilized to start a transaction by specifying features of the subsequent transactions. For instance, using the syntax below, a transaction can be made read and write only:

SET TRANSACTION [READ WRITE | READ ONLY];

SQL BACKUP DATABASE Statement

These statements can be utilized to generate a full back up of a database that already exists on the SQL server, as displayed in the syntax below:

BACKUP DATABASE dbname
TO DISK = 'flpth';

SQL BACKUP WITH DIFFERENTIAL

Statement

A "differential backup" is used to selectively back up the sections of the database which were altered after the last full backup of the database, as displayed in the syntax below:

BACKUP DATABASE dbname
TO DISK = 'flpth'
WITH DIFFERENTIAL;

EXAMPLE

Consider that you have a database called testDB2 and you would like to create a full back up of it. To accomplish this, you can use the query below:

BACKUP DATABASE testDB2
TO DISK = 'c:\backup\testDB2.bak';

Now, if you made modifications to the database after running the query above. You can use the query below to create a backup of those modifications:

BACKUP DATABASE testDB2
TO DISK = 'c:\backup\testDB2.bak'
WITH DIFFERENTIAL;

Chapter 5: Database Security and Administration

MySQL has an integrated advanced access control and privilege system that enables generation of extensive access guidelines for user activities and efficiently prevent unauthorized users from getting access to the database system.

There are 2 phases in MySQL access control system for when a user is connected to the server:

- **Connection verification**: Every user is required to have valid username and password, that is connected to the server. Moreover, the host used by the user to connect must be the same as the one used in the MySQL grant table.

- **Request verification**: After a link has been effectively created for every query executed by the user, MySQL will verify if the user has required privileges to run that` specific query. MySQL is capable of checking user privileges at database, table, and field level.

The MySQL installer will automatically generate a database called mysql. The mysql database is comprised of 5 main grant tables. Using GRANT and REVOKE statements like, these tables can be indirectly manipulated.

- **User**: This includes columns for user accounts and global privileges. MySQL either accepts or rejects a connection from the host using these user tables. A privilege given under the user table is applicable to all the databases on the server.

- **Database**: This comprises of db level privilege. MySQL utilizes the "db_table" to assess the database that can be used by a user to access and to host the connection. These privileges are applicable to the particular database and all the object available in that database, such as stored procedures, views, triggers, tables, and many more.

- **"Table_priv" and "columns_priv"**: This includes privileges at the level of column and table. A privilege given in the "table priv" table is applicable only to that columns of that particular table, on the other hand privileges given in the "columns priv" table is applicable only to that particular column.

- **"Procs_priv"**: This includes privileges for saved functions and processes.

MySQL uses the tables listed above to regulate MySQL database server privileges. It is extremely essential to understand these tables before implementing your own dynamic access control system.

Creating User Accounts

In MySQL you can indicate that the user has been privileged to connect to the database server as well as the host to be used by the user to build that connection. As a result, for every user account a username and a host name in MySQL is generated and divided by the @ character.

For instance, if an admin user is connected from a localhost to the server, the user account will be named as "admin@localhost." However, the "admin_user" is allowed to connect only to the server using a "localhost" or a remote host like mysqlearn.org, which ensures that the server has higher security.

Moreover, by merging the username and host, various accounts with the same name can be configured and still possess the ability to connect from distinct hosts while being given distinct privileges, as needed.

In the mysql database all the user accounts are stored in the "user grant" table.

Using MySQL CREATE USER Statement

The "CREATE USER"is utilized with the MySQL server to setup new user accounts, as shown in the syntax below:

CREATE USER usr_acnt IDENTIFY BY paswrd;

In the syntax above, the CREATE USER clause is accompanied by the name of the user account in username @ hostname format.

In the "IDENTIFIED BY" clause, the user password would be indicated. It is important that the password is specified in plain text. Prior to the user account being saved in the user table, MySQL is required for encryption of the user passwords.

For instance, these statements can be utilized as given below, for creating a new "user dbadmin," that is connected to the server from local host using user password as Safe.

CREATE USER dbadmn@lclhst
IDENTIFY BY 'Safe';

If you would like to check the permissions given to any user account, you can run the syntax below:

SHOW GRANTS FOR dbadmn@localhst and
dbadmn2@localhst2;

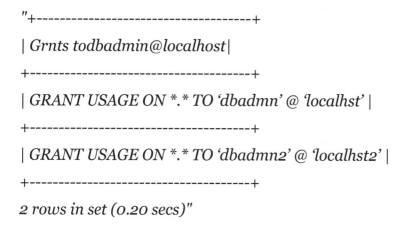

```
"+------------------------------------+
| Grnts todbadmin@localhost|
+------------------------------------+
| GRANT USAGE ON *.* TO 'dbadmn' @ 'localhst' |
+------------------------------------+
| GRANT USAGE ON *.* TO 'dbadmn2' @ 'localhst2' |
+------------------------------------+
```

2 rows in set (0.20 secs)"

The *. * in the output above indicates that the dbadmn and dbadmn2 users are allowed to log into the server only and do not have any other access privileges.

Bear in mind that the portion prior to the dot (.) is representing the db and the portion following the dot is representing the table, for example, db.tab.

The percentage (%) wildcard can be used as shown in the syntax below for allowing a user to create a connection from any host:

CREATE USER supradmn@'%'
IDENTIFY BY 'safe';

The percentage (%) wildcard will lead to identical result as when included in the "LIKE" operator, for example, to enable msqladmn user account to link to the server from any "subdomain" of the mysqlearn.org host, this can be used as shown in the syntax below:

CREATE USER 'msqladmn@' % 'mysqlearn.org'
IDENTIFT by 'safe';"

It should also be noted here, that another wildcard underscore (_) can be used in the CREATE USER statement.

If the host name portion can be omitted from the user accounts, server will recognize them and enable the users to get connected from other hosts. For instance, the syntax below will generate a new remote user account that allows creation of a connection to from random hosts:

CREATE USER remoteuser;

To view the privileges given to the remoteuser and remoteuser2 account, you can use the syntax below:

SHOW GRANTS FOR remoteuser, remoteuser2;

```
+---------------------------------------+
| Grnts for remoteuser@%                |
+---------------------------------------+
| GRANT USAGE ON *.* TO 'remoteuser' @ '%' |
```

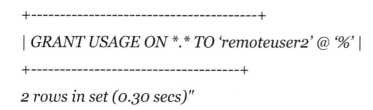

```
+----------------------------------------+
| GRANT USAGE ON *.* TO 'remoteuser2' @ '%' |
+----------------------------------------+
```

2 rows in set (0.30 secs)"

It is necessary to remember that the single quotation (' ') in the syntax above is particularly significant, if the user accounts have special characters like underscore or percentage.

If you inadvertently cite the user account as usrname@hstname, the server will create new user with the name as usrname@hstname and enables it to start a connection from random hosts, that cannot be anticipated.

The syntax below, for instance, can be used to generate a new accountapi@lclhst that could be connected to the server from random hosts.

CREATE USER 'api@lclhst';

SHOW GRANTS FOR 'api@lclhst';

```
+----------------------------------------+
| Grnts for api@lclhst@%                 |
+----------------------------------------+
| GRANT USAGE ON *.* TO 'api@lclhst' @ '%' |
```

```
+---------------------------------------+
```
1 row(s) in set (0.01 sec)

If you accidentally generate a user that has already been created in the database, then an error will be issued by MySQL. For instance, the syntax below can be used to generate a new user account called remoteuser:

CREATE USER remoteuser;

The error message below will be displayed on your screen:

ERROR 1398 (HY0000): Action CREATE USER fails for 'remoteuser'@ '%'

It can be noted that the "CREATE USER" statement will only create the new user but not grant any privileges. The GRANT statement can be utilized to give access privileges to the users.

Updating USER PASSWORD

Prior to altering a MySQL user account password, the concerns listed below should be taken into consideration:

- The user account whose password you would like to be modified.

- The applications that are being used with the user account for which you would like to modify the password. If the password is changed without altering the application connection string being used with that user account, then it would be not feasible for those applications to get connected with the database server.

MySQL offers a variety of statements that can be used to alter a user's password, such as UPDATE, SET PASSWORD, and GRANT USAGE statements.

Let's explore some of these syntaxes!

Using UPDATE Statement

The UPDATE can be utilized to make updates to the user tables in the database. You must also execute the "FLUSH PRIVILEGES" statements to refresh privileges from the "grant table," by executing the UPDATE statement.

Assume that you would like to modify the password for the dbadmn user, which links from the local host to the fish. It can be accomplished by executing the query below:

USE msql;

UPDATE usr

381

SET paswrd = PASWRD ('fish')
WHERE usr = 'dbadmn' AND
    host = 'lclhst';

FLUSH PRIVILEGES;

Using SET PASSWORD Statement

For updating the user password, the user@host format is utilized. Now, imagine that you would like to modify the password for some other user's account, then you will be required to have the UPDATE privilege on your user account.

With the use of the SET PASSOWORD statement, the FLUSH PRIVILEGES statement is not required to be executed, in order to reload privileges to the mysql database from the grant tables.

The syntax below could be utilized to alter the dbadmn user account password:

SET PASSWORD FOR 'dbadmn'@ 'lclhst' =
PASSWORD('bigfish');

Using ALTER USER Statement

Another method to update the user password is with the use of the ALTER USER statements with the "IDENTIFIED BY" clause. For instance, the query below can be executed to change the password of the dbadmn user to littlefish.

ALTER USER dbadmn@lclhst IDENTIFY BY 'littlefish';

USEFUL TIP
If you need to change the password of the "root account," then the server must be force quit and started back up without triggering the grant table validation.

Granting User Privileges

As a new user account is created, there are no access privileges afforded to the user by default. The "GRANT" statement must be used in order for granting privileges to all user accounts. The syntax of these statements are shown below:

GRANT priv,[priv], ... ON priv_level
TO usr [IDENTIFIED BY pswrd]
[REQUIRE tssl_optn]
[WITH [GRANT_OPTION | resrce_optn]];

- In the syntax above, we start by specifying one or more privileges following the GRANT clause. Every privilege being granted to the user account must be isolated using a comma, in case you would like to give the user account more than one privilege at the same time. (The list of potential privileges that may be granted to a user account is given in the table below).

- After that you must indicate the "privilege_level" that will determine the levels at which the privilege is applied. The privilege level supported by MySQL are "global (*. *)," "database (database. *)," "table (database.table)" and "column" levels.

- Next you need to indicate the user that needs to be granted the privileges. If the indicated user can be found on the server, then the GRANT statement will modify its privilege. Or else, a new user account will be created by the GRANT statement. The IDENTIFIED BY clause is not mandatory and enables creation of a new password for the user.

- Thereafter, it's indicated if the user needs to start a connection to the database via secured connections.

- At last, the "WITH GRANT OPTION" clause is added which is not mandatory but enables granting and revoking the privileges of other user, that were given to your own account. Moreover, the WITH clause can also be used to assign the resources from the MySQL database server, for example, putting a limit on the number of links or statements that can be used by the user per hour. In shared environments like MySQL shared hosting, the WITH clause is extremely useful.

Note that the GRANT OPTION privilege as well as the privileges you are looking to grant to other users must already be configured to your own user account, so that you are able to use the GRANT statement. If the read only system variable has been allowed, then execution of the GRANT statement requires the SUPER privilege.

PRIVILE-GE	DESCRI-PTION	LEVEL Global	LEVEL Database	LEVEL Table	LEVEL Column	LEVEL Proce-dure	LEVEL Proxy
"ALL"	Granting all privileges at specific access levels except the GRANT OPTION.						
'ALTER'	Allowing users the usage of ALTER TABLE statement.	Y	Y	Y			
"ALTER ROUTI-NE"	Allowing users to	Y	Y			Y	

	alter and drop saved routines.						
CREATE	Allowing users to generate databases and tables.	Y	Y	Y			
CREATE ROUTI-NE	Allowing users to create saved routines.	Y	Y				
CREATE TABLE-SPACE	Allowing users to generate, modify or remove tables and log file groups.	Y					
CREATE TEMPO-RARY TABLES	Allowing users to generate temp tables with the use of the	Y	Y				

	CREATE TEMPO- RARY TABLE.					
CREATE USER	Allowing users to utilize the CREATE USER, DROP USER, RENAME USER, and REVOKE ALL PRIVI- LEGES state- ments.	Y				
CREATE VIEW	Allowing users to generate or update views.	Y	Y	Y		
DELETE	Allowing users to utilize	Y	Y	Y		

	the DELETE keyword.					
"DROP"	Allowing users to remove databases, tables and views.	Y	Y	Y		
'EVENT'	Enabling the usage of events for the Event Scheduler.	Y	Y			
EXECU-TE	Allowing users for execution of saved routines.	Y	Y	Y		
"FILE"	Allowing users to read the files in the db directories.	Y				

GRANT OPTION	Allowing users privilege for granting or revoking privileges from other users.	Y	Y	Y		Y	Y
'INDEX'	Allowing users to generate or drop indexes.	Y	Y	Y			
INSERT	Allowing users the usage of INSERT state-ments.	Y	Y	Y	Y		
LOCK TABLES	Allowing users the usage of LOCK TABLES on tables that have	Y	Y				

	the SELECT privileges.						
PRO-CESS	Allowing users to view all processes with SHOW PROCESS -LIST state-ments.	Y					
PROXY	Enabling creation of proxy of the users.						
'REFE-RENCES'	Allowing users to generate foreign key.	Y	Y	Y	Y		
RELOAD	Allowing users the usage of the FLUSH operation.	Y					

'REPLI-CATION CLIENT'	Allowing users to query to see where master or slave servers are.	Y				
REPLI-CATION SAVE"	Allowing the users to use replica-ted slaves to read binary log events from the master.	Y				
SELECT	Allowing users the usage of SELECT state-ments.	Y	Y	Y	Y	
"SHOW DATA-BASES"	Allowing users to view all	Y				

	databa-ses.						
"SHOW VIEW"	Allowing users to utilize SHOW CREATE VIEW state-ment.	Y	Y	Y			
"SHUT-DOWN"	Allowing users to use mysqladmin shutdown comman-ds.	Y					
'SUPER'	Allowing users to use other admini-strative operations such as CHANGE MASTER TO, KILL,	Y					

	PURGE BINARY LOGS, SET GLOBAL and mysqladmin commands.						
'TRIG-GER'	Allowing users the usage of TRIGGER operations	Y	Y	Y			
"UPDA-TE"	Allowing users the usage of UPDATE statements.	Y	Y	Y	Y		
'USAGE'	Equivalent to no privilege.						

EXAMPLE

More often than not, the CREATE USER statement will be used to first create a new user account and then the GRANT statement is used to assign the user privileges.

For instance, a new super user account can be created by the executing the CREATE USER statement given below:

CREATE USER super@localhost IDENTIFIED BY 'dolphin';

In order to check the privileges granted to the super@localhost user, the query below with SHOW GRANTS statement can be used.

SHOW GRANTS FOR super@localhost;

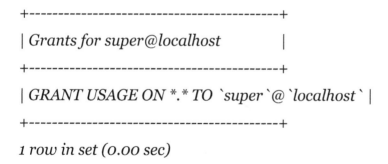

1 row in set (0.00 sec)

Now, if you wanted to assign all privileges to the super@localhost user, the query below with GRANT ALL statement can be used.

GRANT ALL ON *.* TO 'super'@'localhost' WITH GRANT OPTION;

The ON*. * clause refers to all databases and items within those databases. The WITH GRANT OPTION enables super@localhost to assign privileges to other user accounts.

If the SHOW GRANTS statement is used again at this point then it can be seen that privileges of the super@localhost's user have been modified, as shown in the syntax and the result set below:

SHOW GRANTS FOR super@localhost;

```
+----------------------------------------------------------------+
| Grants for super@localhost                                     |
+----------------------------------------------------------------+
| GRANT ALL PRIVILEGES ON *.* TO `super`@ `localhost`
WITH GRANT OPTION |
+----------------------------------------------------------------+
1 row in set (0.00 sec)
```

Now, assume that you want to create a new user account with all the server privileges in the *classicmodels* sample database. You can accomplish this by using the query below:

CREATE USER auditor@localhost IDENTIFIED BY 'whale';

GRANT ALL ON classicmodels.* TO auditor@localhost;

Using only one GRANT statement, various privileges can be granted to a user account. For instance, to generate a user account with the privilege of executing SELECT, INSERT and UPDATE statements against the database *classicmodels*, the query below can be used.

CREATE USER rfc IDENTIFIED BY 'shark';

GRANT SELECT, UPDATE, DELETE ON classicmodels.* TO rfc;

Revoking User Privileges

You will be using the MySQL REVOKE statement to revoke the privileges of any user account(s). MySQL enables withdrawal of one or more privileges or even all of the previously granted privileges of a user account.

The query below can be used to revoke particular privileges from a user account:

REVOKE   privilege_type [(column_list)]
*   [, priv_type [(column_list)]]...*
ON [object_type] privilege_level
FROM user [, user]...

In the syntax above, we start by specifying a list of privileges that need to be revoked from a user account next to the REVOKE keyword. YAs you might recall when listing multiple privileges in a statement they must be separated by commas. Then we indicate the privilege level at which the ON clause will be revoking these privileges. Lastly we indicate the user account whose privileges will be revoked in the FROM clause.

Bear in mind that your own user account must have the GRANT OPTION privilege as well as the privileges that you want to revoke from other user accounts.

You will be using the REVOKE statement as shown in the syntax below, if you are looking to withdraw all privileges of a user account:

REVOKE ALL PRIVILEGES, GRANT OPTION FROM user [, user]...

It is important to remember that you are required to have the CREATE USER or the UPDATE privilege at global level for the mysql database, to be able to execute the REVOKE ALL statement.

You will be using the REVOKE PROXY clause as shown in the query below, in order to revoke proxy users:

REVOKE PROXY ON user FROM user [, user]...

A proxy user can be defined as a valid user in MySQL who can impersonate another user. As a result, the proxy user is able to attain all the privileges granted to the user that it is impersonating.

The best practice dictates that you should first check what privileges have been assigned to the user by executing the syntax below with SHOW GRANTS statement, prior to withdrawing the user's privileges:

SHOW GRANTS FOR user;

EXAMPLE
Assume that there is a user named rfd with SELECT, UPDATE and DELETE privileges on the *classicmodels* sample database and you would like to revoke the UPDATE and DELETE privileges from the rfd user.

To start with we will check the user privileges using the SHOW GRANTS statement below:

SHOW GRANTS FOR rfd;
GRANT SELECT, UPDATE, DELETE ON 'classicmodels'.* TO 'rfc'@'%'

At this point, the UPDATE and REVOKE privileges can be revoked from the rfd user, using the query below:

REVOKE UPDATE, DELETE ON classicmodels.* FROM rfd;

Next, the privileges of the rfd user can be checked with the use of SHOW GRANTS statement.

SHOW GRANTS FOR 'rfd'@'localhost';
GRANT SELECT ON 'classicmodels'.* TO 'rfd'@'%'

Now, if you wanted to revoke all the privileges from the rfd user, you can use the query below:

REVOKE ALL PRIVILEGES, GRANT OPTION FROM rfd;

To verify that all the privileges from the rfd user have been revoked, you will need to use the query below:
SHOW GRANTS FOR rfd;

GRANT USAGE ON *.* TO 'rfd'@'%'

Remember, as mentioned in the privileges description table earlier in this book, the USAGE privilege simply means that the user has no privileges in the server.

Resulting Impact of the REVOKE Auery

The impact of MySQL REVOKE statement relies primarily on the level of privilege granted to the user account, as explained below:

- The modifications made to the global privileges will only take effect once the user has connected to the MySQL server in a successive session, post the successful execution of the REVOKE query. The modifications will not be applicable to all other users connected to the server, while the REVOKE statement is being executed.

- The modifications made to the database privileges are only applicable once a USE statement has been executed after the execution of the REVOKE query.

- The table and column privilege modifications will be applicable to all the queries executed, after the modifications have been rendered with the REVOKE statement.

Conclusion

Thank you for making it through to the end of *SQL Programming: The ultimate guide with exercises, tips and tricks to learn SQL,* Let's hope it was informative and able to provide you with all of the tools you need to achieve your goals whatever they may be.

The next step is to make the best use of your newfound wisdom and learning of the SQL programming language that will help you gain a powerful entry into the world of data analysis. To make the most of your purchase of this book, I highly recommend that you follow the instructions in this book and install the free and open MySQL user interface on your operating system. This will allow you to get hands-on practice so you will be able to create not only correct but efficient SQL queries to succeed at work and ace those job interview questions. The fundamental element of any kind of learning is repeated practice in order to achieve perfection. So let this book be your personal guide and mentor through the journey of learning SQL programming language for relational database management systems. Another tip to make the best use of this book is to try to come up with your own names and labels to be used within the presented examples and verify those result sets obtained with the ones provided in this book, as you read and understand all the concepts and SQL query structures.

Finally, if you found this book useful in anyway, a review on Amazon is always appreciated!

ARDUINO PROGRAMMING

THE ULTIMATE GUIDE FOR MAKING THE BEST OF YOUR ARDUINO PROGRAMMING PROJECTS

By Damon Parker

Table of Contents

413

INTRODUCTION

Thank you for purchasing this book: Arduino Programming—The Ultimate Beginner's Guide. In this book, we are going to give you a summary of the concepts that you have to understand before you begin Arduino programming. We will explain to you the different components that you should learn about before you delve and go into establishing more intricate programs for different operating systems. The Arduino programming language has many benefits.

Nevertheless, it also has various little elements that can leave you perplexed. Not having the ability to comprehend these aspects can trigger some issues in the future. In this book, we're going to talk about what those aspects are. We are also going to talk about what Arduino is, where it originated from, and all of the essential ideas that you have to understand before you begin programming. Additionally, we'll also teach you how to setup and use the Code Blocks IDE, which will assist you significantly when programming Arduino language. We hope you enjoy this book.

CHAPTER ONE
What Is Arduino Programming?

Arduino is a computer software application and hardware business or community that produces and develops microcontroller packages for robotics as well as other digital gadgets.

The name "Arduino" originates from the name of a bar at Ivrea, Italy, where some of the founders of this project used to meet. Nowadays, this is the most favourite tool of modern-day robotics. Before starting with an Arduino microcontroller, one should know the variety of the Arduinos. Some of entry-level Arduino's are:

- UNO

- LEONARDO

- 101

- ROBOT

- ESPLORA

- MICRO

- NANO

- MINI

- MKR2UNO ADAPTER

- STARTER KIT

- BASIC KIT

- LCD SCREEN

These Arduinos are simple to use, and all set to power one's first robot. These boards are the best to begin discovering and to code your bots through the microcontrollers.

These were about the hardware. Now let's consider the Arduino software. Each of these boards is programmable with the Arduino IDE. This is a cross-platform application written in the programming language Java. C and C++ are also supported in this IDE with special rules. A program written in Arduino IDE is called a sketch. These sketches are conserved as the text files with the file extensions.ino and.pde. A minimal Arduino sketch consists of two functions. They are; setup and loop.

Arduino ROBOT is the very first Arduino on wheels. It consists of two boards, and each of the boards has a microcontroller. That indicates that in ROBOT there is an overall of two microcontrollers. One of them is the motor board, which manages the motors, and the other one is the control panel, which oversees the sensors and chooses the operations. It is also programmable with Arduino IDE. Both the microcontroller boards are based on ATmega32u4, which is a low-power CMOS 8-bit microcontroller based on the AVR enhanced RISC architecture. The ROBOT is similar to LEONARDO.

As a novice in robotics, Arduino is the most valuable tool you'll find. It is an open-source electronic devices platform based upon easy-to-use software and hardware. Arduino boards can check out inputs—light on a sensor, a finger on a button, or a Twitter message—and turn it into an output—triggering a motor, turning on an LED. You can instruct your board on what to do by sending out a set of relevant directions to the on-board microcontroller.

To do so, use the Arduino programming language (created on Wiring) and the Arduino Software (IDE), built for Processing.

Over the years, Arduino has been the brain of countless projects, from daily things to complex scientific instruments. An around the world community of makers—students, hobbyists, artists, developers, and specialists—has collected this open-source platform; their contributions have included a fantastic quantity of accessible knowledge that can be of help to professionals and novices.

Arduino was developed at the Ivrea Interaction Design Institute as an easy tool for quick prototyping, focused on trainees without a background in electronic devices and programming. As quickly as it reached a wider community, the Arduino board started changing to adapt to new requirements and challenges, separating its offer from easy 8-bit boards to products for IoT applications, wearable, 3D printing, and ingrained environments. Most Arduino boards are open-source, empowering users to build them independently and eventually adjust them to their specific needs. The software is also open-source, and it is growing through the contributions of users worldwide.

Why Arduino?

Thanks to its available and straightforward user experience, Arduino has been used in countless jobs and applications. The Arduino software application is easy-to-use for beginners yet versatile enough for advanced users. It runs on Mac, Windows, and Linux.

Educators and trainees use it to construct low expense clinical instruments, to show chemistry and physics principles, or to start with programming and robotics.

Architects and designers construct interactive prototypes; artists and workers use it for installations and to experiment with brand-new musical instruments.

Makers, of course, use it to construct many tasks displayed at the Maker Faire, for instance. Arduino is a crucial tool to find out new things. Anybody; children, hobbyists, artists, developers can start playing just following the step by action directions of a kit or sharing concepts online with other members of the Arduino community.

There are lots of other microcontrollers platforms offered for physical computing. Netmedia's BX-24, Phidgets, Parallax Basic Stamp, MIT's Handyboard, and many others provide comparable functionality. All of these tools take the messy information of microcontroller programming and cover it up in a user-friendly plan. Arduino also simplifies the process of dealing with microcontrollers, but it offers some advantage for teachers, trainees, and interested amateurs over other systems:

- **Inexpensive** – Arduino boards are reasonably cheap compared to other microcontroller platforms. The least pricey version of the Arduino module can be assembled by hand, and even the pre-assembled Arduino modules cost less than $50.

- **Cross-platform** – The Arduino Software (IDE) works on Windows, Macintosh OSX, and Linux operating systems. Most microcontroller systems are restricted to Windows.

- **Easy, transparent programming environment** – The Arduino Software (IDE) is easy-to-use for newbies yet versatile enough to benefit innovative users. For teachers, it is suitably based on the programming environment, so trainees discovering to program because the environment will be quite familiar with the way Arduino IDE works.

- **An Open source and extensible software** – The Arduino software is published as open-source tools available for extension by experienced programmers. The language can be broadened through C++ libraries, and individuals desiring to comprehend the technical information can make the leap from Arduino to the AVR Arduino programming language on which it is based. Likewise, you can add AVR-C code directly to your Arduino programs if you wish.

- **Open Source and Extensible Hardware** – The designs of the Arduino boards are available under the Creative Commons license, and professional circuit designers can create their edition of the platform, expand it, and develop it. Even relatively inexperienced users can construct the breadboard version of the module to understand how it works and save cash.

Arduino – The Most Popular Way to Regulate Robots

There are many ways to manage robots. This book will go over one of the most preferred approaches presently used on the planet, the 'Arduino'. It is very basic. It is just a physical computing platform for performing valuable jobs when interfaced (connected) to a computer. 'Arduino' is an open resource project, which means capable individuals in the robotics area can contribute and also enhance the 'Arduino'.

The advantages of using the 'Arduino' atmosphere is that it is extremely user-friendly. Any person with zero levels of electronics and program skills can now find out to program robotics. Incidentally, when it is said that programs robotics, this means composing a specific amount of codes to the 'microcontroller' of the robot. Keep in mind that the 'microcontroller' acts as the mind for the robot.

Generally, when somebody uses 'Arduino' to control robotics, that implies he or she is making use of the software application called 'Arduino IDE', in which 'IDE' means Integrated Growth Atmosphere. This program has been developed extensively and is at no cost. Simply put, it is free software. To compose codes, one will certainly discover the 'Arduino' language. It is mainly based on the currently well known 'C++ programming language'. If you have shown skills or experience in the past, programming robots making use of 'Arduino' is a wind for you.

'Arduino' is well-known until it is commonly manufactured and in some cases made in some variations by third party suppliers. They have acquired broad spread appeal for the last five years. I think the 'Arduino' is an expanding treasure in the eyes of the world today. Check it out and also see it on your own if you are a robotics fan.

Arduino – A Physical Computing Platform for Robotic Programming

'Arduino', is an open-source physical computing system based on the 'Atmel', 'AVR', 'Atmega' mini controller board. It is also a development atmosphere for writing programming codes or software application for the growth board.

The 'Arduino' can be created to interact with objects, inputs, and for this reason, regulating physical outputs like lights and electric motors can be a stand-alone or talk to the computer system.

Its language is an integration of 'Wiring', a comparable physical computer system, based on the 'Processing' multimedia setting atmosphere. The program codes work as if they were C language. 'Arduino' is selected for its many advantages. One would be its price. The 'Arduino' software application can work greater than one system; Windows, 'Macintosh OSX', and also Linux (32bit and 64 bit) operating systems. Its straightforward programming atmosphere ('Handling') is precious to both mini controller novices as well as professionals.

Because of its open resource nature as well as the complimentary integrated established environment ('IDE'), it is a preferred selection worldwide. Improvisations of the boards are continually made by knowledgeable circuit designers, under the Creative Commons license.

The 'Arduino IDE' (version 0018) software application operates to create, put together as postcodes to the microcontroller. The connection from the computer system to the mini controller growth board is by 'USB'. Software programs or codes written in the 'IDE' are called sketches in the text editor. It also a beneficial serial display that acts like Hyper Terminal.

Like the C language, it is comparable. The standard framework of the 'Arduino' programming language is essential; it runs in a minimum of two blocks of codes, the void arrangement, and gap loophole. Whereby the last holes continually, like its said name, and also declarations in the agreement just run as soon as confirmations.

A Short Look at the Arduino System

Arduino is an open-source, programmable microcontroller and software based on the ATMega chip. Although the Arduino is developed as a prototyping platform, it can be used in different electronic devices jobs, whether short-term or ingrained.

The Arduino board can be programmed using the Arduino software application.

The phrase structure for this resembles C/C++ and Java.

It is designed for easy use and can be run by anyone, from novices to professionals alike.

As Arduino is an open-source platform, you can get hold of the source code and schematics for it. This means you can delve right into it as you want, even creating your personal Arduino boards.

How Do I Use Arduino?

If you are looking for motivation, you can discover a great variety of tutorials on Arduino Project Hub.

The Getting Started with Arduino guide is accredited under a Creative Commons Attribution-ShareAlike 3.0 license. Code samples in the book are launched into the public domain.

CHAPTER TWO
Introduction to Arduino Programming Language

Like most new projects, when you set out to do programming, you discover yourself surrounded by weird and possibly odd terms, as well as fancied lingo. In this book, we'll examine those terms in addition to present an introduction of the whole programming process. It is extremely most likely that you're excited to begin writing codes, and you may have currently viewed a later chapter in this book. It is essential to know a few basic terms and programming principles.

History of Arduino Programming Language

Back in 1972, a computer scientist at AT&T's Bell Laboratories started to develop some programs he required for his use. Dennis Ritchie began developing what has progressed into the Arduino programming language.

He was trying to make computing as easy as possible. Dennis Ritchie realized that the then-current assembly language was much intricate. They attempted to reverse this trend by constructing an easy programming language on a minicomputer. What Dennis Ritchie wished to preserve was not only an efficient computer system programming language in which to produce programs, but also a computer system programming language which programming community could form a fellowship. They knew, based on previous experiences that the real nature of joint computing as provided by time-shared, remote accessed systems is not merely to get computer system code into a terminal but to encourage post programming communication. The Arduino Programming language is a primary function and structured programming language.

It is also called a procedural oriented programming language that is not mainly designed for particular application areas. However, it was well matched for business and scientific applications. It has different features like control structures, looping statements, and micros needed for applications.

The Arduino programming language has the following features:

- Portability

- Flexibility

- Effectiveness and efficiency

- Reliability

- Interactivity

What Is Programming?

Programming is where you develop a software application. The software manages hardware, which is the visible part of an electronic gadget such as a computer system, phone, tablet, gaming console, micro-controller, or some other device. Those instructions take the type of programming language. For this book, that language is the Arduino programming language, which was developed back in the early 1970s. It is ancient. In reality, over, time the Arduino programming language has been thought as the Latin of programming languages.

Unlike Latin, Arduino programming is still alive. Great deals of Arduino Programming still goes on despite the recent and fancier programming languages happening. Like Latin, Arduino is the structure on which many other programming languages are constructed. You can quickly discover other languages if you understand Arduino. In a later chapter, we will discuss the programming language's syntax and different rules. For now, know that the code you write is called source code.

What Is a Source Code?

Source code is a plain text file that includes the programming language, all formatted and pretty, as well as written excellently. In Arduino, the file is saved with a.c filename extension. To produce source code, you use a full-screen editor. Any full-screen editor can do, although some editors give handy features like colour coding, line numbers, syntax monitoring, and other tools. The source code is then put together into object code. The program that produces the item code is called a compiler. The traditional name of the Arduino language compiler is CC, which represents C compiler. The compiler reads the source code file and creates an object code file. Object code files have a.o filename extension, and they use the same filename as the initial source code file.

The next action is called Linking. It is frequently forgotten because modern-day compilers link and put together, but connecting is actually a different action. The linker takes the item code file and combines it with Arduino language libraries. The libraries are the workhorse of the language. They consist of routines and functions that manage every gadget you are programming.

If all goes well, the end result is a program file. You can then check run the program to ensure that it works the way you want it. And if not, you start the cycle all over again: modify, compile and connect, or "develop," and evaluate run.

All these tools—the editor, compiler, linker, all came from the command terminal or prompt. You can still discover them there also. Because it is fast, programmers do a lot of coding at the command timely. Commonly, use an IDE, or Integrated Development Environment.

What Is an IDE?

An IDE, or Integrated Development Environment, combines the tools for editing, putting together, connecting, and running. It also includes tools for debugging, producing intricate programs, other functions, and visual tools. Above all, is the humble command line compiler and linker. The process is the same: edit, compile and connect, run. You are going to do many re-working and repeating before you get things right. Fortunately, that is all the tools you need to start your programming journey for free on the internet. The problem being that you need to find the right tools and install them properly.

This is not an issue for you here because in this book, we'll show you how it is done. You will see how to discover a great IDE, or Integrated Development Environment, Arduino language compiler, and get everything setup as well as configured. You will find a horde of IDEs on the internet. Microsoft provides the Visual Studio as its IDE, and Apple has X code. You are welcome to use those tools, particularly if you like them. However for this book, we have chosen the Code Blocks IDE.

The great feature of Code Blocks is that it comes with everything you require. Unlike other IDEs, you don't have to hunt for this or after the IDE is set up. You just need to download, configure, and you are ready to go. Obtain Code Blocks by going to the developer.

Making the Most of Your Arduino Projects

One of the best things about the Arduino platform is that it is open-source; this is a big part of why it is so popular.

Documenting our work is essential so that we can contribute to the growing pool of knowledge. By documentation, I mean more than writing things down.

I want to talk about various tools and resources that you can use for documenting your projects and passing what you have learned on to others, as well as doing it in a manner that doesn't disrupt your work.

The code that you write for the Arduino needs to be well documented.

I feel that the most important thing is to write self-documenting code. By that, I mean that the code has intelligently named variables and functions so that someone reading the system can infer what is going on by reading the code itself.

Of course, comments are necessary and very helpful too, and good commenting practice is essential. If you are doing large projects, then you might want to consider an automated documentation system like Doxygen that has been around for a very long time.

Next, documenting the hardware, the easiest way to do this is to have pictures and videos of your project, but beyond that, some tools are handy for recording the device, such as Fritzing.

If you want to make a circuit diagram, you can also use software like Fritzing. If you are making your circuit boards, this is the way to go; I found it difficult, but a straightforward solution that I rather enjoy doing is to take some graph paper and draw the circuit myself with a pen, then scan it into my computer as an image, that might sound very clunky and old-fashioned, but I find it very efficient. It seems that no matter how hard you try, there is always some little symbol that you can't get right with software, but this is very easy when using pen and paper. I find it to be the most enjoyable part of documenting a project.

If you're writing a lot of programs, you might also want to consider using revision control software, there are many exceptional revision control systems available for free. If you are a single developer, then you may find that the old RCS (revision control system) has everything you need, and often, the simplest solution is the best solution, and it doesn't get much simpler than RCS. I think a better idea is to use something like Git, which although it's intended for large distributed projects, also works for individuals if you're willing to get past the initial learning curve. Git has a significant advantage in that it works seamlessly with Github. Github is a hugely popular source code hosting service that offers unlimited free public repositories and also gives private pools for free. This is how your tools for enabling productive work merge with tools for sharing with others.

If someone wants a copy of your code, you just give them the URL of your Git repository. You can also go with SourceForge, which is the original open-source project hosting site that existed long before Git was popular. Once you've finished a project, have a well-documented source code, and a freely available place to put your source code, you should include your other documentation e.g., circuit diagrams.

CHAPTER THREE
The Arduino Programming Language

Arduino supports a language known as the Arduino programming language, or simply Arduino language.

It is based on the Wiring development platform, which also is based on Processing, and if you are not acquainted with it, is what p5.js is based on. It's a long history of jobs building on other tasks in an extremely Open Source format. The Arduino IDE is mostly based on the Processing IDE and the Wiring IDE, which develops on it.

When we carry out any work with Arduino, we normally use the Arduino IDE (Integrated Development Environment), a software available for all the significant desktop platforms (MacOS, Linux, Windows), which gives us two things: a programming editor with integrated libraries support, a way to quickly assemble and load our Arduino programs to a board linked to the computer.

The Arduino programming language is generally a structure developed on top of C++. You can argue that it's not a genuine programming language in the traditional term, but this helps to avoid confusion for novices.

Any program written in the Arduino programming language is called sketch. A sketch is normally conserved with the .ino extension (from Arduino).

The main distinction from "typical" C or C++ is that you wrap all your code into two main functions. You can have more than two, naturally, but any Arduino program must supply not less than those two.

One is referred to as setup, while the other is called loop.

The first is called as soon as when the program begins; the second is repeatedly called while your program is running.

We don't have a primary function like you are used to in C/C++ as the entry point for a program. The IDE will make the end result is the right C++ application and will essentially add the missing out on glue by pre-processing it as soon as you compile your sketch.

Every other thing is C++ code, and as C++ is a superset of C, any legitimate C is also a valid Arduino code.

One distinction that may cause you troubles is that while you can generate your program over multiple files, those files must all remain in the same folder. Might be an offer breaking limitation if your program will grow very big, but at that, point it will be easy to transfer to a native C++ setup, which is possible.

A section of the Arduino programming language is the built-in libraries that enable you to quickly incorporate the functionality offered by the Arduino board.

Your first Arduino program will definitely include making a led turn on the light and after that switch off. To achieve this, you will use the pinMode, hold-up() and digitalWrite() functions, in addition to some regular functionalities, like HIGH, LOW, OUTPUT.

Always remember that you are not restricted to using this language and IDE to program an Arduino. Projects exist, to name a few, allow you run Node.js code on it using the Johnny

Five task, Python code using pyserial and Go code with Gobot, but the Arduino programming language is definitely the one you'll see most tutorials on, given that it's the native and canonical way to deal with such devices.

The Arduino Programming Language Built-in Constants

Arduino provides two constants we can use to increase corresponds to a high level of voltage, which can vary depending on the hardware (> 2V on 3.3 V boards like Arduino Nano, > 3V on 5V boards like Arduino Uno).

LOW equates to a low voltage point. Again, the fundamental worth depends on the particular board used.

Then we have about three constants we can use in a mix with the pinMode functionality:

- INPUT presents the pin as an input pin.

- OUTPUT displays the pin as an output pin.

- The INPUT_PULLUP sets the pin as an internal pull-up resistor.

The other consistent we have is LED_BUILTIN, which indicates the variety of the on-board pin, which usually relates to the number 13.

We have the C/C++ coefficients true and false.

Arduino Math Constants

- M_PI the continuous(3.14159265358979323846).

- M_LN10 is the traditional logarithm used for the number 10.

- M_LN2 is the traditional logarithm of the number 2.

- M_LOG10E the logarithm From E to Level 10.

- M_LOG2E the logarithm of the base 2.

- M_SQRT2 the square root of 2.

- NAN the NAN (not a number) consistent.

The Arduino Programming Language Built-in Functions

In this section, I am going to refer to the integrated functions supplied by the Arduino programming language.

Program Lifecycle

- **Setup:** This function is called when the program starts, as well as when the Arduino is shut down and restarted.

- **Loop:** This function is called regularly while the Arduino system is working.

Dealing with I/O

The following functions assist with handling input and output from your Arduino gadget.

Digital I/O

- **DigitalRead()** checks out the value from a digital pin. Accepts a PIN as a parameter and returns the LOW or HIGH consistent.

- **DigitalWrite()** writes a HIGH or LOW worth to a digital output pin. You permit the PIN and LOW or HIGH as parameters.

- **PinMode** sets a pin to be an output or an input. You pass the PIN and the OUTPUT or INPUT value as parameters.

- **PulseIn()** reads a digital Pulse from WEAK to MODERATE, and then to SOFT, or from HIGH to LOW and to HIGH again on a pin. The program will block up until the pulse is identified. You specify the PIN and the sort of pulse you wish to determine (LHL or HLH). You can define an optional timeout to stop waiting on that pulse.

- **PulseInLong** is like pulseIn, other than it is implemented differently, and it can't be used if interrupts are shut off. Interrupts are typically shut off to get a more accurate outcome.

- **ShiftIn()** checks out a byte of data one bit at a time from a pin.

- **ShiftOut()** composes a byte of information one bit at a time to a pin.

- **Tone()** sends out a square wave on a pin, used for buzzers/speakers to play sounds. You can specify the frequency, pin, and it works on both analog pins and digital.

- **noTone()** stops the tone() the wave produced on a button.

Analog I/O

- **AnalogRead()** reads the value. The wave is produced on a button.

- **AnalogReference()** configures the value used for the leading input range in the analog input, by default 5V in 5V boards and 3.3 V in 3.3 V boards.

- **AnalogWrite()** writes an analog rate to a pin.

- **AnalogReadResolution()** allows you to replace the default analog bits resolution for analogRead(); by default 10 bits work on specific gadgets (Arduino Fee, No, and MKR).

- **AnalogWriteResolution()** allows you to change the default analog bits resolution to analog Write(), by default 10 bits. It only deals with specific gadgets (Arduino Charge, Zero, and MKR).

Time Functions

- **Delay()** pauses the program for a variety of milliseconds specified as a parameter.

- **DelayMicroseconds()** pauses the program for some split seconds, known as a criterion.

- **Micros()** the number of microseconds from the start of the program. Resets after ~ 70 times due to overflow.

- **Millis()** a variety of milliseconds before the start of the program, resets after ~ 50 days due to overflow.

Mathematics Functions

- **Abs()** the outright value of a number.

- **Constrain()** constrains within some range.

- **Map()** re-maps a number from one set to another; see the use.

- **Max()** the best two numbers.

- **Minutes()** the minimum of two numbers.

- **Pow()** the value and amount arose to energized.

- **Sq()** the square of the amount.

- **Sqrt()** the square root of a number.

- **Cos()** the cosine of an angle.

- **Sin()** the sine of an angle.

- **Tan()** the tangent of an angle.

Dealing with Alphanumeric Characters

- **isAlpha()** checks if a character is alpha (a letter)

- **isAlphaNumeric()** checks if a character is alphanumeric (a letter or number)

- **isAscii()** checks if a character is an ASCII character

- **isControl()** checks if a character is a <u>control character</u>

- **isDigit()** checks if a *'char'* is a number

- **isGraph()** checks if a *'char'* is a printable ASCII character, and contains content (it is not a space, for example)

- **isHexadecimalDigit()** checks if a *'char'* is an hexadecimal digit (A-F 0-9)

- **isLowerCase()** checks if a *'char'* is a letter in lower case

- **isPrintable()** checks if a *'char'* is a printable ASCII character

- **isPunct()** checks if a *'char'* is a punctuation (a comma, a semicolon, an exclamation mark etc)

- **isSpace()** checks if a *'char'* is a space, form feed \f, newline \n, carriage return \r, horizontal tab \t, or vertical tab \v.

- **isUpperCase()** checks if a *'char'* is a letter in upper case

- **isWhitespace()** checks if a *'char'* is a space character or an horizontal tab \t

Random Numbers Generation

- **Random()** generate a pseudo-random number.

- **randomSeed()** initialize the pseudo-random number creator with an arbitrary first figure. In Arduino, like in many languages, it's impossible to get random numbers, and the series is continuously the same, so you seed it with the present time or (in the case of Arduino) you can check out the input from an analog port.

Working with Bytes and Bits

- Bit() computes the worth of a bit (0 = 1, 1 = 2, 2 = 4, 3 = 8 ...).

- BitClear() clears (sets to 0) a small numeric variable, takes a number, and the variety of the bit beginning with the right.

- BitRead() read a little number. It accepts a number and the amount of the bit from the edge.

- BitSet() sets to 1 a little number. It accepts a number and the amount of the bit from the beginning.

- BitWrite() write one or zero to a particular bit of a number Accepts a number, the variety of the bit beginning with the right, and the value to write (zero or one).

- HighByte() get the high-order bit of the term attribute (which has 2 bytes).

- LowByte() get the low-order (rightest) byte of a vector term (comprehension)two bytes).

Disrupts

- NoInterrupts() disables interrupts.

- Disrupts() re-enables disrupts after they've been handicapped.

- AttachInterrupt() allow a digital input pin to be an interrupt. Many boards have different permitted pins; check the primary docs.

- DetachInterrupt() disables an interrupt enabled using attachInterrupt().

CHAPTER FOUR

Arduino Coding Environment and Basic Tools

What Language Is Arduino?

Arduino code is written in C++ with the addition of unique approaches and functions, which we'll mention later. C++ is a human-readable programming language. When you produce a 'sketch' (the name provided to Arduino code files), it is processed and put together to machine language.

Arduino IDE

The Arduino Integrated Development Environment (IDE) is the primary software for editing text used for Arduino programming.

It is where you'll be typing your code before uploading it to the board you want to program. Arduino code is described as sketches.

Arduino Code Example

As you can see, the IDE possesses a minimalist design. There are only five headings on the menu bar, together with a series of buttons that allow you to verify and submit your sketches. Essentially, the IDE translates and assembles your sketches to code that Arduino can understand. As soon as your Arduino code is assembled, it's then uploaded to the board's memory.

All the user needs to do this to start compiling their sketch is press the button.
If there are any mistakes in the Arduino code, a warning message will flag up, prompting the user to make changes. The majority of new users typically experience difficulty with compiling because of Arduino's stringent syntax requirements. The code won't assemble, and you'll be satisfied with an error message if you make any mistakes in your punctuation when using Arduino.

Serial Monitor and Serial Plotter

The Arduino serial monitor can be started by clicking on the magnifying glass icon on the upper left side of the IDE or under tools. The serial screen is used purposely for engaging the Arduino board using the computer and is a considerable tool for real-time monitoring and debugging. To use the monitor, you will have to use the serial class.

The code you download from circuito.io possesses a position of authentication that helps you to evaluate each part using the serial display.

Arduino Serial Plotter

This is another element of the Arduino IDE, which allows you to generate a real-time chart of your serial information. The serial plotter makes it a lot easier for you to examine your information through a visual display. You're able to create graphs, negative worth charts, and conduct waveform analysis.

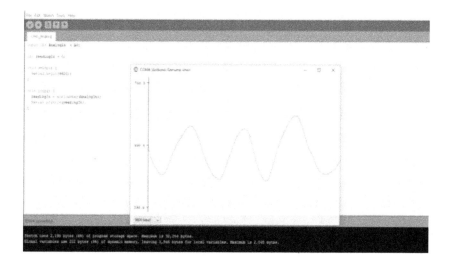

Debugging Arduino Code and Hardware

Unlike other software programming platforms, Arduino does not have an on-board debugger. Users can either use a third-party software application or serial display to print Arduino's active processes for monitoring and debugging.

By using the serial level to print, a serial programming debugs its remarks and values of variables. On many Arduino models, this will be using serial pins 0 and 1, which are connected to the USB port.

Code Structure

Libraries

In Arduino, similar to other leading programming platforms, there are built-in libraries that give basic functionality. Also, it's possible to bring in other libraries and broaden the Arduino board's abilities and functions. These libraries are approximately divided into libraries that engage with an element or those that carry out new services.

To import a brand-new library, you need to go to Sketch > Import Library on your PC.

Also, at the peak of your.ino file, you need to use '#include', which consists of external libraries. You can also create custom-made libraries to use isolated sketches.

Pin Definitions

To use the Arduino pins, you would need to identify which pin is being used and its performance. A practical way to specify the used pins is by using:

'#define pinNamepinNumber'.

The performance is either input or output and is defined by using the pinMode() technique in the setup section.

Variables

You need to declare worldwide variables and instances to be used whenever you're using Arduino.

In a nutshell, a variable enables you to name and keep a value to be used in the future. You would store data obtained from a sensor to use it later.

To declare a variable, you merely define its type, name, and initial value.

It's worth pointing out that stating global variables isn't an outright requirement, it's advisable that you declare your variables to make it easy to use your values more down the line.

Instances

In software programming, a class is a compilation of functions and variables that are kept together in one place. Each class has a particular function known as a contractor, which is used to develop an example of the class. To use the purposes of the course, we need to declare a situation for it.

Setup()

Every Arduino sketch needs to have a setup function. Once this function defines the preliminary state of the Arduino on boot and runs.

Here we'll specify the following:

- Initialize classes.

- Initialize variables.

- Preliminary state of pins.

- Pin functionality using the pinMode function.

- Code logic.

Loop()

Once setup() is done, the loop function is a must for every Arduino sketch and dos. It is the primary function, and as its name tips, it runs in a loop over and over again. The loop explains the fundamental reasoning of your circuit.

How to Configure Arduino

The basic Arduino code reasoning is an "if-then" structure and can be divided into four blocks:

1. **Setup** –Will generally be written in the setup section of the Arduino code and carries out things that need to be done as soon as possible, such as sensing unit calibration.

2. **Input** –At the start of the loop, checked out the information. These values will be applied as conditions ("if") such as the ambient light reading from an LDR using analogRead().

3. **Manipulate Data** –This is used to change the information into a more convenient form or carry out estimations. For example, the analog read() gives a reading of 0-1023,

which can be mapped to a range of 0-255 to be used for PWM.

4. **Output** – This area specifies the final result of the logic ("then") according to the information determined in the previous step. Looking at an example of the LDR and PWM, switch on an LED when the ambient light level goes down with a specific limit.

Arduino Code Libraries
Library Structure

A library is a folder consisted of files with C++ (.CPP) code files and C++ (.h) header files.

- The .h file explains the structure of the library and states all its functions and variables.

- The .cpp file holds the function application.

Importing Libraries

The first thing you need to do is identify the library you intend to use out of the many libraries available online. After downloading it to your computer, you need to open Arduino IDE and click Sketch > Include Library > Manage Libraries.

You can then select the library that you would like to import into the IDE. Once the process is complete, the library will be provided in the sketch menu.

In the code supplied by circuito.io, instead of including external libraries, as discussed previously, we provide them with the firmware folder. In this case, the IDE knows the method of finding them when using #include.

From Software to Hardware

There is a lot to be stated about Arduino's software application capabilities, but it's crucial to remember that the platform consists of both software and hardware. The two operate in tandem to run a complicated operating system.

Code > Compile > Upload > Run.

At the core of Arduino is the capability to run the code and compile.

After writing the code in the IDE, you need to release it to the Arduino. Clicking the Upload button (the right-facing arrow icon) will compile the code and upload it if it passed collection.

As soon as your upload is complete, the program will start running automatically.

You can also do this action by step:

1. First of all, assemble the code. To do this, click the check icon (or click on sketch)> Verify/Compile in the menu bar.

2. When you've done this, Arduino will begin to compile. Once it's finished, you'll get a completion message.

3. If your code fails to run, you'll also be informed, and the problematic code will be highlighted for editing.

4. As soon as you've compiled your sketch, it's time to upload it.

5. Pick the serial port your Arduino is currently connected to. To do this, click on "Tools">"Serial Port" in the menu to select it; you can then publish the assembled sketch.

6. To submit the sketch, click on the upload icon next to the tick. Additionally, you can go to the menu and click File >Upload. When the data is being moved, your Arduino LEDs will flicker.

7. When complete, you'll be greeted with a conclusion message that tells you Arduino has ended up uploading.

Establishing Your IDE

To link an Arduino board to your computer, you need a USB cable. When using the Arduino UNO, the USB transmits the data in the program straight to your board. The USB cable is used to power the Arduino. You can also run your Arduino effectively through an external source of energy.

Before you can upload the code, there are specific settings that you would need to configure.

Choose your board –You have to designate which Arduino board you're going to be using. Do this by clicking Tools > Board > Your Board.

Select your processor, there are specific boards (for example Arduino pro-mini) of which you need to define which processor you will use. Under tools >Processor >Choose the plan you have.

Pick your port – To select the port to which your board is linked, go to Tools > Port > COMX Arduino (this is Arduino's serial port).

How to Install Non-Native Boards

Some board types and designs are not pre-installed in the Arduino IDE; therefore, you'll need to install them before you can upload code.

To install a non-native board such as NodeMCU, you would need to:

1. Click on tools > Boards > Boards Manager.

2. Look for the board you wish to add the search bar and click "install".

Some boards cannot be found through the Board Manager. In this case, you'll need to include them manually. To do this:

1. Click on Files > Preferences.

2. In the Additional Boards Supervisor field, paste the URL of the installation bundle of your board. For instance, for NodeMCU, add the following: URL:http://arduino.esp8266.com/stable/package_esp8266 com_index.json.

3. Click OK.

4. Go to tools > Boards > Boards Manager.

Search for the board you wish to add in the search bar and click "install".

When you've completed this step, you will see the setup boards in the boards' list under tools.

Note: The process may vary a little for different boards.

Arduino: An Extremely Versatile Platform

Arduino is far more than a simple microcontroller. With an expansive IDE and a wide variety of hardware setups, Arduino is genuinely a diverse platform. The type of its libraries and its instinctive style make it a preferred for new users and knowledgeable makers alike. There are countless community resources to assist you in getting started with both hardware and software applications.

As you advance your abilities, you may face problems that require debugging, which is a weak area of the Arduino IDE. Thankfully, there are several methods and tools to debug any Arduino hardware and software application.

CHAPTER FIVE
Why We Choose Arduino, What Can We Do with It?

Arduino is a rapid electronic prototyping platform made up of the Arduino board and the Arduino IDE.

What Is Arduino?

It is an open-source task; software/hardware is very available and very flexible to be tailored and extended.

It is versatile, uses a range of digital and analog inputs, SPI, serial user interface, digital and PWM outputs.

It is simple to use, connects to the computer through USB and communicates using the basic serial procedure, runs in standalone mode and as interface linked to PC/Macintosh computer systems.

It is economical, around 30 euros per board and comes with a free authoring software application.

Arduino is backed up by a developing online community, many source code is already offered, and we can share and post examples for others to use, too!

I ought to note that many of the developers of Arduino are based in Ivrea, merely 40 minutes from Torino, where we lie: calling, networking, and collaborating with them in the future can be pretty straightforward.

What Can I Make with an Arduino?

Practically anything you want! It has been made use of in so many ways as the alternatives are virtually unlimited.

i. Past tasks included robotics, art setups, in-car computer systems, MIDI controllers, cocktail makers, human-computer user interfaces, Facebook 'Like' counters, marketing screens, clocks, song instruments, customized computer mouse and keyboard, home automation... The list continues!

ii. The highlights of an Arduino board are its capacity to review information from sensing units, to send out and get digital signals as well as attach using serial to your computer system.

iii. You can manage many things, from LEDs and LCDs to electric motors and relays.

iv. You can also read values from sensors such as potentiometers, light-dependent resistors (LDRs), and piezos.

v. The digital pins on an Arduino allow you to check out or compose 5Vvalues.

vi. You can use a pin to switch on an LED (with a resistor).

vii. You can send a signal to a relay to run higher voltage home appliances like televisions and house lights. You can send messages to electric motors to switch on and off.

viii. You can inspect to see if a button has been pressed.

ix. You can even send and get serial data, identical information, and electronic pulse width inflection, virtually anything that can be regulated via a little current.

The analog pins permit you to review an incoming voltage between 0V and 5V. This will be exactly how you check out from sensing units. There are a plethora of sensing units readily available, from accessible, hands-on pressure sensing units and rotary potentiometers, to environment sensors such as pressure, gas, temperature level, and alcohol. If you have, for example, a slider set to exactly half of its variety, it ought to result in a voltage of 2.5V. The Arduino can read this and use the value to control another object.

You do not have to stop with merely regulating electronic circuits. You can send data back to the computer to manage software such as Handling and Max/MSP. You can send out the data on USB with most designs. Some models have Bluetooth and Ethernet ports, together with an extra shield (like an add-on device) you can communicate through Wi-Fi and other methods.

What Can We Finish with Arduino?

Arduino is a terrific tool for establishing interactive items, taking inputs from a variety of switches or sensing units, and managing a range of lights, motors, and other outputs. Arduino projects can stand-alone, or they can be connected to a computer system using USB.

The Arduino will be regarded as a simple serial user interface (do you remember the COM1 on Windows?). There are serial communication APIs on many programming languages, so interfacing Arduino with a software application running on the computer system should be quite straightforward.

The Arduino board: A microcontroller module, a little circuit board(the board) that contains a whole computer system on a bit of chip (the microcontroller). There are various versions of the Arduino board; they are different in components, objective and size, etc. Some examples of Arduino boards include Arduino Diecimila, Arduino Duemilanove, Freeduino, Arduino NG, and many more. Arduino schematics are distributed using a free certificate to make someone complimentary to build his Arduino compatible board. The Arduino name is a registered trademark; this will disallow you from calling your hacked board Arduino.

Arduino Duemilanove

I was given an Arduino Duemilanove board, which is, according to the Arduino developers, the most basic one to use and the best one for learning.

A vital element of the Arduino board is the number of connectors readily available. These are the components which allow circuitry the Arduino boards to other parts (sensors, resistors, buttons, and more) that can be connected: reading, composing, moving, etc.

Arduino Duemilanove board has the following connectors (noted clockwise beginning from the leading left):

AREF: Analog Reference Pin

The voltage at this pin figures out the voltage at which the analog-to-digital converters (ADC) will report the decimal worth 1023, which is their highest level output. This suggests that using this pin, you'll have the ability to change the maximum value readable by the analog in nails; this is a way to change the scale of the analog in pins.

The AREF pin is, by default, connected to the 5V AVCC voltage (unless you are running your Arduino at a lower voltage).

GND: Digital Ground

Used as ground for digital inputs/outputs.

DIGITAL 0-13: Digital Pins

Used for digital I/O.

Digital pins have different uses.

TX/RX Pins 0-1: Serial In/Out

These pins can be used for digital I/O just like it's done with digital pins 2-13, but they can't be used for serial communication.

If your work uses serial communication, you might wish to use the one for Serial interaction instead of using the USB to the serial user interface. This can be useful while using the serial user interface to interact with a no PC gadget (e.g., another Arduino or a robot controller).

External Interrupts Pins 2-3

These pins can be configured to set up an interrupt on different input conditions. I still did not know how to use these pins, but more information is readily available on the attachInterrupt() function referral.

PWM Pins 3, 5, 6, 9, 10, 11.

Provide 8-bit PWM output alongside the analogWrite() function.

LED: 13

There is an integrated LED linked to digital pin 13. When the pin is HIGH value, the LED is switched on; when the pin is LOW, it's off.

ICSP: In-circuit Serial Programmer

Arduino comes with a bootloader, which makes it possible for program uploading through the USB to the serial interface. Advanced users can also directly submit programs to the Arduino board using an external programmer. This is done using the ICSP header, by doing so you save the ~ 2KB memory used in submitting sketches logic.

ANALOG IN 0-5: Analog Input Pins

They are used to read from an analog source (for example, a pressure sensing unit or potentiometer).

POWER Pins

Used to get or supply power to the Arduino board.

Vin

When using an external power supply, this offers the same current, which is showing up from the power supply. It's likewise possible to give voltage through this pin.

Grand (2 Pins)

Used as ground pins for your tasks.

While searching for the distinctions between the digital ground and the other two ground pins, I discovered that all the three ground pins on the Arduino board are connected; therefore the digital ground pin and the two ground pins under the power section are the same. I didn't examine the Arduino Duemilanove interior style on this.

- **5V:** This is used to acquire 5V power from the board. This is the same thing that powers the microcontroller. This can be as a result of USB or Vin (external power supply).

- **3V3:** A 3.3V power supply which is created from the FTDI chip. The optimum existing draw is 50mA. If subjected to small or large current draws, as read in the forum, it shows that the FTDI chip is quite a delicate part that can quickly burn. The consensus is to prevent using this pin source of power.

- **RESET:** By bringing this line to LOW, you can reset the board; there is also a button for doing so on the board but, as additional guards (e.g., Ethernet shield) may make the button unreachable, this can be used for resetting the board.

- **External Power Supply In:** With this, we can link an external power supply to Arduino. A 2.1 mm centre-positive plug connected to a battery or an AC-to-DC adapter. The current range can be 6 to 20 volts, however in order not to get too hot and stability problems, the advised variety is seven to twelve volts.

- **USB:** Used for publishing sketches (Arduino binary programs) to the board and serial interaction between the board and the computer system. Arduino can be powered from the USB port.

What Can't I Perform with One?

The Arduino doesn't have a great deal of processing power, so virtually any kind of significant intensive task is out of the inquiry. You will not have the ability to process, document, or output video or audio (although you can output graphics to TFT or LCD screens). It is not like a computer system. You will not be able to connect your webcam or keyboard to it. There is no operating system with a GUI (like a Raspberry Pi). It is a different quiet monster.

Can Anyone Make Use of One?

That's the charm of it. Even if you have no understanding or experience with electronic devices or shows, you can get a primary job and run in one or two hours.

Getting a result in a flash on and off in a pattern is as simple as adding an LED and resistor to a breadboard, connecting some cables, and composing some code lines. Arduinos are used in classrooms throughout the globe as a starter in programming and electronics.

The Arduino KIT

Arduino Board is pretty useless until we connect it to different electrical components. Usually, coupled with an Arduino board, stores also give Arduino KITs, which consists of many useful elements for developing circuits with Arduino.

I was supplied with an Arduino Base Workshop KIT, which contains:

- 1 x Straight single line pinhead connectors 2,54 40x1.

- 1 x Arduino Duemilanove board.

- 5 x 10K Ohm Resistors 1/4W (brown, orange, black, gold).

- 1 x USB cable.

- 5 x 2.2K Ohm Resistor 1/4 W (red, red, red, gold).

- 10 x 220 Ohm Resistors 1/4W (red, red, gold brown).

- 5 x 100nF capacitor polyester.

- 5 x 10nF capacitor polyester.

- 3 x 100uF electrolytic capacitor 25Vdc.

- 1 x 4,7K Ohm Thermistor.

- 5 x 330K Ohm Resistors 1/4W (orange, orange, yellow, gold).

- 1 x 10..40K Ohm LDR VT90N2.

- 3 x 5mm RED LED.

- 1 x 5mm GREEN LED.

- 1 x 5mm YELLOW LED.

- 1 x 10K Ohm linear potentiometer, PCB terminals.

- 2 x BC547 Transistor in TO92 Package.

- 1 x Set of 70 breadboard jumper wires.

- 1 x Piezo buzzer.

- 5 x PCB Pushbutton, 12x12mm size.

- 2 x 4N35 Optocoupler DIL-6 bundle.

- 1 x Breadboard, 840 tie points.

- 2 x Tilt sensor.

- 1 x Diode 1n4007.

- 1 x MOS Irf540.

Arduino IDE

The other part of the Arduino forum is Arduino IDE. This includes all the software which will run a computer to program and interact with an Arduino board.

The Arduino IDE contains an editor that is used for sketching (that's the name of Arduino programs); in short, the Arduino programming language imitated the processing language.

Using the IDE, the program we composed is converted to C language and then compiled using Avr-GCC. This procedure produces binary code which the microcontroller on the Arduino board will be able to perform and understand.

When the Arduino board is linked to a computer using the USB cable, by using the IDE, we can compile and upload to the jury the program.

Arduino and Linux

Archlinux system had no problems in the Arduino board when connected to a PC.A new Linux device called /dev/ttyUSB0 is produced.

If you have other devices linked using USB, which uses serial communication (e.g., a 3G UMTS USB dongle), you should carefully check the gadget name that your Arduino gets (you can use does for this). Other USB devices will also get a /dev/tty USBX gadget, so the Arduino may end up using a different gadget name (e.g., /dev/ttyUSB5) if/ dev/USB0 is not given (use mesg after plugging Arduino to check how Arduino was named).

In this case, perhaps you want a checklist for the Arduino board always ends up called with the same name.

CHAPTER SIX
A Tour of the Arduino UNO Board

You can try various electronic parts but don't have adequate knowledge, then Arduino is what you need to proceed.

So what is Arduino?

Arduino is a microcontroller-electronic prototyping platform based on open software that can be set with a user-friendly Arduino IDE.

This chapter will discuss what's on the Arduino UNO board and what it can do. UNO is not the only board in the Arduino collection. There are some other boards like Arduino Mega, Arduino Lilypad, Arduino Mini, and Arduino Nano.

However, the Arduino UNO board ended up being more popular than other boards in the household because it has more comprehensive documentation. This led to high adoption for electronic prototyping, producing a large neighborhood of electronic geeks and hobbyists.

In recent times, the UNO board is known as Arduino.

Components of Arduino UNO Board

The significant parts of the Arduino UNO board are as follows:

- USB adapter

- Power port

- Microcontroller

- Reset switch

- Crystal oscillator

- Analog input pins

- Digital pins

- USB interface chip

- TX RX LEDs

Now let's take a better look at each part:

USB adapter: This is a printer USB port used in loading a program from the Arduino IDE to the Arduino board. The board can likewise be powered through this port.

Power port: An AC-to-DC adapter or a battery can power the Arduino board. The power supply can be connected by plugging in a 2.1 mm centre-positive plug into the power jack of the board. The Arduino UNO board runs at a voltage of 5 volts, but it can endure a maximum voltage of 20 volts. If the board is provided with a higher voltage, there is a voltage regulator (it sits between the power port and USB port) that safeguards the board from stressing out.

Microcontroller: An Atmega328P microcontroller. It is the most prominent black rectangular chip, which comprises twenty-eight pins. Consider it as the brain behind your Arduino. The microcontroller used on the UNO board is Atmega328P by Atmel (major microcontroller producer).

Atmega328P has the following components in it:

- Flash memory of 32KB. The program loaded from Arduino IDE is kept here.

- RAM of 2KB. This is a runtime memory.

CPU: It manages everything that goes on within the gadget. It fetches the program instructions from flash memory and executes them with the help of a RAM.

Electrically Erasable Programmable Read-Only Memory (EEPROM) of 1 KB: This is a form of non-volatile memory, and it keeps the data after the device restarts and resets.

Atmega328P is pre-programmed with a bootloader. This allows you to directly submit a new Arduino program into the gadget without using any external hardware developer, making the Arduino UNO board easy to use.

Analog input pins: The Arduino UNO board has six analog input pins, known as "Analog 0 to 5."

These pins can read the signal from an analog sensing panel as a temperature level sensing unit and convert it to a digital value so that the system understands. These pins determine voltage and not the present because they have a very high internal resistance. Hence, just a percentage of present circulations through these pins.

These pins are identified as analog inputs by default. These pins can also be used for digital input or output.

Digital pins: You can discover these pins identified "Digital 0 to 13." These pins can be used as either output or input pins. When used as an output, these pins function as a power supply source for the components connected to them. When used as input pins, they check out the signals from the part attached to them.

When digital pins are used as output points, they contain forty milliamps of current at five volts, which is sufficient to light an LED.

Some of the digital pins are identified with the tilde (~) symbol next to the PINs (PINs 3, 5, 6, 9, 10, 11).

These pins act as optical sticks but can be used for Pulse-Width Modulation (PWM), which mimics analog output like fading an LED in and out.

Reset switch: When this switch is clicked, it gives a sound vibration to the reset pin of the Microcontroller and runs the program from the start. This can be extremely helpful if your code doesn't repeat, but you wish to evaluate it several times.

Crystal oscillator: This is a quartz crystal oscillator which ticks sixty million times in a second. On each tick, the microcontroller does one operation, for instance, addition, subtraction, and so on.

USB user interface chip: Consider this as a signal translator. It transforms signals in the USB level to a level that an Arduino UNO board understands.

TX-RX LEDs: TX means transmit, and RX for receive. These are indicator LEDs that blink anytime the UNO board is sending or getting data.

Now that you have explored the Arduino UNO board, you have started your journey towards developing your first IoT prototype.

CHAPTER SEVEN

Arduino – Overview

Arduino is a prototype platform (open-source) based on user-friendly hardware and software. It includes a circuit board, which can be programmed (referred to as a microcontroller) and a ready-made software called Arduino IDE (Integrated Development Environment), which is used to write and publish the computer system code to the physical board.

Key Function of Arduino

The essential functions are:

- Arduino boards can read analog or digital input signals from various sensing units and turn it into an output such as triggering a motor, turning LED on/off, connect to the cloud, and many other actions.

- You can control your board functions by sending some instructions directly to the microcontroller located on the board via Arduino IDE (described as uploading software application).

- Unlike many previous programmable circuit boards, Arduino does not need an extra piece of hardware (called a programmer) to pack a brand-new code into the board. You can simply use a USB cable.

- Additionally, the Arduino IDE makes use of a simplified version of C++, making it easier to discover the program.

- Finally, Arduino provides a standard type element that breaks the functions of the micro-controller into a more available plan.

Board Types

Various kinds of Arduino boards are readily available, depending on the different microcontrollers used. However, all Arduino boards have one thing in common; they are known to be programmed through the Arduino IDE.

The differences are the variety of outputs and inputs (the number of buttons, LEDs, and sensing units you can use on a single board), speed, running voltage, kind aspect, etc. Some boards are designed to be ingrained and have no programming interface (hardware), which you would need to buy personally.

Some can run directly from a 3.7V battery, and others require a minimum of 5V.

Here is a list of several Arduino boards available:

- Arduino boards based on ATMEGA328 microcontroller
- Arduino boards based on ATMEGA32u4 microcontroller
- Arduino boards based on ATMEGA2560 microcontroller
- Arduino boards based on AT91SAM3X8E microcontroller

496

CHAPTER EIGHT

Arduino – Board Description

In this chapter, we will discover the different parts contained on the Arduino board. Since it is the most widely known board in the Arduino board family, we will study the Arduino UNO board.

In addition, it is the best board to begin coding and electronics. Some boards look a bit different from the one given in the next page; however, many Arduinos have a lot of these parts in common.

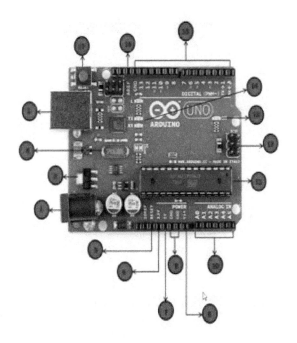

Power USB

Arduino board can be driven by using the USB cable from your computer system. All you need to do is connect the USB cable properly to the USB connection.

Power (Barrel Jack)

Arduino boards can be powered right from the air conditioner's main power supply by connecting it to the barrel jack (2).

Voltage Regulator

The function of the voltage regulator is to control the voltage given to the Arduino board and stabilize the DC voltages used by the processor and other elements.

Crystal Oscillator

The crystal oscillator assists Arduino in dealing with time concerns.

How Does Arduino Compute Time?

The answer is by using the crystal oscillator. The number printed on the Arduino time is 16,000H9H. It tells us that the frequency is 16 MHz or 16,000,000 Hertz.

The Arduino Reset

You can reset your Arduino board, that is, begin your program from the beginning. You can reset the UNO board in two ways.

- By using the reset control (17) on the screen.

- By connecting an external reset button to the Arduino pin labeled RESET (5).

Pins (3.3, 5, GND, Vin)

- 3.3 V (6)—Supply 3.3 output volt.

- 5V (7)—Supply 5 output volt.

- Most of the parts used with the Arduino board work better with 3.3 volts and 5 volts.

- GND (8)(Ground)—There are many GND pins on the Arduino, any of which can be used to ground your circuit.

- Vin (9)—This pin also can be used to power your Arduino board right from an external power source, like air conditioner's main power supply.

Analog Pins

The Arduino UNO board has six analog input pins A0 through A5. The volts can check out the signal from an analog sensing unit like the humidity sensor or temperature level sensor and transform it into a digital value that can be checked by the microprocessor.

Main Microcontroller

Each Arduino board has its microcontroller (11). You can take it as the brain of your board. The main IC (integrated circuit) on the Arduino is a little different from one board to another. The microcontrollers are generally from the ATMEL Company. You must know what IC your board has before filling up a new program from the Arduino IDE. This detail is available on the top of the IC. For more information about the IC building and functions, you can refer to the information sheet.

ICSP Pin

Mainly, ICSP (12) is an AVR, a small programming header for the Arduino consisting of MOSI, MISO, SCK, RESET, VCC, and GND. It is typically described as an SPI (serial peripheral interface), which could be considered as the "growth" of the output. You are working the output device to the master of the SPI bus.

Power LED Indication

When you plug your Arduino into a power source to confirm that your board is well powered up, this LED ought to light up.

There is something wrong with the connection if this light does not switch on.

AREF

AREF stands for analog reference. It is often used to set an external referral voltage (between 0 and 5 volts) as the upper limit for the analog input pins.

Arduino – Installation

After discovering the main parts of the Arduino UNO board, we are all set to learn how to set up the Arduino IDE. Once we learn this, we will be ready to upload a program properly on the Arduino board.

Ways to Set up the Arduino IDE on Your Computer

In this section, you have the opportunity to learn how to set up the Arduino IDE on our computer system and prepare the board to receive the program through USB cable.

Step 1 – Firstly, you should have your Arduino board (you can choose your favourite board) and a USB cable. In case you use Nano, Arduino Mega 2560, Arduino UNO, Arduino

Duemilanove, or Diecimila, you will need a standard USB cable (A plug to B plug).

Step 2 – Download Arduino IDE Software. You can get different varieties of Arduino IDE from the download page on the Arduino official website. You must choose your software application, which works with your OS (Windows, IOS, or Linux). After your file download is done, unzip the file.

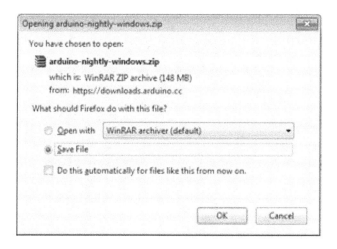

Step 3– Power up your board. The Arduino Uno, Arduino Nano Mega, Duemilanove, and immediately draw power from either the USB connection to the computer or an external power supply. If you are using an Arduino Diecimila, you have to make that the board is set up to draw power from the USB

connection. The source of energy is chosen with a jumper, a small piece of plastic that fits two of the three pins between the USB and power jacks. Examine that it is on the two pins closest to the USB port.

Link the Arduino board to your computer using the USB cable. The green power LED (labeled PWR) should be radiant.

Step 4 – Launch Arduino IDE. After your Arduino IDE software is downloaded, you need to unzip the folder. Inside the folder, you can discover the application icon with an infinity label (application.exe). Double-click the image to start the IDE.

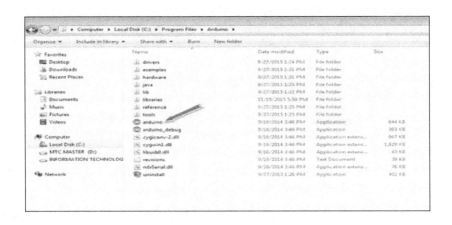

Step 5 – Open your first task. When the software starts, you have two alternatives:

- Create a new task.

- Open an existing task example.

To create a brand-new job, select File > New.

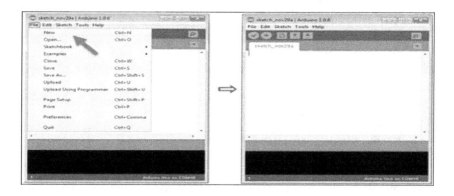

To open an existing project example, choose File > Example > Basics > Blink.

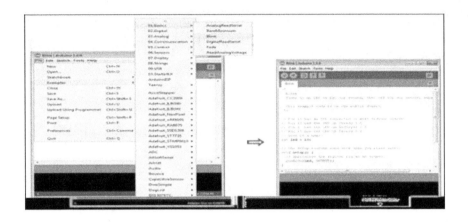

Here, we are choosing among the examples with the name Blink. It turns the LED off and on with some hold-up. You can pick any other instance from the list.

Step 6– Select your Arduino board.

To avoid any error while submitting your program to the board, you should choose the appropriate Arduino board name, which matches with the board connected to your computer system.

Go to Tools > Board and choose your board.

Here, we have selected the Arduino Uno board; however, you should choose the name matching the board that you are using.

Step 7 – Select your serial port. Select the serial gadget of the Arduino board. Go to Tools > Serial Port menu. This is likely to be COM3 or greater (COM1 and COM2 are usually reserved for hardware serial ports). To find out, you can disengage your Arduino board and re-open the menu, the entry that disappears need to be of the Arduino board. Reconnect the board and select that serial port.

Step 8 – Upload the program to your board. Before highlighting how we can publish our application to the board, we should demonstrate the function of each symbol appearing in the Arduino IDE toolbar.

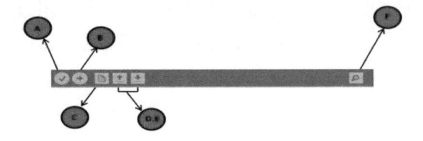

A – Used to check any compilation error.

B – Used to upload programs to the Arduino board.

C – Shortcut used to produce a new sketch.

D – Used to straight open among the example sketch.

E – Used to save your sketch.

F – Serial screen used to receive serial information from the board and send the following information to the board.

Now, merely click the "Upload" button in the environment. Wait a few seconds; you will see the TX LEDs and RXbon on the board flashing. If the upload achieves success, the message "Done publishing" will appear in the status bar.

Note: If you have an Arduino Micro or other board, NG, you need to press the reset button physically on the board right away before clicking the upload button on the Arduino software.

Arduino – Program Structure

In this session, we will study the Arduino program structure, and we will discover more new terminologies used in the Arduino world. The Arduino software application is open-source. The source code for the Java environment is launched below the GPL, and the C/C++ microcontroller libraries are under the LGPL.

Sketch

The first brand-new term in the Arduino program is "sketch".

Arduino programs can be split into three main parts:

1. Structure

2. Values (variables and constants)

3. Functions

In this session, we will learn more about the Arduino software application program, step by step, and how we can write the program without any syntax or collection mistake.

Let us begin with the structure. The software application structure consists of two primary functions:

- Setup() function

- Loop() function

PURPOSE

The **setup()** function is called when a sketch starts. Use it to initialize the variables, pin modes, start using libraries, etc. The setup function will only run once, after each power up or reset of the Arduino board.

After creating a **setup()** function, which initializes and sets the initial values, **the loop()** function does precisely what its name suggests, and loops consecutively, allowing your program to change and respond. Use it to actively control the Arduino board.

Arduino – Data Types

Information types in Arduino refer to a comprehensive system used for stating variables or functions of various kinds. The type of variable identifies how much space it occupies in the storage and how the bit pattern saved is analyzed.

Below are the data types that you need during Arduino programming:

Void

The space keyword is used only in function declarations. It shows that the function is anticipated to return no details to the role from which it was called.

Example

Space Loop

Boolean

A Boolean holds one of two values, right or wrong. Each Boolean variable inhabits one byte of memory.

Example

boolean value = incorrect;// declaration of variable with type boolean and initialize it with falseboolean state = real;// declaration of variable with type boolean and initialize it with true

Char

An information type that takes one byte of memory that saves a character worth, character literals are written in single quotes.

However, characters are saved as numbers. You can see the particular encoding in the ASCII chart. This indicates that it is possible to do math operations on aspects in which the ASCII worth of the role is used. For example, 'A' + 1 has worth 66 because the ASCII value of the uppercase A is 65.

Example

Char chr_a='a';// statement of a variable with type char and initialize it with a character a.

Char chr_c = 97;// declaration of a variable with type char and initialize it with character 97.

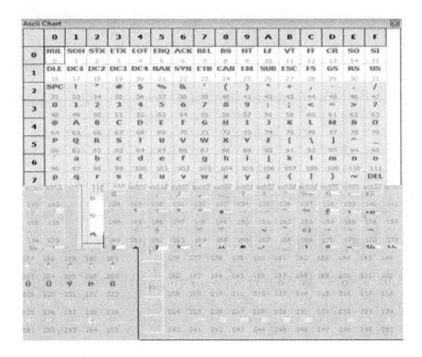

Unsigned Char

Anonymous char is an unsigned data type that occupies one byte of memory. The unknown char data type encodes numbers from 0 to 255.

Example

Anonymous Char chr_y = 121;// statement of the variable with type Unsigned char and initialize it with character y.

Byte

A byte stores an 8-bit unknown number, from 0 to 255.

Example

Byte m = 25;// declaration of a variable with type byte and initialize it with 25.

Int

Integers are the main data-type for number storage. Int stores a 16-bit (2-byte) worth. This yields a series of -32,768 to 32,767 (minimum value of $-2 \wedge 15$ and a maximum amount of $(2 \wedge 15) - 1$).

The intsize varies from one board to another. On the Arduino Due, for instance, an int shops a 32-bit (4-byte) worth. This yields a series of -2,147,483,648 to 2,147,483,647 (minimum worth of $-2 \wedge 31$ and an optimum value of $(2 \wedge 31) - 1$).

Example

int counter = 32;// declaration of a variable with type int and initialize it with 32.

Unsigned Int

Anonymous ints (unsigned integers) are the same as an int in the manner in which they store a 2-byte value. Instead of keeping negative numbers, nevertheless, they only stay positive values, yielding a beneficial series of 0 to 65,535 (2 ^ 16) - 1). The Due stores a 4 byte (32-bit) value, within the zero to four,294,967,295 (2 ^ 32 - 1).

Example

Anonymous int counter = 60;// declaration of a variable with type unsigned int and initialize it with 60.

Word

On the Uno and other ATMEGA based boards, a word becomes a 16-bit unsigned number. On the Due and Zero, it keeps a 32-bit unsigned number.

Example

Word w = 1000;// declaration of a variable with type word and initialize it with 1000.

Long

Long variables are extended size variables adopted for number storage, and store 32 bits (4 bytes), from -2,147,483,648 to 2,147,483,647.

Example

High speed = 102346;// statement of a variable with type Long and initialize it with 102346.

Anonymous Long

Unsigned long variables are extended size variables for number storage and shop 32 bits (4 bytes). Compare to longs, and anonymous longs will not save negative numbers, making their range from 0 to 4,294,967,295 ($2 \wedge 32 - 1$).

Example

Anonymous Long speed = 101006;// declaration of a variable with type Unsigned Long and initialized it with 101006.

Short

A petite one is a 16-bit data-based on every Arduino. (ATMega and ARM-based), a small stores a 16-bit (2-byte) value. This results a variety of -32,768 to 32,767 (minimum value of $-2 \wedge 15$ and an optimum worth of ($2 \wedge 15$) - 1).

Example

Brief Val = 13;// statement of a variable with type short and initialize it with 13.

Float

Information type for the floating-point number is a number that has a decimal point. Floating-point names are frequently used to approximate the analog and constant values because they have higher resolution than integers.

Floating-point numbers can be as small as -3.4028235 E +38 and as large as 3.4028235 E +38. They are stored as 32 bits (4 bytes) of details.

Binary

Other ATMEGA based and Uno boards.

Double-precision floating-point number occupies four bytes. That is, the dual implementation is the same as the float, without benefits in precision. On the Arduino Due, doubles have 8-byte (64 bit) accuracy.

Example

Statement of variable double num = 45.352;// with type double and start it with 45.352.

CHAPTER NINE
Arduino–Variables and Constants

Before we begin discussing the variable types, there is a crucial subject we need to make sure you understand quite well; this is called the variable scope.

What Is a Variable Scope?

The variables in Arduino programming language, those that Arduino uses, have a residential or commercial property called scope. A scope is a region of the program, and there are three locations where the declaration of variables can be made. They are:

- Inside a block or a function, which is called regional variables.

- In the definition of function parameters, which is called formal places.

- Outside every feature, which is called global variables.

Regional Variables

The variables that are stated inside a function or block are regional variables. They can be used by the statements that are inside that function or block of code. Local variables are not known to function outside their own.

Following is the example using local variables:

- Void setup ()

- Space loop ()

```
Void setup (){



}




Void loop (){

intx, y ;

intz;Local variable declaration

x =0;
```

```
y =0; actual initialization

z =10;

}
```

Global Variables

Global variables are defined beyond all the functions, generally at the top of the program. The global variables will hold their worth throughout the lifetime of your plan.

Any function can access a global variable; that is, you can use the above during your entire program after its declaration.

The following example uses regional and global variables:

```
IntT, S ;

float c =0;Global variable declaration



Void setup (){
```

```
}

Void loop (){

intx, y ;

intz;Local variable declaration

x =0;

y =0; actual initialization

z =10;}
```

Int T, S;

float c = 0; Global variable declaration

Space setup ()

Void loop ()

Arduino – Operators

An operator is a sign that informs the compiler to carry out specific mathematical or sensible functions. C language is rich in integrated operators and provides the following kinds of operators:

- Arithmetic Operators

- Comparison Operators

- Boolean Operators

- Bitwise Operators

- Substance Operators

Arduino –Control Structures

Decision making structures need that the developer specifies one or more conditions to be evaluated or checked by the program. It must be along with a declaration or statements to be executed if the state is determined to be real, and additionally, other announcements to be carried out if the state is determined to be false.

Following is the essential kind of a typical choice-making structure found in most of the programming languages:

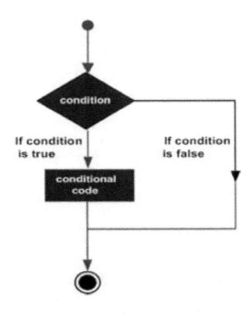

Control structures are elements in the source code that control already made program.

They comprise of:

Arduino – Loops

Languages in programming give different control structures that provide more complicated execution paths.

A loop declaration allows us to carry out a statement or group of accounts many times, and the following is the basic form of a loop declaration in the majority of the programming languages:

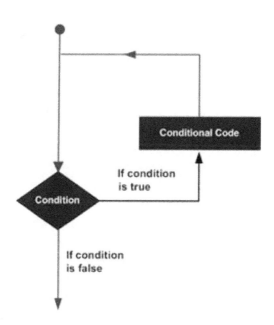

Arduino – Functions

Functions allow structuring the programs in sectors of code to carry out private jobs. The typical case for creating a service is when one needs to carry out the same action many times in a program.

- Functions codify one step in one place so that the roles need to be considered once.

- Standardizing code fragments into services has many benefits.

- Features help the programmer stay arranged. Often this helps to conceive the program.

- This also reduces possibilities for mistakes in adjustment if the code needs to be altered.

- Functions make the whole sketch smaller and more compact.

There are two functions in an Arduino sketch, i.e., setup () and loop(). Other features should be created outside the brackets of these two functions.

The most common syntax to specify a function is:

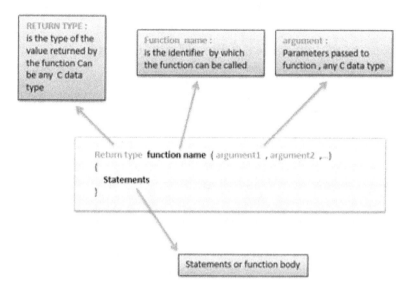

Function Declaration

A function is declared outside any other features.

Which are:

Firstly, writing the part of the function known as a function prototype above the loop function, which consists of:

- Function return type.

- Function name.

- Function argument type, no requirement to write the argument name.

Function model should be followed by a semicolon (;).

The copying reveals the presence of the function declaration using the first method.

The second part, which is called the function definition or statement, needs to be declared below the loop function, which consists of:

- Function return type.

- Function name.

- Function argument type, here you need to include the argument name.

- The function body (declarations inside the function are carrying out when the function is called).

Low Power Arduino

A usual Arduino, for example, the Mini does not consume much power, commonly 40 MA when connected to a USB cable. If you're going to be powering your Arduino on something aside from batteries, the power requirements usually aren't a concern; it will undoubtedly be inadequate to make any type of distinction. Once you start something like a remote monitoring application where you are needed to run with battery power, power consumption can become substantial.

In my functioning experience, hoping to calculate the number of time an Arduino will continue with a battery pack is reasonably tight because there are many variables included, types of alkaline, nickel-metal hydride, lithium-ion, rechargeable, non-rechargeable for a specific kind of battery state triple-A, there will be widely varying storage abilities depending on the design of battery it is (nickel-metal hydride or lithium-ion). There is irregularity amongst the different brands (usually you obtain what you spend for). When your batteries depleted, the voltage provided decreases; if you are using four three-way A batteries, which supply six volts to operate an Arduino which calls for at least 5V, the Arduino might effectively stop working when the voltage provided dips and low, even when there is a substantial amount of power remaining in the batteries.

I will not be doing any kind of details computations below for the reason that I discover the figures are not sensible. I have to state that batteries typically are defined in regards to milliampere hours. So anytime your Arduino is connected through USB, it's working at 5 volts; if it is attracting forty milliamperes, that isn't the same action of wattage as requiring forty milliamperes from a 9V battery. Moreover, it depends on what your application is. Are you just taking input from some kind of analog surveillance tool, or are you using it on a servo? These have drastically different power requirements, and again in my experience, you'll discover it not helpful to determine. I place the most effective method is to find some batteries you have around the house and also see how long they last after used those dimensions to make empiric calculations.

Presume you're dealing with a remote monitoring device, and you need to have the Arduino to gauge something for some significant time continuously. I did something comparable with a DS18B20 sensor that was within one of the cold frames in my lawn; it would have been a discomfort drawing an expansion cable bent on the park, and not an excellent suggestion to leave it outdoors revealed, so I pick operating on a battery.

The ATmega, as well as SAM processors that come on an, Arduino contain some extremely advanced power administration functionality that you can play with. Still, before we review the techniques which you can make your Arduino preserve power, we need to analyze some simple direct services. Most importantly, it would be to use a different Arduino that is feasible. The 3.3 volt Arduinos will use less energy than a 5V Arduino for a specific kind of application. The Arduino Nano and Arduino Micro will use less power than a Uno and Mega, and if they benefit your demands, this alone may be enough.

Another point to think of is using a different kind of battery. Currently, when we mention batteries, it occasionally seems as if there is this attitude that lithium-ion batteries are the best for anything. Lithium-ion batteries are lovely for possessing a very high power/weight ratio.

This is wonderful for tasks like robots and various other things that move. If your battery isn't going to move, a better option might be a lead-acid battery, similar to the one in your vehicle or truck; this is what I decided on in my yard cold frame.

What if you still want to conserve power and a different Arduino or larger sized battery will not meet your requirements? Then there are lots of approaches we can try out to get the Arduino to conserve power.

One technique is to bypass everything except the processor chip; you do this by avoiding the power connector but directly give energy to the processor with power. You must be careful here that you stay inside the operating limitations of the given chip which is on your Arduino, that voltage regulator is for a reason! This will save significant power. The processor chip consumes much less energy than the entire Arduino board; this is typically in the form of heat lost by the regulator and objects like the LED.

- Another way to reduce power consumption is to lower the clock speed. If you're running a program like monitoring the temperature of your frame every thirty seconds, there's no need for the Arduino to perform at its maximum clock rate. This can be accomplished with the pre-scaler library. You can reduce the clock speed by a factor as much as 256; this will decrease a sixteen megahertz Arduino to a 62.5 kHz one, but when you find yourself just checking a measurement every 25 seconds or so, this is more than enough, and this will decrease consumption significantly.

- For a remote monitoring project, the most effective technique you could do to improve efficiency is to put Arduino to sleep. There is a library called narcoleptic, which allows you to hold the Arduino in a minimal consumption mode, and just a single timer is functioning. This timer can be used to awaken the Arduino every 20 seconds, as I needed to do. Many of the smaller 3.3V Arduino's will consume under 1 MA while asleep.

Adding Ethernet, Wi-Fi, and Other Communications to Your Arduino (or Other PIC) – Including the NSLU2

The Arduino is a small programmable device that can hold a short program and perform tasks such as reading temperature sensors, turning on or off switches, and can serve as the 'brain' for a robot. I have used the Arduino (actually freeArduino) for projects related to HVAC and hydroponics automation.

It is often useful to communicate with the Arduino—for example, everyday use of an Arduino is for data collection. You may have a temperature sensor wired to the Arduino and interface with flash storage to log the temperature data. Later you have to remove the flash storage and transfer it to your computer.

What If You Can Communicate with the Arduino?

With Ethernet or wireless connectivity, you could simply connect to the Arduino with a computer and capture the data in real-time. This gives more automation and opens a world of possibilities; real-time alerts, real-time adjustments (have the Arduino switch something on/off), and many more.

There Are Some Choices Available for Communications

Serial: The Arduino has TTL lines, not traditional RS232, but it is possible for a reasonable cost to use a conversion/level adapter or circuit. You could then run a serial line to a computer. This is acceptable in many cases but restricts you to using one network, and in the case of my home, the wiring is not as convenient. I have Ethernet cat5 running all over the place, so if I am going to use a wired solution, Ethernet is the best.

Wi-Fi: For some, this may be the best solution. If you cannot or do not want to run wires of any kind, solutions are ranging from 400/900 MHz transceivers that use 4-6 pins for simple communications to more powerful XBee, ZigBee, and even 802.11 Wi-Fi. The primary issue I have found with these solutions is the cost or the technical expertise required. Also, double-check if the interface you are using requires any libraries or interface code that will use space within the Arduino. The RFM units are promising as they are low cost, though I have not successfully interfaced them as of yet.

Ethernet: There are some solutions for adding Ethernet capabilities such as shields and serial to Ethernet bridges/adapters. Some require a 'TCP/IP stack' to be written to the Arduino—consider this as it uses many storage spaces.

NSLU2 or Computer: For my application, I chose to use some NSLU2 units I had (these are often available via online auction). The NSLU2 is a network-attached storage device (NAS) that is frequently changed (hacked) to run other operating systems and improve its functionality at the hardware level. In my case, I overclocked mine and installed Debian Linux using an 8GB flash drive. The NSLU2 also uses a TTL interface, though at 3.3V instead of 5V. Interfacing is done with three simple wires, and a resistor is needed on one line for the 3.3V to 5V conversion.

This book has presented several options for adding communications capabilities to the Arduino.

CHAPTER TEN

Arduino – Strings

This is used to store text. They can be used to show text on an LCD or in the Arduino IDE serial monitor window. Strings are also helpful for keeping user input.

- Two kinds of strings in Arduino programming.

- The Arduino String, which gives room for sketching.

- Arrays of characters, which are the same as strings.

String Arrays Character

The first type of string that we will find out is the string that is a series of characters of the type char. In the previous chapter, we learned what an array is, a consecutive sequence of the same kind of variable saved in memory. A string is a variety of char variables.

A string is a unique range that has one additional component at the end of the series, which always has a value of 0 (absolutely no). This is referred to as a "null ended string".

String Character Array Example

This will demonstrate how to make a string and print it to the serial display window.

void loop()

The following example reveals what a string is made up of; a character selection with characters 0 as the last component of the range to show that this is where the string ends. The string can be printed out to the Arduino IDE serial monitor window by using Serialprintln() and passing the name of the string.

Example

charmy_str[]="Hello";.

Serial.begin(9600);.

void setup()

Serial.println(my_str);.

space loop()

In this sketch, the compiler determines the string size, string selection, and the string null terminations. A selection that is six aspects long and includes five characters followed by an absolutely no is produced with the same method as in the previous sketch.

Manipulating String Arrays

We can modify a string array within a sketch, as revealed in the following illustration.

Example

```
voidsetup(){

charlike[]="I like coffee and cake";// create a string

Serial.begin(9600);

// (1) print the string

Serial.println(like);

// (2) delete part of the string

like[13]=0;
```

```
Serial.println(like);

// (3) substitute a word into the string

like[13]=' ';// replace the null terminator with a space

like[18]='t';// insert the new word

like[19]='e';

like[20]='a';

like[21]=0;// terminate the string

Serial.println(like);

}


voidloop(){


}
```

Result

I like coffee and cake.

I like coffee.

I like coffee and tea.

The sketch operates in the following way:

Producing and Printing the String

In the sketch given above, a new string is produced and printed for the screen in the serial monitor window.

Shortening the String

The string is shortened by replacing the 14th character in the chain together with a valueless terminating zero (two). This is component number 13 in the string variety counting from 0.

When the string is printed, all the characters are written to the new null ending.

Other characters do not disappear; they still exist in memory, and the string selection remains the same size. The only difference is that any function that works with strings will only see the chain up to the first null terminator.

Changing a Word in the String

Finally, the sketch changes the word "cake" with "tea" (3). It first has to replace the null terminator at like [thirteen] with a place where the string is brought back to the initially developed format.

New characters overwrite "cak" from the word "cake" with the "tea".

This is done by excessive writing of specific characters in ex. The 'e' of "cake" is replaced with a brand-new null ending character. The outcome is that it ended with two invalid characters, the original one at the end of the string and the new one that changes the 'e' in "cake". This makes no difference when the unique chain is printed because the function that writes the string stops printing the string characters when it comes across the very first null terminator.

Functions to Manipulate String Arrays

The previous sketch manually manipulated the string by accessing special characters in the chain. To make it much easier to control string arrays, you can compose your functions to do so or use some of the string operations from the C language library.

Provided Below Is the List of Functions to Manipulate String Arrays

The next sketch uses some Arduino string functions.

Example

```
voidsetup(){

charstr[]="This is my string";// create a string

charout_str[40];// output from string functions placed here

intnum;// general purpose integer

Serial.begin(9600);
```

```
// (1) print the string

Serial.println(str);



// (2) get the length of the string (excludes null terminator)

num=strlen(str);

Serial.print("String length is: ");

Serial.println(num);



// (3) get the length of the array (includes null terminator)
num=sizeof(str);// sizeof() is not a C string function
Serial.print("Size of the array: ");
Serial.println(num);
// (4) copy a string

strcpy(out_str,str);

Serial.println(out_str);
```

```
// (5) add a string to the end of a string (append)

strcat(out_str," sketch.");

Serial.println(out_str);

num=strlen(out_str);

Serial.print("String length is: ");

Serial.println(num);

num=sizeof(out_str);

Serial.print("Size of the array out_str[]: ");

Serial.println(num);

}


voidloop(){}
```

Result

This is my string.

String length is 17.

Size of the selection: 18.

This is my string.

This is my string sketch.

String length is25.

Size of the range out_str []: 40.

The sketch operates in the following method:

Print the String

The newly developed string is printed to the serial monitor window, as carried out in previous sketches.

Get the Length of the String

The string line() function is used to get the string length, which is used for the printable characters only and not the null terminator.

The string contains 17 characters.

Get the Length of the Range

The operator sizeof() is used to get the string length. The length includes the null terminator, so the distance is more than the length of the string.

Sizeof() appears like a function; however, technically is an operator. It is not part of the C string library but was used in the sketch to indicate the distinction between the size of the range and the size of the string (or string length).

The string was copied to the range for us to have an extra space in the selection to use in the next part of the sketch that is including a string to the end.

Add a String to a String (Concatenate)

The sketch joins one string to another. This is done by using the string() function. The chain() feature puts the second string passed to it to the end of the first team.

Concatenation, the length of the string is printed to show the brand-new string length. The length of the range is then written to show that we have a 25-character long line in a 40 aspect long range.

Bear in mind that the 25-character long string uses up 26 characters of the array due to the null ending zero.

Selection Bounds

When dealing with strings and varieties, it is essential to work within the bounds of chains or selections. In the example sketch, a variation was created, which was 40 characters long to allocate the memory that could be used to manipulate strings.

If the selection was made smaller and we tried to copy a string that is larger than the range to it, the chain would be replicated at the end of the selection. The memory beyond the end of the collection could include other relevant information used in the sketch, which would then be overwritten by our string. If the mind beyond completion of the chain is overrun, it could crash the design or cause unanticipated behavior.

Arduino – String Object

The second type of string is object string, which can be used in Arduino programming as well.

What Is an Object?

An object is a construct that contains both data and functions. A String object can be produced merely like a variable and assigned a value or string. The String object includes features (which are called "approaches" in objects oriented programming 'OOP') that run on the string information contained in the String object.

The following sketch and explanation will make it clear what an item is and how the String object is used.

Example

```
voidsetup(){

Stringmy_str="This is my string.";

Serial.begin(9600);



// (1) print the string
```

```
Serial.println(my_str);


// (2) change the string to upper-case

my_str.toUpperCase();

Serial.println(my_str);



// (3) overwrite the string

my_str="My new string.";

Serial.println(my_str);



// (4) replace a word in the string

my_str.replace("string","Arduino sketch");

Serial.println(my_str);
```

```
// (5) get the length of the string

Serial.print("String length is: ");

Serial.println(my_str.length());

}


voidloop(){}
```

Result

This is my string.

THIS IS MY STRING.

My brand-new string.

My new Arduino sketch.

String length is 22.

A string object is developed and appointed a worth (or string) at the top of the sketch.

String my_str="This is my string.";.

This develops a String object with the name my_str and gives it a value of "This is my string".

This can be compared to creating a variable and assigning a worth to it such as an integer:

intmy_var = 102;.

The sketch works in the following way.

Printing the String

The string can be printed to the serial monitor window just like a character array string.

Change the String to Uppercase

The String objectmy_str that was created has a variety of functions or ways that can be run on it. These methods are invoked by using the object's name followed by the dot operator (.) and the name of the function to use.

my_str. toUpperCase();.

The toUpperCase() function runs on the string consisted of my_str object, which is of type String and transforms the string information (or text) that the objects contain to upper-case characters. A list of the functions that the String class consists of can be found in the Arduino String reference. Technically, String is called a level and is used to create String objects.

Overwrite a Series

The job operator is used to appoint a brand-new string to the my_strobjects that replace the old string.

my_str="My brand-new string.";.

The project operator cannot be used on character variety strings, however, it deals only with String objects.

Changing a Word in the String

The replace() function is used to replace the first string passed to it by the second string pass. return() is another function that is constructed to the String class and is readily available to use on the String objectsmy_str.

Getting the Length of the String

This is very easy to do with the uses of length().

In the sample sketch, the result returned by length() is passed directly to Serial.println() without using an intermediate variable.

When You Can Use a String Object

A String object is easier to use than a string character array. The objects have integrated functions that can perform a variety of operations on strings.

The primary downside of using the String object is that it uses a great deal of memory and can rapidly use up the Arduinos RAM, which might cause Arduino to hang and crash all of a sudden. If a sketch on an Arduino is little and limits making use of objects, then there ought to be no problems.

Character array strings are more challenging to use, and you may need to compose your functions to run these types of lines. The advantage is that you have control over the size of the string ranges that you make, so you can keep the fields small to save memory.

You need to make sure that you do not compose beyond the end of the range bounds with string varieties. The String object does not have this problem and will look after the string bounds for you, providing enough memory for it to run on. The String object can attempt to write memory that does not exist when it lacks memory but will not write on the end of the string that it is operating on.

CHAPTER ELEVEN

Stating Arrays

Ranges inhabit an area in memory. To define the type of aspects and the number of components required by a range, use a declaration of the following:

Type arrayName [arraySize];

The compiler reserves the proper quantity of memory. (Recall that a declaration, which reserves memory is more meaning).

The array size must be an integer consistent greater than nothing. To tell the compiler to reserve 11 aspects for integer variety C, use the statement:

int C [12];// C is a variety of 12 integers

Selections can be declared to contain the values of a non-reference data type. A range of type string can be used to keep character strings.

Examples Using Arrays

This section offers many examples that show how to state, start, and control varieties.

Example 1: Declaring an array and using a loop for array's elements.

Lines a—b is the use or statement to initialize the selection components to nos. Like other automated variables, automatic arrays are not implicitly initialized to absolutely no. The first output declaration (line c) displays the column headings for the columns printed in the subsequent for a confirmation (lines e), which writes the selection in tabular format.

Pins Configured as INPUT

Arduino pins are configured as inputs, so they do not need to be called data with pinMode() when you are using them as inputs. Pins configured by doing this are stated to be in a high-impedance state. Input pins make minimal demands on the circuit equals to a series of 100 megaohms in front of the nail.

This suggests that it takes minimal current to change the input pin from one state to another. This makes the pins beneficial for such jobs as carrying out a capacitive touch sensing unit or reading an LED as a photodiode.

Pins set up as pinMode(pin, INPUT) with a wire that is not connected to other circuits, or without anything to connect them, report seemingly random changes in the state of the pins, getting electrical noise from the environment, or capacitive coupling the state of a neighboring pin.

Pull-up Resistors

If no input is present, pull-up resistors are typically useful to steer an input pin to a known state. This can be done by adding a pull-up resistor (to +5V)on the input.

Important Features

Here are some crucial functions about disrupts:

- Most Arduino styles have two hardware interrupts (described as "interrupt0" and "interrupt1") hard-wired to digital I/O pins 2 and 3, respectively.

- The Arduino Mega has six hardware disrupts, including the extra disrupts ("interrupt2" through "interrupt5") on pins 21, 20, 19, and 18.

- You can specify a routine using a particular function called "Interrupt Service Routine" (generally referred to as ISR).

- Interrupts can originate from various sources. In this case, we are using a hardware interrupt that is generated by a state change in the digital pins.

- You can define the regular and specify conditions at the rising edge, falling edge, or both. At these specific conditions, the interrupts would be addressed.

Types of Interrupts

We have two types of disrupts:

- Hardware Interrupts – They occur in response to an external occasion, like an external interrupt pin going low or high.

- Software Interrupts – They occur in action to a guideline sent out in software. The only kind of interrupt that the "Arduino language" supports is the attachInterrupt() function.

Using Interrupts in Arduino

Interrupts are beneficial in Arduino programs as it assists in resolving timing problems. A useful application of an interrupt reads a rotary encoder or observing a user input. Generally, an ISR must be fast and as brief as possible. If your sketch uses several ISRs, only one can perform at a time. Other interrupts will be carried out after the current one finishes in an order that depends upon the concern they have.

Usually, global variables are used to pass data between an ISR and the main program. To ensure variables shared between an ISR and the first program are updated properly, declare them as unstable.

attachInterrupt Statement Syntax

attachInterrupt(digitalPinToInterrupt(pin), ISR, mode);// suggested for Arduino board

attachInterrupt(pin, ISR, mode);// suggested Arduino Due, Zero only

// argument pin: the PIN

// argument ISR: the ISR to call when the interrupt happens

// This function is often referred to as an interrupt service regimen.

// argument mode: defines when the interrupt ought to be activated.

The following three constants are predefined as legitimate values:

- FALLING anytime the pin goes from high to low.

- LOW to activate the interrupt whenever the pin is low.

- CHANGE to trigger the interrupt whenever the pin changes its value.

Communication in Arduino

Many communication methods have been specified to achieve this data exchange. Each procedure can be classified into one of the two classifications: parallel or serial.

Identical Communication

The same connection between the Arduino and peripherals using input/output ports which is the suitable option for much shorter distances to longer meters. Nevertheless, in other cases, when it is needed to develop interaction between two gadgets for longer distances, it is not possible to use a parallel connection. Identical user interfaces move multiple bits at the same time. They typically call for buses of information— sending across eight, sixteen, or more cables. Data is transferred in quantum, collapsing waves of both 1 as well as 0.

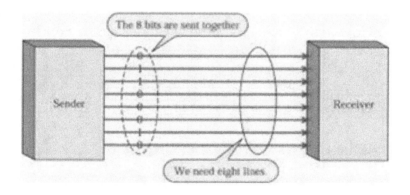

Benefits and Disadvantages of Identical Communication

Identical communication has its advantages. It is much faster than serial, uncomplicated, and relatively simple to carry out. However, it calls many input/output (I/O) ports and lines. If you needed to relocate a project from a fundamental Arduino Uno to a Mega, you recognize that the I/O lines on a microprocessor can be valuable.

Therefore, we like serial communication, compromising prospective speed for the pins.

Serial Interaction Components

Today, a lot of Arduino boards are built with some systems for serial interaction as conventional equipment.

Any of the systems used depends on the elements listed below:

- How many tools the microcontroller has to exchange data with?

- How fast the data exchange needs to be?

- What is the range between these devices?

- Is it required to send and receive information simultaneously?

Among the essential things worrying serial interaction is the protocol, which needs to be strictly observed. It is a set of regulations, which need to be used such that the devices can appropriately translate the information they mutually exchange. Luckily, Arduino makes sure that the work of the programmer/user is decreased to simple create (information to be sent out) and read (received data).

Types of Serial Communications

Serial communication can be additional categorized as:

- **Synchronous** – Tools that are synchronized using the same clock, and their timing is in synchronization with each other.

- **Asynchronous** –Tools that are asynchronous have their own clocks and are caused by the result of the previous state.

It is easy to know if a tool is synchronous or not. If the same clock is given to all the connected devices, then they are synchronous. If there is no clock line, it is asynchronous.

The asynchronous serial method has some built-in policies.

These policies are nothing but systems that ensure robust and error-free data transfers. These systems, which we get for eschewing the exterior clock signal, are:

- Synchronization bits

- Information bits

- Parity bits

- Baud rate

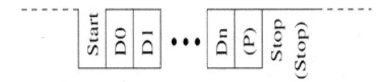

Synchronization Bits

The little synchronization bits are two or three individual bits transferred with each packet of information. They are the start and the stop bits. According to their name, these little bits note the beginning and the end of a package specifically.

There is continuously one start bit; however, the variety of stop bits is configurable to either one or two (though it is usually left at one).

To start small is always shown by an idle information line going from one to zero, while the stop bits will shift back to the idle state by holding the line at one.

Information Bits

The amount of data in each packet can be set to any size from five to nine little bits. The standard information size is your primary 8-bit byte; however other dimensions have their uses. A 7-bit information package can be much more reliable than 8, especially if you are simply transferring 7-bit ASCII personalities.

Parity Bits

The user can choose whether there should be a parity bit or not, and if so, whether the equality should be rare or not. The parity bit is 0 if the variety of 1 is among the information bits as well. Odd parity is just the contrary.

Baud Rate

The term baud rate is used to denote the variety of bits moved every second [bps];note that it refers to little bits, not bytes. It is generally called for by the protocol that each byte is transferred together with several control bits. It indicates that byte in serial data stream might include 11 little bits. For instance, if the baud rate is 300 bps, then the maximum 37 and also minimal 27 bytes may be moved per second.

Arduino – Inter-Integrated Circuit

Inter-integrated circuit (I2C) is a system for serial data exchange between the specialized integrated circuits and microcontrollers of a brand-new generation. It is used when the distance between them is short, and the connection is established via two conductors. One is used for data transfer and the other is used for synchronization (clock signal).

As seen in the adhering number, one device is constantly a master. It performs addressing of one slave chip before the communication begins. This way, one microcontroller can communicate with 112 various gadgets. The baud rate is 100 KB/s (typical setting) or 10 KB/s (slow-moving baud rate mode). Solutions with the baud rate of 3.4 MB/s have lately shown up. The range between tools, which communicate over an I2C bus is restricted to numerous meters.

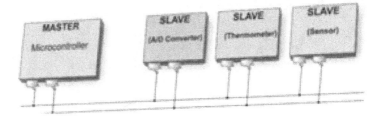

Board I2C Pins

The I2C bus comprises of two signals—SCL and also SDA. SCL is the clock signal, and also SDA is the data signal. The current bus master always produces the clock signal. Some slave tools may require the clock low sometimes to delay the master sending extra information (or to need even more time to prepare data before the master attempts to clock it out). This is called "clock stretching".

Adhering to the pins for different Arduino boards:

- Uno, Pro Mini A4 (SDA), A5 (SCL).

- Huge, Due 20 (SDA), 21 (SCL).

- Leonardo, Yun 2 (SDA), 3 (SCL).

Arduino I2C

We have two modes; master code and slave. They are:

- Master Transmitter/Slave Receiver.

- Master Receiver/Slave Transmitter.

Master Transmitter/Slave Receiver

Let us see what master transmitter and slave receiver is.

Master Transmitter

The following functions are used to boot up the cord collection and also sign up with the I2C bus as a master or servant. This is normally called just once.

- Wire.begin(address) – Address is the 7-bit slave address in our situation as the master is not stated, and it will sign up with the bus as a master.

- Wire.beginTransmission(address) – Begin a transmission to the I2C slave gadget with the given address.

- Wire.write(worth) – Queues bytes for transmission from a master to servant device (in-between calls to beginTransmission() and end transmission()).

- Wire.endTransmission()–Ends a transmission to a slave device that was begun by beginTransmission() as well as transmits the bytes that were queued by wire.write().

Example

#include <Wire.h>// consist of cord library.

void arrangement()// this will certainly run just as soon as

Wire.begin();

brief age = 0;.

void loop()

Slave Receiver

```
#include<Wire.h>//include wire library


voidsetup()//this will run only once {

Wire.begin();// join i2c bus as master

}
```

```
short age =0;

voidloop(){

Wire.beginTransmission(2);

// transmit to device #2

Wire.write("age is = ");

Wire.write(age);// sends one byte

Wire.endTransmission();// stop transmitting

delay(1000);

}
```

The complying with features are used:

- **Wire.begin(address)** –Address is the 7-bit servant address.

- **Wire.onReceive(gotten data trainer)** – Feature to be called when a servant gadget obtains information from the master.

- **Wire.available()** – Returns the variety of bytes available for retrieval with Wire.read(). This need to be called inside the Wire.onReceive() handler.

Master Receiver/Slave Transmitter

Let's see what a master receiver and slave transmitter is.

Master Receiver

The master is set to request and then reads bytes of information that are sent from the distinctively addressed Servant Arduino.

The following function is used:

Wire.requestFrom(address, variety of bytes) –Used by the master to request bytes from a servant gadget. The bytes may be gotten afterward with the wire.available() and wire.read() functions.

Slave Transmitter

The following feature is used:

Wire.onRequest(handler) – A function is called when a master needs information from the servant device.

Arduino – Serial Peripheral User Interface

A Serial Peripheral User Interface (SPI) bus is a system for serial communication, which uses four conductors, commonly three. One conductor is used for getting information, one for sending out data, one for synchronization, and one alternatively for selecting a tool to interact with. It is a full-duplex connection, which shows that the data is sent and obtained at once. The maximum baud rate is more than that in the I2C communication system.

Board SPI Pins

SPI uses the complying with four cords:

- **SCK** – This is the serial clock driven by the master.

- **MISO** – This is the master input/slave output driven by the master.

- **SS** –This is the slave-selection cable.

The following features are used:

You have to include the SPI.h.

- **SPI.begin()** –Initializes the SPI bus by establishing SCK, MOSI, and SS to outcomes, pulling SCK and also MOSI reduced, and SS high.

- **MOSI** – This is the master-slave/output input driven by the master.

- **SPI.setClockDivider(divider)**–To establish the SPI clock divider panel relative to the system clock. On AVR based boards, the dividers available are 2, 4, 8, 16, 32, 64,and 128. The default setup is SPI_CLOCK_DIV4, which sets the SPI clock to one-quarter of the frequency of the system clock (5 MHz for the boards at 20 MHz).

- **SPI.beginTransaction(SPISettings(speedMaximum, data order, data mode))**–Speed maximum is the clock, data order(MSBFIRST or LSBFIRST), data model(SPI_MODE0, SPI_MODE1, SPI_MODE2, or SPI_MODE3).

- **Divider panel–** It could be (SPI_CLOCK_DIV2, SPI_CLOCK_DIV4, SPI_CLOCK_DIV8, SPI_CLOCK_DIV16, SPI_CLOCK_DIV32, SPI_CLOCK_DIV64, SPI_CLOCK_DIV128).

- **SPI. Transfer (Val)** – SPI transfer is based on a synchronized send as well as obtainment: the obtained information is returned in received Val.

We have four modus operandi in SPI as follows:

- **Setting 0 (the default)** – Clock is generally reduced (CPOL = 0), and the data is tasted on the transition from reduced to high (leading edge) (CPHA = 0).

- **Setting 1** –Clock is generally reduced (CPOL = 0), and the information is experienced on the shift from high to reduced (tracking side) (CPHA = 1).

- **Setting 2** – Clock is usually tall (CPOL = 1), and the data is tasted on the change from high to reduced (leading edge) (CPHA = 0).

- **Setting 3** – Clock is typically tall (CPOL = 1), as well as the information is tested on the change from low to high (routing edge) (CPHA = 1).

- **SPI.attachInterrupt(handler)** – Feature to be called when a slave gadget gets information from the master.

Now, we will undoubtedly connect two Arduino UNO boards, one as a master and the other as a servant.

- **(SS):** pin 10.

- **(MOSI):** pin 11.

- **(MISO):** pin 12.

- **(SCK):** pin 13.

The ground is common. Following is the diagrammatic representation of the connection between both the boards.

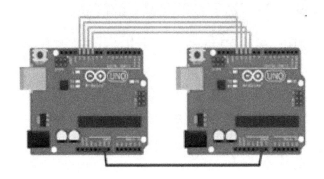

Arduino – Attaching Switch Over

Pushbuttons or switches connect two open terminals in a circuit. This instance activates the BAITED pin 2 when you press the pushbutton connected to pin 8.

Pull-down Resistors

Pull-down resistors are made use of in electronic logic circuits to make sure that inputs to Arduino work out at expected logic levels if external gadgets are separated or are at high-impedance. As nothing is attached to an input pin, it does not mean that it is an absolute no. Pull-down resistors are connected between the appropriate pin on the device and the ground.

An instance of a pull-down resistor in an electronic circuit is shown in the following figure. A pushbutton switch is connected between the supply voltage and a microcontroller pin. In such a course, when the button is shut, the micro-controller input is at a high rational worth. Yet, when the switch is open, the pull-down resistor pulls the input voltage to the ground (logical zero value), preventing an undefined state at the input.

The pull-down resistor should have a more significant resistance than the resistance of the logic circuit; otherwise, it may pull the voltage down, and the input voltage at the pin would undoubtedly continue to be at a continuous logical reduced value, despite the button position.

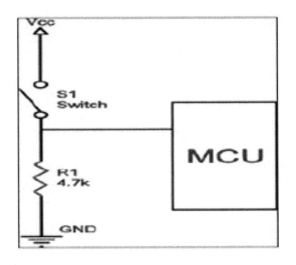

Parts Required

You will need the following components:

- One × Arduino UNO board.

- One × 330 ohm resistor.

- One × 4.7K ohm resistor (pull-down).

- One × LED.

Procedure

Adhere to the circuit layout and make the connections, as shown in the image below.

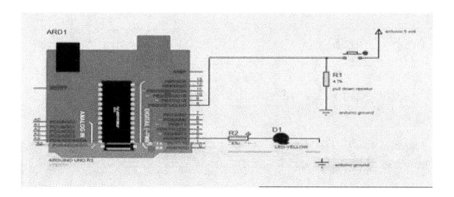

Sketch

Open the Arduino IDE software program on your computer, the coding in the Arduino language will undoubtedly manage your circuit. Open a new illustration document by clicking "New".

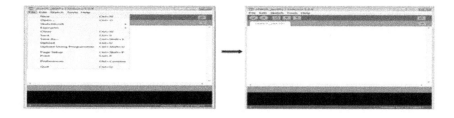

Arduino Code

```
// constants won't change. They're used here to

// set pin numbers:

constintbuttonPin=8;// the number of the pushbutton pin

constintledPin=2;// the number of the LED pin

// variables will change:

intbuttonState=0;// variable for reading the pushbutton status


voidsetup(){

// initialize the LED pin as an output:

pinMode(ledPin, OUTPUT);

// initialize the pushbutton pin as an input:

pinMode(buttonPin, INPUT);

}
```

```
voidloop(){

// read the state of the pushbutton value:

buttonState=digitalRead(buttonPin);

// check if the pushbutton is pressed.

// if it is, the buttonState is HIGH:

if(buttonState== HIGH){

// turn LED on:

digitalWrite(ledPin, HIGH);

}else{

// turn LED off:

digitalWrite(ledPin, LOW);

}}
```

Code to Note

When the switch is open (pushbutton is not pressed), there is no connection between the two terminals.

So the pin is connected to the ground (through the pull-down resistor), and we read a LOW. When the switch is closed (pushbutton is pressed), it makes a connection between its two terminals, attaching the pin to 5 volts, to make sure that we read a HIGH.

Result

LED is switched on when the pushbutton is pressed and switch off when it is launched.

Arduino – DC Motor

In this phase, we will use various kinds of electric motors with the Arduino board (UNO) and show how to connect the engine as well as drive it from your board.

There are three different types of motors:

- DC motor.

- Servo motor.

- Stepper electric motor.

1. A DC electric motor (direct current electric motor) is one of the most common types of engines. DC electric motors usually have two leads, one favourable and one adverse. If you connect these two leads straight to a battery, the driver will rotate.

If you change the leads, the electric motor will rotate in the contrary direction.

The pull-down resistor needs to have a more significant resistance than the impedance of the logic circuit; otherwise, it could draw the voltage down, and the input voltage pin would remain at a consistent logical low value, despite the switch setting.

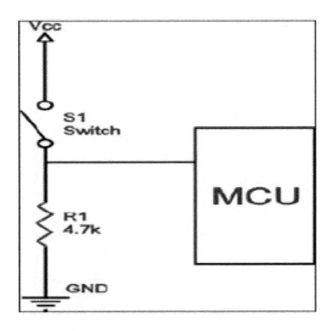

Parts Required

You will require the adhering to elements:

- One × Arduino UNO board.

- One × 330 ohm resistor.

- One × 4.7 K ohm resistor (pull-down).

- One × LED.

Procedure

Adhere to the circuit layout as well as make the links as displayed in the photo given listed below.

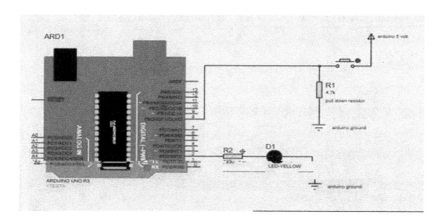

Sketch

Open up the Arduino IDE software program on your computer system. Coding in the Arduino language will regulate your circuit. Open a brand-new sketch document by clicking "New".

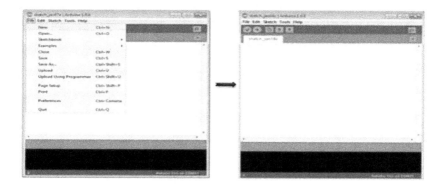

Warning: Do not drive the electric motor directly from Arduino board pins. This might damage the board. Use a chauffeur circuit or an IC.

We will split this chapter right into three parts:

- Just make your motor spin.

- Control electric motor rate.

- Control the instructions of the turn of DC electric motor.

Components Required

You will undoubtedly need to comply with these elements.

- 1x Arduino UNO board.

- 1x PN2222 Transistor.

- 1x Little 6V DC Electric Motor.

- 1x 1N4001 diode.

- 1x 270 Ω Resistor.

Treatment

Comply with the circuit representation and make the connections as displayed in the image provided below.

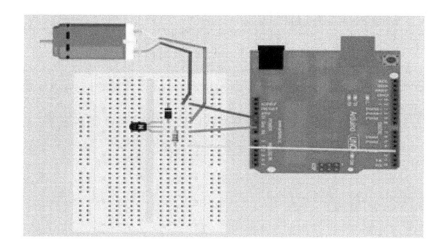

Safety Measures

Take the following preventative measures while making the connections.

- Firstly, ensure that the transistor is connected correctly. The flat side of the transistor should encounter the Arduino board as displayed in the arrangement.

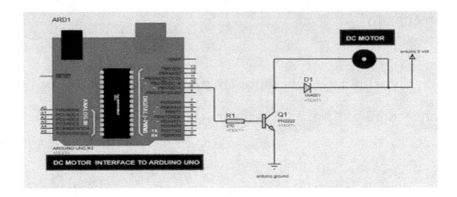

Secondly, the striped end of the diode ought to be towards the +5V power line according to the setup shown in the photo.

Spin Control Arduino Code

```
intmotorPin=3;

voidsetup(){

}

voidloop(){

digitalWrite(motorPin, HIGH);}
```

Code to Note

The transistor imitates a switch, managing the power to the motor. Arduino pin three is used to turn the transistor on and off and is named 'motorPin' in the illustration.

Result

The motor will ultimately rotate the speed when the Arduino pin three goes high.

Electric Motor Rate Control

Below is the schematic representation of a DC electric motor connected to the Arduino board.

Arduino Code

```
intmotorPin=9;


voidsetup(){

pinMode(motorPin, OUTPUT);

Serial.begin(9600);

while(!Serial);
```

```
Serial.println("Speed 0 to 255");

}

voidloop(){

if(Serial.available()){

int speed =Serial.parseInt();

if(speed >=0&& speed <=255){

analogWrite(motorPin, speed);

}

}}
```

When the program begins, it motivates you to offer the values

to manage the speed of the motor. You need to go into a value

between 0 and 255 in the serial monitor. In the 'loophole'

feature, the command 'Serial.parseInt' is used to check out the

number went into the message in the serial monitor as well as

transform it right into an 'int'. You can use any kind of number

here. The 'if' statement in the following line merely does an analog compose with this number if the number is between 0 and 255.

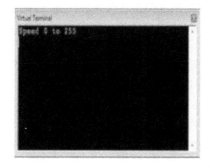 

Result

The DC electric motor will spin with various rates according to the value (0 to 250) obtained using the serial port.

Rotate Instructions Control

To manage the direction of the spin of the DC electric motor without interchanging the leads, you can use a circuit called an H-Bridge. An H-bridge is a digital circuit that can drive the automobile in both instructions. H-bridges are made used indifferent applications. One of the most usual forms is to manage motors in robots. It is called an H-bridge because it makes use of four transistors attached in such a way that the schematic diagram appears like an "H".

We will be using the L298 H-Bridge IC here. The L298 can control the instructions and the speed of DC electric motors and stepper electric motors, as well as can control two electric motors all at once. Its current score is 2A for each motor. At these currents, nevertheless, you will need to make use of warmth sinks.

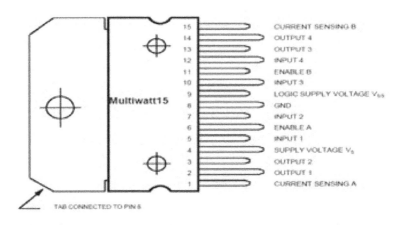

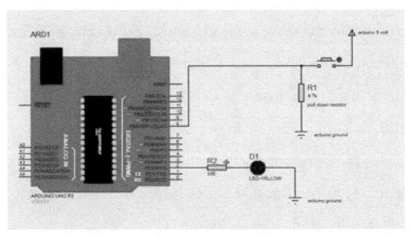

Components Required

You will certainly need the adhering parts:

- One × L298 bridge IC.

- One × DC motor.

- One × Arduino UNO.

- One × breadboard.

- 10 × jumper cables.

Procedure

Following is the schematic representation of the DC electric motor interface to the Arduino Uno board.

The above diagram shows how to attach the L298 IC to regulate two electric motors. There are three input pins for each electric motor, Input1 (IN1), Input2 (IN2), and Enable1 (EN1) for Motor1 as well as Input3, Input4, and Enable2 for Motor2.

Given that we will be managing one motor in this instance, we will attach the Arduino to IN1 (pin 5), IN2 (pin 7), and Enable1 (pin 6) of the L298 IC. Pins 5 and 7 are electronic, i.e., ON or

OFF inputs, while pin 6 needs a pulse-width regulated (PWM) signal to control the electric motor speed.

IN1	IN2	Motor Behavior
		BRAKE
1		FORWARD
	1	BACKWARD
1	1	BRAKE

The table shows the instructions in which the electric motor will transform based on the digital values of IN1 and IN2.Pin IN1 of the IC L298 is connected to pin 8 of Arduino when IN2 is linked pin 9. These two electronic pins of Arduino regulate the direction of the motor. The EN-A pin of IC is attached to the PWM pin 2 of Arduino. This will control the rate of the engine.

To set the value of the Arduino pins 8 and 9, we have to use the digitalWrite() function, and to establish the value of pin 2, we have to use the analogWrite() capacity.

Connection Steps

- Connect 5V and the ground of the IC to 5V and the ground of Arduino, respectively.

- Connect the motor to pins 2 and 3 of the IC.

- Connect the IC's IN1 to pin 8 of Arduino.

- Attach IN2 of the IC to pin 9 of Arduino.

- Connect EN1 of IC to pin 2 of Arduino.

- Connect SENS A pin of IC to the ground.

- Attach Arduino using the Arduino USB cable and publish the program to Arduino making use of Arduino IDE software application.

- Provide power to the Arduino board making use of a power supply, battery, or USB cable.

Arduino – Servo Electric Motor

A servo motor is a tiny gadget that has an output shaft. This shaft can be placed in particular angular positions by sending the servo a coded signal. As long as the coded signal feeds on the input line, the servo will preserve the angular placement of the shaft. If the coded signal changes, the lean setting of the shaft changes. In practice, servos are used in radio-controlled aircraft to position control surface areas like the elevators and rudders. They are also used in radio-controlled vehicles, puppets, and robots.

Servos are exceptionally valuable in robotics. The motors are tiny, have built-in control wiring, and are very useful for their dimension. A standard servo such as the Futaba S-148 has 42 oz-in of torque, which is substantial for its size. It also attracts power proportional to the mechanical tons.

A gently packed servo, consequently, does not take in much energy.

The parts of a servo motor are displayed in the following picture. You can see the control circuitry, the electric motor, a collection of gears, and the case. You can also see the three cables that connect to the outside. One is for power (+5 volts), ground, and the white cord is the control cable.

The Work of a Servo Electric Motor

The servo-electric motor has some control circuits and a potentiometer (a variable resistor, also known as the pot) connected to the outcome shaft.

Take note of the above; the pot can be seen on the right side of the circuit board. This pot enables the control wiring to monitor the current angle of the servo motor.

If the shaft is at the correct angle, after which the heater and the generator were turned off, the circuit discovers that the corner is not right; it will change the electric motor until it is at a preferred angle. The resulting shaft of the servo is capable of taking a trip around 180 levels. Typically, it is somewhere in the 210-degree variety; however, it differs depending on the manufacturer. A regular servo is used to control an angular movement of zero to one hundred and eighty degrees. It is mechanically not capable of turning continuously because a mechanical quit has improved to the leading output equipment.

The power put on the electric motor is symmetrical to the range it needs to travel. So, if the shaft needs to transform a significant distance, the electric motor will go for full speed. If it needs to turn just a small amount, the engine will perform at a slower rate. This is called proportional control.

How Do You Communicate the Angle at Which the Servo Turn?

The control cable is used to link the angle. The angle is determined by the duration of a pulse connected to the control cable. This is called pulse-code modulation (PCM).

The servo expects to see a pulse every 20 nanoseconds.

The duration of the pulse will certainly identify how much the electric motor transforms. A 1.5-millisecond pulse, for example, will undoubtedly make the electric motor rest on the ninety-degree location(called the neutral setting). If the vibration is much shorter than 1.5 nanoseconds, then the motor will turn the shaft more detailed to 0 degrees. If the pulse is longer than 1.5 milliseconds, the shaft changes closer to 180 levels.

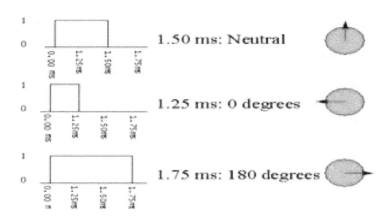

Requirement

- You will need the following elements:

- One × Arduino UNO board

- One × Servo Motor

- One × ULN2003 driving IC

- One × 10 KΩ Resistor

Procedure

Follow the circuit representation and also make the links as displayed in the photo offered below.

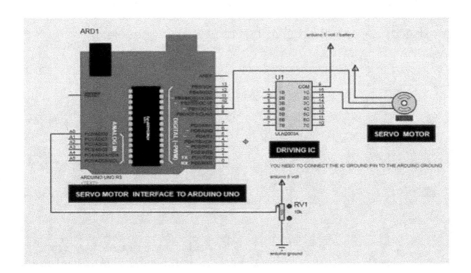

Sketch

Open up the Arduino IDE software program on your computer. Coding in the Arduino language will control your circuit. Open a new sketch data by clicking on "New".

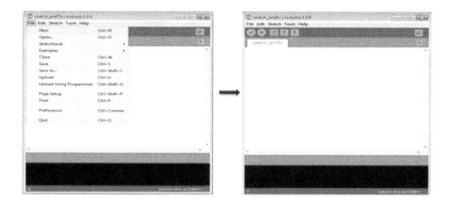

Code to Keep in Mind

Servo motors have three terminals—power, ground, and signal. The power wire is ordinarily red and should be connected to the 5V pin on the Arduino. The ground wire is typically black or brown and should be connected to one terminal ULN2003 IC (10 -16). To secure your Arduino board from damages, you will need some vehicle driver IC. Right, here we have made use of ULN2003 IC to drive the servo motor. The signal pin is yellow or orange and must be connected to the Arduino PIN 9.

Connecting the Potentiometer

A voltage divider or potential divider panel are resistors in a series circuit that scale the resulting voltage to a specific ratio of the input voltage applied. Following is the circuit representation:

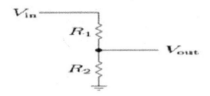

$$ V\_out = (V\_in \times R\_2)/ (R\_1 + R\_)$$.

Vout is the production power that depends on the used input voltage (Vin) and resistors (R1 andR2) in the collection. It suggests that the existing flow through R1 will likewise flow through R2 without being split. In the above equation, as the value of R2 changes, the Vout is appropriately scaled in relation to the input voltage, Vin.

Generally, a potentiometer is a prospective divider, which can scale the output voltage of the circuit based on the value of the variable resistor, which is making use of the handle.

It has three pins: GND, Signal, and also +5V, as shown in the diagram below:

Result

By changing the pot's NOP placement, the servo motor will change its angle.

Arduino – Stepper Electric Motor

A stepper motor or a step electric motor is a brushless, simultaneous electric motor, which splits a full turning into several actions. Unlike a brushless DC motor, which turns when a deal with DC voltage is related to it, a step motor revolves in distinct action angles.

The stepper motors, for that reason, are produced with steps per change of 12, 24, 72, 144, 180, and200, leading to tipping angles of 30, 15, 5, 2.5, 2, and 1.8 levels per step. The stepper motor can be controlled with or without comments.

Find the Electric Motor on the RC Aircraft

The electric motor rotates very fast in one direction or another. You can differ the speed with the amount of power provided to the engine, yet you cannot tell the propeller to stop at a specific setting.

Currently Envision a Printer

There are lots of moving components inside a printer consisting of motors. One electric motor functions as the paper feed, rotating rollers run the paper as ink is being printed on it. This motor needs to be able to relocate the article at the same range to be able to publish the following line of the message or the next line of a picture.

There is another electric motor connected to a threaded rod that moves the print head to and fro. Again, that threaded pole needs to be moved a precise amount to print one letter after another. This is where the stepper motors have been available.

How a Stepper Electric Motor Works?

A routine DC electric motor rotates based on a direction, whereas a stepper electric motor can rotate in specific increments.

Stepper motors can turn a specific quantity of degrees (or actions) as wanted. This gives you overall control over the engine, enabling you to move it to an exact location and also hold that placement. It does so by powering the coils inside the motor for a short time.

The drawback is that you need to power the electric motor always to keep it in the placement that you prefer.

All you need to know is to move a stepper motor; you tell it to run a particular step in one direction or the other and show it the speed at which to act by following those instructions. There are numerous varieties of stepper electric motors. The techniques defined below can be used to infer how to use various other motors or vehicle engines, which are not discussed in this book. However, it is always recommended that you get in touch with the datasheets and overviews of the specific engines of the models you have.

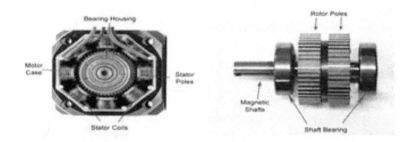

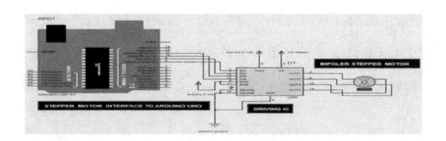

Components Required

You will certainly need the following components:

- One × Arduino UNO board.

- One × little bipolar stepper motor as received the photo offered below.

- One × LM298 driving IC.

Procedure

Comply with the circuit diagram and make the connections, as shown in the photo provided below.

Sketch

Open the Arduino IDE software application on your computer system. Coding in the Arduino language will manage your circuit. Open a brand-new illustration file by clicking "New".

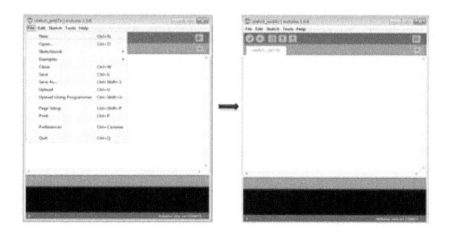

Code to Note

This program drives a unipolar or bipolar stepper motor. The electric motor is committed to digital pins 8–11 of Arduino.

Result

The motor will take one transformation in one direction, then one change in the other instructions.

Arduino – Tone Library

In this area, we will make use of the Arduino Tone collection. It is an Arduino Library, which produces a square-wave of a defined regularity (and 50% duty cycle) on any Arduino pin. A period can additionally be specified; otherwise, the wave continues until the stop() function is called. The nail can be connected to a piezo buzzer or an audio speaker to play the tones.

Warning: Do not connect the pin straight to any kind of audio input. The voltage is considerably higher than the standard line-level voltages and can harm audio card inputs, etc. You can use a voltage divider to bring the energy down.

Parts Required

You will need the following elements:

- One × 8-ohm speaker.

- One × 1k resistor.

- One × Arduino UNO board.

Procedure

Adhere to the circuit layout and make the links as displayed in the image given below.

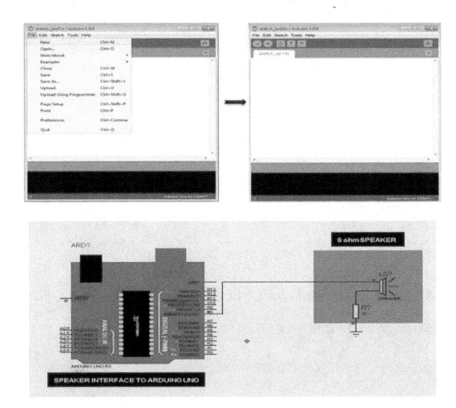

Sketch

Open up the Arduino IDE software on your computer system.

Coding in the Arduino language will manage your circuit.

Open a new illustration Data by clicking "New".

To make the pitches.h documents, either click the switch simply listed below the serial display symbol and also choose "New Tab", or make use of Ctrl+ Shift + N.

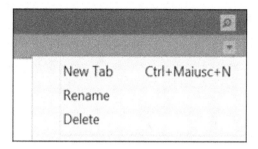

Then paste the following code:

```
/***********************************************

* Public Constants

**********************************************/


#define NOTE_B0 31

#define NOTE_C1 33

#define NOTE_CS1 35

#define NOTE_D1 37

#define NOTE_DS1 39
```

```
#define NOTE_E1 41

#define NOTE_F1 44

#define NOTE_FS1 46

#define NOTE_G1 49

#define NOTE_GS1 52

#define NOTE_A1 55

#define NOTE_AS1 58

#define NOTE_B1 62

#define NOTE_C2 65

#define NOTE_CS2 69

#define NOTE_D2 73

#define NOTE_DS2 78

#define NOTE_E2 82

#define NOTE_F2 87
```

```
#define NOTE_FS2 93

#define NOTE_G2 98

#define NOTE_GS2 104

#define NOTE_A2 110

#define NOTE_AS2 117

#define NOTE_B2 123

#define NOTE_C3 131

#define NOTE_CS3 139

#define NOTE_D3 147

#define NOTE_DS3 156

#define NOTE_E3 165

#define NOTE_F3 175

#define NOTE_FS3 185

#define NOTE_G3 196
```

```c
#define NOTE_GS3 208

#define NOTE_A3 220

#define NOTE_AS3 233

#define NOTE_B3 247

#define NOTE_C4 262

#define NOTE_CS4 277

#define NOTE_D4 294

#define NOTE_DS4 311

#define NOTE_E4 330

#define NOTE_F4 349

#define NOTE_FS4 370

#define NOTE_G4 392

#define NOTE_GS4 415

#define NOTE_A4 440
```

```
#define NOTE_AS4 466

#define NOTE_B4 494

#define NOTE_C5 523

#define NOTE_CS5 554

#define NOTE_D5 587

#define NOTE_DS5 622

#define NOTE_E5 659

#define NOTE_F5 698

#define NOTE_FS5 740

#define NOTE_G5 784

#define NOTE_GS5 831

#define NOTE_A5 880

#define NOTE_AS5 932

#define NOTE_B5 988
```

```c
#define NOTE_C6 1047

#define NOTE_CS6 1109

#define NOTE_D6 1175

#define NOTE_DS6 1245

#define NOTE_E6 1319

#define NOTE_F6 1397

#define NOTE_FS6 1480

#define NOTE_G6 1568

#define NOTE_GS6 1661

#define NOTE_A6 1760

#define NOTE_AS6 1865

#define NOTE_B6 1976

#define NOTE_C7 2093

#define NOTE_CS7 2217
```

```c
#define NOTE_D7 2349

#define NOTE_DS7 2489

#define NOTE_E7 2637

#define NOTE_F7 2794

#define NOTE_FS7 2960

#define NOTE_G7 3136

#define NOTE_GS7 3322

#define NOTE_A7 3520

#define NOTE_AS7 3729

#define NOTE_B7 3951

#define NOTE_C8 4186

#define NOTE_CS8 4435

#define NOTE_D8 4699

#define NOTE_DS8 4978
```

Conserve the above-given code as pitches.

Code to Note

The code uses additional documents, pitches.h. This data contains all the pitch values for standard notes. For instance, NOTE_C4 is middle C. NOTE_FS4 is F sharp, etc. This note table was initially written by Brett Hagman, on whose work the tone() command was based. You may locate it useful whenever you intend to make musical notes.

Result

You will certainly listen to musical notes conserved in the pitches.hdata.

Arduino – Wireless Communication

The wireless transmitter and receiver components operate at 315 MHz. They can easily suit a breadboard and work well with microcontrollers to develop an essential wireless information link. With one set of the transmitter and the receiver, the components will communicate information one-way; nonetheless, you would need two pairs (of various regularities) to function as a transmitter/receiver pair.

Note: These modules are unplanned and get a fair quantity of sound. Both the transmitter and receiver operate at usual regularities and do not have IDs.

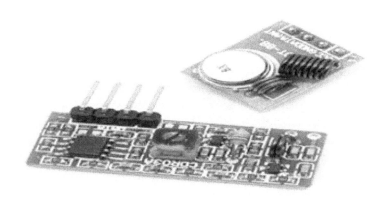

Receiver Component Specifications

- **Item Design** – MX-05V

- **Operating Voltage** – DC5V

- **Quiescent Existing** – 4mA

- **Getting Frequency** – 315Mhz

- **Receiver level of sensitivity** – -105 DB.

- **Dimension** – 30 * 14 * 7mm.

Transmitter Module Requirements

- **Item Version** – MX-FS-03V.

- **Introduce range** – 20-200 meters (various voltage, different results).

- **Operating voltage** – 3.5-12V.

- **Dimensions** – 19 * 19mm.

- **Operating setting** – AM.

- **Transfer price** – 4 KB/S.

- **Transferring power** – 10mW.

- **Transmitting frequency** – 315MHz.

- **An exterior antenna** – 25cm regular multi-core or single-core line.

- **Pin out from left > ideal** – (DATA; VCC; GND).

Components Required

You will need to comply with these elements:

- Two × Arduino UNO board.

- One × Rf wireless transmitter.

- One × Rf link receiver.

Treatment

Follow the circuit diagram and also make the links as received in the picture provided listed below.

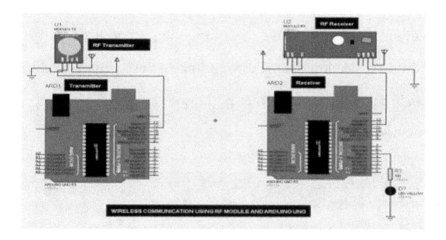

Sketch

Open the Arduino IDE software program on your computer system. Coding in the Arduino language will regulate your circuit. Open up a new illustration data by clicking "New".

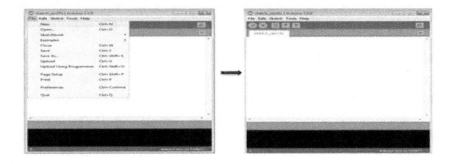

Keep in mind – You have to include the keypad library in your Arduino collection data. Copy and paste the VirtualWire.lib data in the libraries folder, as highlighted in the screenshot provided below.

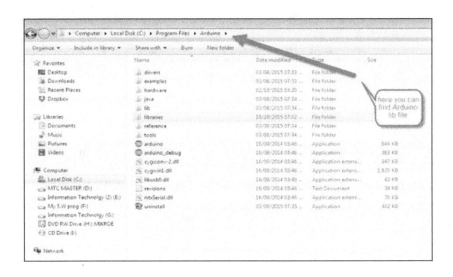

Code to Keep in Mind

The LED attached to PIN 5 on the Arduino board is switched on when personality '1' is gotten and shut off when character '0' is obtained.

Arduino – Network Interaction

The CC3000 Wi-Fi component from Texas Instruments is a little silver bundle, which finally brings user-friendly, affordable Wi-Fi performance to your Arduino jobs.

It uses SPI for communication (not UART!), so you can press information as rapidly as you want or as slow as you want. It has an appropriate interrupt system with an IRQ pin so you can have asynchronous links. It sustains 802.11 b/g, open/WEP/WPA/ WPA2 protection, TKIP and AES. A built-in TCP/IP pile with a "BSD outlet" user interface sustains TCP and also UDP in both the customer and the web server setting.

Parts Required

You will need the following components:

- One × Arduino Uno.

- One × Adafruit CC3000 breakout board.

- One × 5V relay.

- One × Rectifier diode.

- One × LED.

- One × 220 Ohm resistor.

- One × Breadboard, as well as some jumper cables.

For this task, you just need the typical Arduino IDE, the Adafruit's CC3000 collection, and also the CC3000 MDNS library. We are also likely to use aREST library to send commands to the relay using Wi-Fi.

Procedure

Adhere to the circuit representation and make the connections as displayed in the photo given listed below.

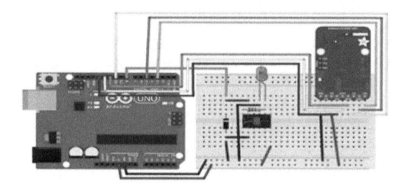

The hardware setup for this job is easy.

- Link the IRQ pin of the CC3000 board to PIN 3 of the Arduino board.

- VBAT to pin 5, and CS to pin 10.

- Connect the SPI pins to Arduino board: MOSI, MISO, and CLK to pins 11, 12, and 13, respectively.

- Vin is attached to Arduino 5V and GND to GND.

Now connect the relay.

After positioning the relay on the breadboard, you can start recognizing the two fundamental parts on your relay: the coil component that commands the relay, and the button component where we will connect the LED.

- First, connect PIN 8 of the Arduino board to one coil pin.

- Connect the other pin to the ground of the Arduino board.

You additionally need to put the rectifier diode (anode linked to the ground pin) over the nails of the coil to shield your circuit when the relay is switching.

- Link the +5V of the Arduino board to the standard pin of the relay's switch.

- Lastly, attach some other pins of the button (usually, the one which is not connected when the relay is off) to the LED in series with the 220 Ohm resistor, and compare the opposite side of the result the ground of the Arduino board.

Checking Individual Elements

You can test the relay with the following sketch:

```
const

{

Serial.begin(9600);

pinMode(relay_pin,OUTPUT);

}



voidloop(){

// Activate relay

digitalWrite(relay_pin, HIGH);

// Wait for 1 second

delay(1000);

// Deactivate relay
```

```
digitalWrite(relay_pin, LOW);

// Wait for 1 second

delay(1000);}
```

Code to Keep in Mind

The code is self-explanatory. You can simply upload it to the board and the relay will switch over states every second, and the LED will undoubtedly turn on and off appropriately.

Adding Wi-Fi Connectivity

Let us now manage the relay wirelessly using the CC3000 Wi-Fi chip. The software application for this task is based on the TCP procedure. Nonetheless, for this task, the Arduino board will be running a little internet server, so we can "pay attention" to commands coming from the computer. We will initially take care of the Arduino illustration, and then we will certainly see just how to compose the server-side code and develop a friendly user interface.

First, the Arduino sketch. The goal here is to connect to your Wi-Fi network, create a web server, see if there is a server inbound TCP connect, and after that, change the state of the relay as necessary.

Vital Parts of the Code

```
#include<Adafruit_CC3000.h>

#include<SPI.h>

#include<CC3000_MDNS.h>

#include<Ethernet.h>

#include<aREST.h>
```

You need to define inside the code what specifies to your arrangement, that is, Wi-Fi name and password, and also the port for TCP interactions (we have made use of 80 below).

```
// WiFi network (change with your settings!)

#define WLAN_SSID "yourNetwork"// cannot be longer than 32 characters!

#define WLAN_PASS "yourPassword"
```

> #define WLAN_SECURITY WLAN_SEC_WPA2 // This can be WLAN_SEC_UNSEC, WLAN_SEC_WEP,
>
> // WLAN_SEC_WPA or WLAN_SEC_WPA2
>
> // The port to listen for incoming TCP connections

#define LISTEN_PORT 80

We can then create the CC3000 instance, web server, and REST circumstances:

// Web server circumstances.

Adafruit_CC3000_Server restServer(LISTEN_PORT);// DNS - responder instance.

MDNSRespondermdns;// Create aREST circumstances.

aREST rest = aREST();.

In the setup() part of the sketch, we can now connect the network to the CC3000 chip:

```
// Server instance

Adafruit_CC3000_ServerrestServer(LISTEN_PORT);// DNS
responder instance

MDNSRespondermdns;// Create aREST instance

aREST rest =aREST();
```

Exactly how will the computer system recognize where to send out the data? One way would certainly be to run the illustration when the IP address of the CC3000 board is obtained. However, we can do much better, and that is where the CC3000 MDNS collection comes into play. We will assign a set name to our CC3000 board with this library so that we can make a note of this name straight right into the server code.

This is made with the following code:

```
if(!mdns.begin("arduino", cc3000)){

while(1);

}
```

We additionally require to listen for inbound links.

restServer.begin();.

Next off, we will undoubtedly code the loop() feature of the illustration that will indeed be implemented. We first have to update the DNS server.

DNS.update();.

The server operating on the Arduino board will wait for the incoming links and also deal with the demands.

It is now quite simple to examine the projects using Wi-Fi. Ensure you upgraded the sketch with your very own Wi-Fi name and password and post the illustration to your Arduino board. Open your Arduino IDE serial monitor, and also look for the IP address of your board.

Let us think for the rest right here that it is something like 192.168.1.103.

Then, just most likely to your preferred internet browser, and type:

192.168.1.103/digital/8/1.

You ought to see that your relay immediately activates.

Developing the Relay Interface

We will currently code the user interface of the project. There will be two components below: HTML documents containing the interface and client-side Javascript documents that will take care of the clicks in the interface. The user interface here is based on the aREST.js task, which was made to manage Wi-Fi gadgets from your computer conveniently.

Let us initially the HTML documents, called interface.html. The initial part consists of importing all the needed libraries for the user interface:

```
<head>

<metacharset=utf-8/>

<title> Relay Control </title>

<linkrel="stylesheet"type="text/css"

href="https://maxcdn.bootstrapcdn.com/bootstrap/3.3.4/css/
bootstrap.min.css">

<linkrel="stylesheet"type="text/css"href="style.css">

<scripttype="text/javascript"

src="https://code.jquery.c the CC3000 chip to om/jquery-
2.1.4.min.js"></script>

<scripttype="text/javascript"

src="https://cdn.rawgit.com/Foliotek/AjaxQ/master/ajaxq.js"
></script>
```

```
<scripttype="text/javascript"

src="https://cdn.rawgit.com/marcoschwartz/aREST.js/master
/aREST.js"></script>

<scripttype="text/javascript"

src="script.js"></script>

</head>
```

Then, we define two switches inside the user interface, one to turn the relay on and the other to turn it off once again.

Relay Control Relay

```
<divclass='container'>

<h1>Relay Control</h1>

<divclass='row'>

<divclass="col-md-1">Relay</div>

<divclass="col-md-2">

<buttonid='on'class='btnbtn-block btn-success'>On</button>
```

```
</div>

<divclass="col-md-2">

<buttonid='off'class='btnbtn-block btn-danger'>On</button>

</div>

</div></div>
```

Client-side Javascript data is needed to take care of the clicks on the switches. We will as well produce a device that we will certainly link to the DNS of our Arduino device. If you changed this in the Arduino code, you would need to change it below.

```
// Create device

var device =newDevice("arduino.local");

// Button

$('#on').click(function(){device.digitalWrite(8,1);});

$('#off').click(function(){device.digitalWrite(8,0);});
```

Finally, if you've found this book helpful in any way, an Amazon review is always welcome!